Now You Try It Do this exercise to practice applying the tip to recognize and correct the error. You can check your answers to the first two sets against the answer key.

Now You Try It,

Find the fragments b[illegible] e sentence and *frag* ab[illegible] it with the complete se[illegible] d group is a complete [illegible]

I rea[illegible] g

EXAMPLE: I started a poem but couldn't finish, ~~Because~~ I ran out of ideas.

1. We heard a noise. A loud, frightful noise.
2. The bull charged. What happened next is too horrible to tell.
3. A river runs through San Antonio. A peaceful, beautiful river.

Editing Practice Do this exercise to practice recognizing and correcting the error in a brief sample essay similar to one you might write. You can check your answers to the first two editing practices against the answer key.

Editing Practice, 1 **(Corrected sentences appear on page 297.)**

Correct all errors in the following paragraph using the first correction as a model. The number in parentheses at the end of the paragraph indicates how many errors you should find.

Many cities played an important role in the forming of the United States, ~~Especially~~ *, especially* Philadelphia. Which has some of the nation's most important historical treasures. Most of them found around Independence Mall. The most famous is Independence Hall. Where the Declaration of Independence was signed. The Liberty Bell was, at one time, located there as well, but it was moved. Because it was not very accessible. (4)

Writing Practice Do this activity to demonstrate your ability to avoid the error in your own writing.

Writing Practice

On your own paper, write a paragraph or two describing a work of art (sculpture, photograph, painting, and so on) that you like or dislike. Use the Proofreading Checklist to make sure there are no fragments.

Proofreading Checklist Refer to this summary of the lesson when you do the Writing Practice or whenever you need to refresh your memory about the error.

PROOFREADING CHECKLIST

Using Complete Sentences in Your Writing

- Some people detect fragments by reading backward, sentence by sentence. Read each sentence in a normal fashion, but start at the *end* of your paper.
- See whether *I realize* can be placed before any group of words that you have questions about. If it can't go there, then the words may be a fragment.
- Also see whether the group of words can be turned into a yes-no question. You shouldn't have to make any major additions to do so. If the test fails, you probably have a fragment.
- To correct a fragment, try combining it with the sentence immediately before it or after it (or add whatever words are necessary to make it complete). Double-check your correction with one or both of the tests mentioned above.

The Bottom Line Here is a final reminder of the main point of the lesson. The sentence is written so that it is an example of the concept it discusses.

THE BOTTOM LINE

I realize you can place *I realize* in front of a complete sentence.

NOW I GET IT

A COMMONSENSE GUIDE TO GRAMMAR AND USAGE

LARRY BEASON
Eastern Washington University

MARK LESTER
Eastern Washington University

ST. MARTIN'S PRESS NEW YORK

Sponsoring editor: Barbara A. Heinssen
Development editor: Sylvia L. Weber
Managing editor: Patricia Mansfield Phelan
Project editor: Diana M. Puglisi
Production supervisor: Scott Lavelle
Art director and cover designer: Lucy Krikorian
Text design: Leon Bolognese & Associates, Inc.
Composition: Ewing Systems

Library of Congress Catalog Card Number: 96-67029

Manufactured in the United States of America.

1 0 9 8 7
f e d c b a

For information, write:
St. Martin's Press, Inc.
175 Fifth Avenue
New York, NY 10010

ISBN: 0-312-13359-6

CONTENTS

PREFACE

The need for effective writing is always with us. Most people need to write well throughout their lives—from passing proficiency exams in school to writing clear, concise business letters. Part of being an effective writer is making appropriate choices in grammar and usage—the rules and conventions that govern formal writing. This book helps people produce writing that is free of the grammar and usage errors that are likely to distract and confuse their readers.

At the core of our approach is the conviction that errors can be signs of risk taking, experimentation, and growth. Once students understand that errors are part of the learning process and do not necessarily reflect sloppiness or unsound thinking, they can develop the confidence to move toward the recognition and correction of errors in their own writing.

Now I Get It is intended for a range of students who need a firmer foundation in the grammar and usage of formal writing. These students might be enrolled in a beginning writing course, a freshman composition course, or even a course in a field such as business, history, or science. Some sections, indicated by , are particularly useful for non-native speakers of English.

Regardless of the students' level of expertise in writing, *Now I Get It* offers practical, concrete strategies for solving common problems with the rules and conventions of academic English. Indeed, flexibility is a key feature of this book. It can be used as a major text for an entire class or as a self-paced supplemental text. It can be read sequentially but need not be.

WHAT DOES THIS BOOK COVER—AND WHY?

To be concise and accessible, this book focuses on solutions to thirty-five errors in written academic English chosen on the basis of research, experience, and feedback from students and teachers. We concentrate on errors which appear most often in freshman composition. Other research according to a comprehensive study by Robert Connors and Andrea Lunsford ("Frequency of Formal Errors in Current College Writing, or Ma and Pa Kettle Do Research," *College Composition and Communication* 39, 1988, pp. 395–409) revealed errors which are considered particularly distracting even though they might not appear often. In testing our book in classrooms, we gathered feedback from students of diverse backgrounds—including students in developmental writing courses and students whose first language is not English—as well as from teachers.

We wrote *Now I Get It: A Commonsense Guide to Grammar and Usage* because we found no textbook with the following combination of features.

- *Commonsense tips.* We center each lesson on at least one *tip*—a commonsense way of looking at an error. These tips rely not on complex grammatical rules but on intuitive, practical strategies that people actually use when writing. Our text uses some grammatical terms, but we keep these to a minimum and provide definitions as needed.

- *A developmental sequence of hands-on activities.* The hands-on activities allow students to focus on skills that are different yet developmentally related. Brief diagnostic exercises in each unit overview and each lesson allow the students and teacher to consider whether or not the students need to complete a given lesson.
  - After reading the information and commonsense tips of each lesson, students apply the tips by completing three *Now You Try It* exercises. Thus, students master a core idea or strategy before moving on to more extended pieces of writing.
  - Next, the students complete three *Editing Practice* exercises. Here, they apply the editing skills they developed from the *Now You Try It* exercises. They progress from examining independent sentences to examining a mini-essay and correcting the errors.
  - Finally, the *Writing Practice* section of each lesson asks students to compose their own writing and correctly use the punctuation or grammatical item covered in the lesson. In this way, students learn about errors in the context of their own writing.

- *An emphasis on the positive.* This text focuses on errors because we want to provide a concise way to deal with problems in usage or grammar that interfere with the communication of ideas. We avoid a pessimistic, negative, or belittling approach to error.
  - First, we provide *both incorrect and corrected versions of the sample errors.* Errors are marked with an ✘, and corrections are clearly labeled.
  - Second, we explain *why* each error occurs.
  - Third, we offer *correction strategies.* This book not only helps students identify an error but also provides them with options for revising their writing to make it error-free.

- *A consistent framework.* All lessons are based on a similar organization. *How to Use This Book,* a model on the inside front cover and first page, guides students through a sample lesson. They know what to expect in each lesson, so information is easier to locate and understand.

- *A user-friendly format.* The text is designed around the way people will actually use the book. The *Table of Contents* offers a sample error for each lesson so that students do not have to rely on technical terms to locate a given lesson or issue. The *Guide to Grammar Terminology* presents a glossary where readers need it—before rather than after the lessons. *Consistent tabs* and a *comprehensive index* help students to locate information quickly. The *spiral binding* enables students to lay the book flat while writing in it or consulting it in a computer lab.

- *Handy references.* Finally, because we realize people often need to remind themselves of the most essential information, for each lesson we have provided a *Proofreading Checklist* that itemizes the commonsense tips, correction strategies, and rules. *The Bottom Line* feature, the last item in each lesson, demonstrates, as well as describes, how to avoid a particular error.

HOW TO USE THIS BOOK

The text is intended to be flexible and to fit various needs and situations.

- Each lesson can stand on its own. When reading a particular lesson, the student should complete the diagnostic exercise. If this work shows a need for further study, the student should then read the information provided and do the remaining exercises.

  It is also useful to complete the *Overview* for each unit for additional diagnostic work for a group of related lessons. Similarly, *Putting It All Together* at the end of each unit synthesizes and summarizes the lessons.

- The teacher can assign exercises as homework or as classwork. The text can also be a *self-paced reference* that students use on their own. Answers are provided for all exercises except the following: *Now You Try It, 3*; *Editing Practice, 3*; *Writing Practice*; and the unit *Review*.

Language is a dynamic, flexible system and not just a set of absolute rules. We encourage students not to assume that any textbook is adequate by itself. Students also need to be involved in reading, writing, receiving feedback, and reflecting on their own writing processes. However, we believe that there is still a place in the curriculum for students to study the conventions of academic writing and to incorporate them into their own writing.

We offer, then, a foundation for dealing with problems of concern to both writers and readers. Such a starting point is essential for reaching a goal, but it is not an end unto itself. Our hope is that we offer some valuable resources that assist in a lifelong attempt to communicate effectively.

INSTRUCTIONAL RESOURCES

The *Instructor's Resource Manual* for *Now I Get It* offers suggestions, including sample syllabi for using the text in a variety of situations and environments. Tips for teaching each unit and lesson, answer keys for the text, and supplemental exercises with answers are also provided. We invite you to visit our home page at **http://www.smpcollege.com/get_it/** for access to the authors, additional exercises, and links to related sites.

ACKNOWLEDGMENTS

We would like to thank the following instructors for their reviews of the manuscript and suggestions for its improvement: Beth Camp, Linn-Benton Community College; Diana Cox, Amarillo College; J. S. Cofer, Atlantic Community College; Harold Derderian, Henry Ford Community College; Gretchen Flesher, Gustavius Adolphus College; Judith Funston, SUNY-Potsdam; Susanmarie Harrington, Indiana University–Purdue University; Rebecca Munshaw Heintz, Polk Community College; Franklin Horowitz, Columbia University Teachers College; Wanda R. Larrier, Rowan College of New Jersey; Joan Latchaw, North Dakota State University; Mary McGann, University of Indianapolis; Rita M. Mignacca, SUNY College at Brockport; Mark Newman, Scott Community College; Troy D. Nordman, Butler County Community College; Penny Shively, Edmonds Community College; Rod Siegfried, American River College; Isara Kelley Tyson, Manatee Community College; Wanda Van Goor, Prince George's Community College; and Susan H. Young, LaGuardia Community College.

We also thank the following teachers for their suggestions and for field-testing our lessons in their classes: Cheryl Elsmore, Antelope Valley College; Susan Moore, Scottsdale Community College; Isara Kelley Tyson, Manatee Community College; and Susan H. Young, LaGuardia Community College.

In addition, we thank the following teachers for responding to a questionnaire that allowed us to develop our book: Gwendolyn Anderson-Walitho, Delaware County Community College; Jo Ann Buck, Guilford Technical Community College; Nancy Carriuolo, University of New Haven; Lisa Ede, Oregon State University; Toni Empringham, El Camino College; Judy A. Harris, Rochester Community College; Michael Mackey, Community College of Denver; John A. Marsyla, Inver Hills Community College; Susan Miller, University of Utah; Guy Nishimoto, Kapiolani Community College; Maureen Hogan O'Brien, Springfield Technical Community College; Nell Ann Pickett, Hinds Community College; Lawrence D. Thompson, Kingsborough Community College; and Carol Wershoven, Palm Beach Community College.

We extend special thanks to the people at St. Martin's Press for their significant contributions to the planning, drafting, and revising of this book. In particular, we thank Barbara A. Heinssen, executive editor; Sylvia L. Weber, development editor; Anne Dempsey, associate development editor; Diana M. Puglisi, project editor; Lucy Krikorian, art director; and Scott Lavelle, production supervisor.

Finally, we wish to thank our wives, Colleen Beason and Mary Ann Lester, for their unwavering support and patience.

Larry Beason
Mark Lester

Guide to Grammar Terminology

This guide is an alphabetical listing of all the grammar terms used in this book. Each term is defined with an example. For some grammar terms, there are also helpful hints and suggestions. Anytime you encounter a grammar term you are not 100 percent sure about, look it up in this guide.

> NOTE: Examples of the term being defined are in ***bold italic*** type. References to important related terms are underlined. Ungrammatical phrases or sentences are indicated by an **✗**.

Active The term *active* or *active voice* refers to sentences in which the subject plays the role of the actor, or the "doer" of the action, as opposed to passive sentences, in which the subject is the person or thing *receiving* the action of the verb. For example, in the active sentence ***Sandy saw Pat,*** the subject *Sandy* is doing the seeing, whereas in the corresponding passive sentence *Pat was seen by Sandy*, *Pat* is the person being seen. Also see passive.

Adjective Adjectives play two different roles: (1) they modify the nouns that they precede (a ***young*** *tree*); or (2) after certain verbs like *be*, *seem*, and *become*, adjectives describe the subject of the sentence. For example, in the sentence *The tree is* ***green***, the adjective *green* describes the subject *tree.* Also see article and proper adjective.

Adjective clause An adjective clause (also called a relative clause) always modifies the noun it follows. In the sentence *The tree* ***that we planted*** *is getting leaves*, the adjective clause *that we planted* modifies the noun *tree.* An adjective clause begins with a relative pronoun (*that* in the example sentence is a relative pronoun). There are two types of adjective clauses. Depending on the relation of the adjective clause to the noun it modifies, the clause is either a restrictive adjective clause or a nonrestrictive adjective clause.

Adverb An adverb modifies a verb (*walked* ***briskly***), an adjective (***pretty*** *tall*), another adverb (***very*** *badly*), or a sentence (***Truthfully***, *I do not know the answer*). Adverbs that modify verbs give *when*, *where*, *why*, and *how* information. Such adverbs normally occur at the end of a sentence, but can usually be moved to the beginning; for example: *I got a ticket* ***yesterday***. ***Yesterday****, I got a ticket.* An adverb prepositional phrase or an adverb clause also modifies a verb and may move to the beginning of the sentence.

Adverb clause An adverb clause modifies a verb, giving *when*, *where*, *why*, or *how* information. Adverb clauses are easily moved to the beginning of the main clause from their normal position after the main clause; for example: *I was at the office* ***when you called. When you called****, I was at the office.*

Agreement Some words in a sentence are so closely related that the shape of one determines the shape of another. When such words are correctly chosen in relation to one another, they are in *agreement*. A pronoun should agree with its antecedent in terms of gender and number (*The* ***boy*** *ate* ***his*** *food*), and a subject should agree with its verb in terms of number (***He was*** *hungry*). Also see subject-verb agreement.

Antecedent See pronoun antecedent.

Appositive An appositive is a noun (or a noun and its modifiers) that renames (further identifies) a preceding noun. For example, in *My English teacher,* ***Ms. Smith****, also teaches Spanish, Ms. Smith* is an appositive that renames (further identifies) the noun *teacher*. Usually, two commas set off the appositive from the rest of the sentence, as in the example here.

Article Articles are a special kind of adjective that come before all other types of adjectives. For example, in the phrase ***the*** *tall trees*, the article *the* must come before the adjective *tall*; that is, we cannot say ✘ *tall the trees*. There are two types of articles: definite (*the*) and indefinite (*a* and *an*).

Clause A clause contains at least one subject and one verb. A clause that stands alone as a complete thought is called an independent clause or a main clause. All sentences must contain at least one main clause. For types of clauses that cannot stand alone, see dependent clause.

Comma splice A comma splice is the incorrect use of a comma to join two sentences or two independent clauses (✘ *Angela answered the phone, she was the only person in the office*). Also see fused sentence and run-on sentence.

Common noun A common noun refers to categories of people, places, things, and ideas—as opposed to a proper noun, which names particular individual people or places. For example, *reporter* is a common noun, but *Lois Lane* is a proper noun. Common nouns can be identified by their use of the definite article *the*. For example, *replace* and *replacement* are related words, but you can tell that *replacement* is a common noun because you can say *the replacement*. *Replace* is not a common noun, because you cannot say ✘ *the replace*.

Complete sentence A complete sentence is an independent clause that can be correctly punctuated with a terminal punctuation mark: a period, a question mark, or an exclamation point. The opposite of a complete sentence is a fragment, which is only part of a sentence and which cannot be punctuated correctly with a terminal punctuation mark.

Compound A compound consists of two or more grammatical units of the same type that are joined by a coordinating conjunction. For example, in the sentence ***Thelma and Louise*** *went for a trip*, the phrase *Thelma and Louise* is a compound subject.

Compound sentence When two or more sentences (independent clauses) are combined into one, the result is a compound sentence. A compound sentence is usually created by inserting a coordinating conjunction between the two "former" sentences, as in *I left the party early,* ***but*** *Angie refused to leave.*

Conjunction The term *conjunction* means "join together." Conjunctions are words that join grammatical elements together. There are two types of conjunctions: (1) coordinating conjunctions—words like *and*, *but*, and *or*; and (2) subordinating conjunctions—words like *when*, *since*, *because*, and *if*, which begin adverb clauses.

Conjunctive adverb A conjunctive adverb shows how the meaning of a second sentence is related to the meaning of the first sentence. For example, in the pair of sentences *I had planned to leave at noon.* ***However,*** *my flight was delayed*, the conjunctive adverb *however* signals to the reader that the second sentence will contradict the first sentence in some way. Some other conjunctive adverbs are *nevertheless*, *moreover*, and *therefore*.

Contraction A contraction is the shortened form of a word that results from leaving out some letters or sounds. In writing, the missing letters in contractions are indicated by an apostrophe ('); for example, *I'll* is the contracted form of *I will*. This use of the apostrophe in contractions is different from its use to indicate possession; see possessive apostrophe.

Coordinating conjunction A coordinating conjunction joins grammatical units of the same type, creating a compound. There are seven coordinating conjunctions, which can be remembered by the acronym *FANBOYS: for, and, nor, but, or, yet, so.*

Count noun A count noun is a common noun that can be counted: ***one cat/two cats.*** Nouns that have irregular plural forms—such as *one child/two children, one goose/two geese,* and *one deer/two deer*—are also count nouns. For nouns that cannot be counted, see noncount noun.

Dangling modifier A dangling modifier is a noun modifier (usually a participial phrase) that does not actually modify the noun that it is intended to modify. The modifier is said to be "dangling" because the noun it is supposed to modify is not in the sentence. For example, in the sentence ***Based on the evidence,*** *the jury acquitted the defendant,* the phrase *based on the evidence* is a dangling modifier because it does not really modify *jury.* (You cannot say that *the jury was based on the evidence.*) Also see misplaced modifier.

Definite article The definite article is *the*, which can be used either with a singular or with a plural common noun. Use the definite article when referring to a specific object or thing that is also known to the reader or listener. For example, in the sentence *Please hand me the cup,* you can assume that the speaker is referring to a specific cup which the reader or hearer can also identify. When not referring to anything specific, or when referring to something that is *not* known to the listener, use an indefinite article: *a* or *an.*

Dependent clause A dependent clause is a clause that cannot be used as a complete sentence by itself, as opposed to an independent clause, which can stand alone. There are three types of dependent clauses: (1) an adjective clause modifies a noun (*I read the book* ***that you recommended***); (2) an adverb clause modifies a verb (*I was in the shower* ***when the telephone rang***); and (3) a noun clause plays the role of subject or object (***What you see*** *is* ***what you get***). A dependent clause is also called a subordinate clause.

Direct quotation A direct quotation uses quotation marks (" ") to show the reader that the words inside the marks are *exactly* what the person said or wrote; for example: *Tina said, "I know where we can borrow a flügelhorn."* The opposite of a direct quotation is an indirect quotation, which does not use quotation marks, as in the following sentence: *Tina said that she knew where they could borrow a flügelhorn.*

Faulty parallelism The term *faulty parallelism* refers to a series of two or more grammatical elements in which not all the elements are in the same grammatical form. For example, the sentence ✗ *Senator Deadlock is* ***loud, pompous,*** *a* ***fraud,*** *and* ***talks too much*** presents a series of four elements, but there is faulty parallelism because the first two elements (*loud* and *pompous*) are adjectives; the third element (*fraud*) is a noun; and the fourth element (*talks too much*) is a verb phrase.

Fragment A fragment is only part of a sentence that is punctuated as though it were a complete sentence. Typically, fragments are pieces cut off from the preceding sentence; for example: *The computer lost my paper.* ✗ ***Which I had worked on all night.*** One way to recognize a fragment is to test it with the yes-no question. A complete sentence can always be turned into a question that can be answered "yes" or "no," but a fragment can never be. Thus, the first example sentence can be turned into the yes-no question *Did the computer lose my paper?*

But there is no yes-no question that corresponds to the fragment ✘ *Which I had worked on all night.*

Fused sentence A fused sentence is a type of run-on sentence in which two complete sentences (or independent clauses) are joined together without any mark of punctuation. ✘ *My brother caught a cold he has been out of school for a week* is an example of a fused sentence because it consists of two complete sentences (*My brother caught a cold* and *He has been out of school for a week*) that are joined without proper punctuation. A comma splice is a similar type of error that incorrectly joins complete sentences with only a comma.

Gender Certain third-person personal pronouns are marked for gender: *she, her,* and *hers* refer to females; *he, him*, and *his* refer to males. The third-person plural pronouns *they* and *them* are not marked for gender; that is, these pronouns can refer to males, females, or both. *They* and *them* are sometimes called "gender-neutral" or "gender-exclusive" pronouns. The third-person singular pronoun *it* refers to things that do not have gender, such as concrete objects and abstractions; so do the third-person plural pronouns *they, them,* and *their.*

Gerund A gerund is the *-ing* form of a verb (the present participle) that is used as a noun. For example, in the sentence *I like* ***taking*** *the bus to work, taking* is the gerund. The term *gerund* can also refer to the *-ing* verb together with all the words that go with it (in what is technically called a *gerund phrase*). In the example sentence, the whole phrase ***taking the bus to work*** is a gerund phrase.

Helping verb When two or more verbs are used together in a string, the last verb in the sequence is called the main verb. All the other verbs that come before the main verb are called *helping verbs.* For example, in the sentence *We* ***should have been*** *tuning our flügelhorn,* the last verb (*tuning*) is the main verb, and all the preceding verbs (*should have been*) are the helping verbs. The first helping verb in the sequence is the only verb that agrees with the subject. The most important helping verbs are *be* and *have* (in all their different forms), plus *can, could, may, might, must, shall, should, will,* and *would.*

Indefinite article Indefinite articles appear in two forms, depending on the initial sound of the following word: *a* is used before words beginning with a consonant sound (***a*** *yellow banana*), and *an* is used before words beginning with a vowel sound (***an*** *old banana*). An indefinite article is used when mentioning something that the reader or listener does not already know about; after that point, use the definite article *the.* For example: *I bought* ***an*** *Apple computer.* ***The*** *computer has* ***a*** *built-in modem.* ***The*** *modem is connected to my telephone line.*

Independent clause An independent clause (also called a main clause) can always stand alone as a complete sentence. Every sentence must contain at least one independent clause. One way to recognize independent clauses is by turning them into questions answered by "yes" or "no." For example, the yes-no question for the independent clause *This is the beginning of a beautiful friendship* is *Is this the beginning of a beautiful friendship?* Also see yes-no question.

Indirect quotation An indirect quotation is a paraphrase of the writer or speaker's actual, verbatim words. For example, if Mr. Lopez said, "We are going to Florida tomorrow," the indirect quotation might be the following: *He said that he and his family were going to Florida the next day.* One of the distinctive features of indirect quotation is the use of *that* before the paraphrase of the writer or speaker's words. Also notice that, unlike direct quotation, an indirect quotation uses no quotation marks.

Infinitive An infinitive is the form of a verb as it appears in the dictionary. For example, the infinitive form of *is, am, was,* and *were* is *be.* Like the *-ing* present participle form of verbs (gerunds), infinitives are often used as nouns. When serving as nouns, infinitives almost always are used with *to*; for example, *I like **to eat** pizza with my fingers.* As with gerunds, the term *infinitive* can also be used more broadly to include both the infinitive and the words that go with it (together called an *infinitive phrase*). In this broader sense, the infinitive in the example sentence is ***to eat pizza with my fingers.***

Introductory element An introductory element is any kind of word, phrase, or clause that has been placed at the beginning of a sentence rather than in its expected position in the middle or at the end of the sentence. Introductory elements are usually set off from the rest of the sentence by a comma (especially if the introductory element is a phrase or a clause); for example: ***Feeling a little down***, *Scrooge left the party early.*

Main clause See independent clause.

Main verb The main verb is the rightmost verb in a string of verbs. All the verbs that precede the main verb are helping verbs. For example, in the sentence *Cinderella must have **eaten** all the chilidogs,* the main verb is *eaten.* The other two verbs (*must* and *have*) are helping verbs.

Mass noun See noncount noun.

Misplaced modifier A misplaced modifier is any type of modifier that has been placed so far away from the word it modifies that it appears to modify the wrong word. For example, in the sentence *I saw the car at the station **with the flat tire,*** the modifier *with the flat tire* appears to modify *station.* When the modifier is placed next to the word it modifies, the problem disappears: *I saw the car **with the flat tire** at the station.*

Noncount noun A noncount noun (also called a mass noun) is a common noun that cannot be used in the plural or with number words (✗ *one homework/*

✗ *two homeworks*; ✗ *one dirt*/✗ *two dirts*). A noun that can be used in the plural and with number words is called a count noun.

Nonrestrictive adjective clause Every adjective clause modifies a noun, but different types of adjective clauses have different relations with the nouns they modify. Nonrestrictive clauses do not narrow or limit the meaning of the nouns they modify. Like appositives, nonrestrictive clauses rename the nouns they modify, and, like appositives, they are always set off with commas. For example, in the sentence *My mother,* ***who was born in Tonga,*** *came to the United States as a child,* the relative clause *who was born in Tonga* is nonrestrictive because it does not narrow or limit the meaning of *my mother.* My mother is my mother no matter where she was born. A clause that defines or limits the meaning of the noun it modifies is called a restrictive adjective clause.

Noun Nouns are names of people, places, things, and ideas. A noun that refers to categories (*teacher, city*) is a common noun; a noun that refers to actual individual persons or places (*Mr. Smith, Chicago*) is a proper noun. See also count noun and noncount noun.

Noun clause A noun clause is a group of words that work together to function as a noun, as in ***Whether you go or not*** *is up to you.* If you look at the noun clause by itself, you will always find a word acting like a subject and a word serving as its verb. In the example above, *you* is acting like a subject, and *go* is its verb.

Object When a noun or a pronoun follows certain verbs or any preposition, it is called an *object.* For example, in the sentence *Kermit kissed* ***Miss Piggy,*** the object of the verb *kissed* is *Miss Piggy.* Most pronouns have distinct object forms. Thus, to replace *Miss Piggy* with a pronoun in the example sentence, we would have to use the object form *her* rather than the subject form *she*: *Kermit kissed* ***her.*** Prepositional phrases consist of prepositions and their objects. For example, in the prepositional phrase *on the* ***ladder***, the object of the preposition *on* is the noun *ladder.*

Parallelism The term *parallelism* refers to a series of two or more elements of the same grammatical type, usually joined by a coordinating conjunction. For example, in the sentence *I love* ***to eat, to drink,*** *and* ***to dance*** *the polka,* there are three parallel forms—all infinitives: *to eat, to drink,* and *to dance.* Failure to express parallel elements in the same grammatical form is called faulty parallelism.

Paraphrase To *paraphrase* means to rephrase something in a different grammatical form or with different wording while keeping the meaning of the original. For example, the passive sentence *I was given a present by Mary* is a paraphrase of the corresponding active sentence *Mary gave me a present.* Paraphrase is common in indirect quotation.

Participle Participles are verb forms. There are two types of participles: (1) present participles (the *-ing* form of verbs such as *seeing*, *doing*, and *having*); and (2) past participles (for example, *seen*, *done*, and *had*). Both types of participles can be used as verbs (following certain helping verbs). For example, in the sentence *Senator Deadlock is **watching** the movie*, the word *watching* is in the present participle form. In the sentence *Senator Deadlock has **watched** the movie*, the word *watched* is in the past participle form.

Both present participles and past participles can also be used as adjectives. For example, in the saying *A **watched** pot never boils*, the past participle *watched* functions as an adjective modifying the noun *pot*.

Passive The term *passive* or *passive* voice describes sentences in which the subject is not the "doer" of the action but instead *receives* the action of the verb. For example, in the passive sentence *Sandy **was seen** by Pat*, the subject *Sandy* is not the person doing the seeing but instead is the person being seen. The passive voice can always be recognized by a unique sequence of verbs: the helping verb *be* (in some form) followed by a past participle verb form. In the example above, *was* is the past tense form of *be*, and *seen* is the past participle form of *see*. Sentences that are not in the passive voice are said to be in the active voice.

Past participle Past participle verb forms are used in the perfect tenses after the helping verb *have* (as in *Thelma has **seen** that movie*) or after the helping verb *be* in passive sentences (*That movie was **seen** by Thelma*). The past participle form of most verbs ends in *-ed*—as do most past tense forms of most verbs. How, then, can we tell a past participle from a past tense? The difference is that the past participle form of a verb always follows a helping verb. For example, in the sentence *Thelma has **loved** the movies*, *loved* is a past participle because it follows the helping verb *has*. In the sentence *Thelma **loved** the movies*, however, *loved* is a past tense verb because it does *not* follow a helping verb. Past participles can also be used as adjectives (*The car **seen** in that commercial belongs to my uncle*).

Past tense The past tense is used to describe an action that took place at some past time; for example, *Carlos **borrowed** my car last night*. For regular verbs, the past tense form ends in *-ed*. However, there are a large number of irregular verbs that form their past tense in different ways. The most unusual past tense is found in the verb *be*, which has two past tense forms: *was* in the singular and *were* in the plural.

Perfect tenses The perfect tenses refer to action that takes place over a period of time or is frequently repeated. There are three perfect tenses: (1) present perfect (*Louise **has seen** Thelma twice this week*); (2) past perfect (*Louise **had seen** Thelma two times last week*); and (3) future perfect (*Louise **will have seen** Thelma twice by Friday*). Notice that all the perfect tenses use *have* (in some form) as a helping verb, followed by a verb in the past participle form (*seen*, in all these examples).

Personal pronoun There are three sets of personal pronouns: (1) first-person pronouns refer to the speaker (*I, me, mine; we, us, ours*); (2) second-person pronouns refer to the hearer (*you, yours*); and (3) third-person pronouns refer to another person or thing (*he, him, his, she, her, hers, it, its; they, them, theirs*). A personal pronoun can also be categorized by the role it plays in a sentence: subject (*I, we, you, he, she, it, they*) or object (*me, us, you, him, her, them*).

Phrase In grammatical terminology, a *phrase* is a group of related words that act as a single part of speech. The most common type is the prepositional phrase. For example, in the sentence *Kermit kissed Miss Piggy* ***on the balcony***, the prepositional phrase is *on the balcony,* here acting as an adverb.

Plural Referring to more than one. Plural nouns are usually formed by adding *-s* to the singular form of the noun. *Also see* agreement; subject-verb agreement.

Possessive apostrophe Possessive nouns (***John's*** *book*) and possessive indefinite pronouns (***one's*** *ideas,* ***somebody's*** *book,* ***anybody's*** *guess*) are spelled with an apostrophe (') to show that the *-s* added at the end of the word is a "possessive *-s*," as opposed to a "plural *-s*." When an *-s* at the end of a word is both possessive *and* plural, the apostrophe goes after the *-s* (*The* ***girls'*** *dresses*). This use of the apostrophe to indicate possession is different from its use to indicate a contraction.

Preposition Prepositions are such words as *on, by, with, of, in, from, between,* and *to.* A preposition is used with a noun or a pronoun object to make a prepositional phrase. Certain prepositions (sometimes called *particles*) can be combined with verbs to create new verbs. For example, in the sentence *John should* ***give up***, the combination of the verb *give* with the preposition (or particle) *up* creates a new verb: *give up*, which means "surrender." New verbs created in this manner are sometimes called *two-word verbs.*

Prepositional phrase A prepositional phrase is a phrase consisting of a preposition and its object; for example: *on the beach, at noon, by Shakespeare.* Prepositional phrases function as adverbs or adjectives. For example, in the sentence *I got a message* ***at my office***, the prepositional phrase *at my office* functions as an adverb telling where I got the message. In the sentence *The chair* ***at my office*** *is not very comfortable*, the prepositional phrase *at my office* is an adjective modifying *chair.*

Present participle Present participle verb forms are used in the progressive tenses after the helping verb *be*, in some form. For example, in the sentence *Thelma and Louise were* ***practicing*** *their duets, were* is a form of the helping verb *be*, and *practicing* is in the present participle form. The present participle form is completely regular because it always ends in *-ing*; for example: *doing, being, seeing, helping*. Present participles can also be used as adjectives (*The car* ***turning*** *at the signal is a Buick*) or as nouns (***Seeing*** *is* ***believing***).

Present tense Despite its name, the most common use of the present tense is not to describe present time but, rather, timeless generalizations (*The earth* ***is*** *round*) or habitual, repeated actions (*I always* ***shop*** *on Saturdays*).

Present tense verb forms have an added *-s* when the subject is a third-person singular pronoun (*he*, *she*, or *it*) or when the subject is a noun that can be replaced with a third-person pronoun. See subject-verb agreement.

Progressive tenses Progressive tenses are used to refer to actions that are ongoing at the time of the sentence—as opposed to the present tense, which is essentially timeless. The term *progressive* refers to three related verb constructions that employ *be* (in some form) as a helping verb. If *be* is in the present tense (*am*, *is*, *are*), then the construction is called the *present progressive*; for example: *Thelma* ***is visiting*** *Louise now*. If *be* is in the past tense (*was*, *were*), then the construction is called the *past progressive*; for example: *Thelma* ***was visiting*** *Louise last week*. If *be* is used in the future (*will be*), then the construction is called the *future progressive*; for example: *Thelma* ***will be visiting*** *Louise next week*.

Pronoun A pronoun can replace a noun either as a subject or as an object. Among the many different types of pronouns, the most important is the personal pronoun. Also discussed in this book is the relative pronoun, which is the kind that begins an adjective clause. Also see gender, pronoun antecedent, and vague pronoun.

Pronoun antecedent Many pronouns refer back to a person or persons or to a thing or things mentioned earlier in the sentence or even in a previous sentence. For example, in the sentences *My* ***aunts*** *live next door.* ***They*** *are my mother's sisters*, the antecedent of the pronoun *they* is *aunts*. When a pronoun might refer to more than one antecedent, it is said to exhibit "ambiguous pronoun reference." For example, in the sentence *Aunt Sadie asked Mother where* ***her*** *keys were*, the pronoun *her* is ambiguous because it might refer either to Aunt Sadie or to Mother. A pronoun that has no real antecedent is called a vague pronoun. For example, in the sentence ***They*** *shouldn't allow smoking in restaurants*, the pronoun *they* is vague because it does not have any actual antecedent—it does not refer to any identified individuals.

Pronoun-antecedent agreement See agreement.

Proper adjective A proper adjective is derived from a proper noun. For example, the adjective *Jamaican* in ***Jamaican*** *coffee* is the adjective form of the proper noun *Jamaica*. Proper adjectives are always capitalized.

Proper noun Proper nouns are the names of specific individual persons, titles, or places. Proper nouns are always capitalized; for example: *Queen Elizabeth*, *Harry Truman*, *New York Times*, *Vancouver*. When a noun refers to a category rather than to a specific individual, it is called a common noun.

Quotation There are two types of quotation: (1) direct quotation, which uses quotation marks to report exactly what someone said, with word-for-word accuracy; and (2) indirect quotation, which paraphrases what a person said without using the writer or speaker's exact words. Indirect quotations are not set within quotation marks.

Relative clause See adjective clause.

Relative pronoun A relative pronoun begins an adjective clause. The relative pronouns are *who*, *whom*, *whose*, *which*, and *that*. Relative pronouns must refer to the noun in the independent clause that the adjective clause modifies. For example, in the sentence *I got an offer* ***that*** *I can't refuse*, the relative pronoun *that* refers to *offer*. The relative pronouns *who*, *whom*, and *whose* are used to refer to people. For example, in the sentence *He is a man* ***whom*** *you can rely on*, the relative pronoun *whom* refers to *man*. Using *that* to refer to people is incorrect in formal writing; for example: ✘ *He is a man* ***that*** *you can rely on*.

Restrictive adjective clause Every adjective clause (also called a relative clause) modifies a noun, but different types of adjective clauses have different relations with the nouns they modify. Restrictive adjective clauses narrow or limit the meaning of the nouns they modify. For example, in the sentence *All students* ***who miss the test*** *will fail the course*, the adjective clause *who miss the test* narrows or limits the meaning of the noun *students*. The students who are threatened with failure are only the ones who miss the test. Since restrictive adjective clauses "restrict" the meaning of the nouns they modify, these adjective clauses are never separated from their nouns by commas. A clause that does *NOT* define or limit the meaning of the noun it modifies is called a nonrestrictive adjective clause.

Run-on sentence A run-on sentence consists of two sentences or more (independent clauses) that are joined together without adequate punctuation. Joining two sentences together with only a comma is called a comma splice. Joining two sentences together with no punctuation at all is called a fused sentence.

Sentence A sentence consists of at least one independent clause (with or without an accompanying dependent clause) that is punctuated with a period, an exclamation point, or a question mark.

Sexist language Language that stereotypes, demeans, or unfairly excludes men or women is referred to as sexist language. One of the most common forms is the sexist or gender-exclusive use of pronouns. In this example, notice how it appears that only men vote: *Everybody should vote for* ***his*** *favorite candidate for governor.*

Singular Referring to one. Also see agreement; subject-verb agreement.

Subject The subject of a sentence is the doer of the action or what the sentence is about. The term *subject* has two slightly different meanings: (1) the *simple subject* is the noun or pronoun that is the doer or the topic of the sentence, and (2) the *complete subject* is the simple subject together with all its modifiers. For example, in the sentence *The book on the shelf belongs to my cousin*, the simple subject is *book*, and the complete subject is *the book on the shelf.*

Subject-verb agreement This term refers to the matching of the number of a present tense verb (or a present tense helping verb if there is more than one verb) with the number of the subject of that verb. Following are three examples with different subjects: (1) *Aunt Sadie* ***lives*** *in Denver.* (2) *My aunts* ***live*** *in Denver.* (3) *Aunt Sadie and Uncle Albert* ***live*** *in Denver.*

If the subject is a third-person singular personal pronoun (*he, she, it*) *or* if the subject is a noun that can be replaced by a third-person singular personal pronoun (as is the case with *Aunt Sadie* in example 1), then it is necessary to add an *-s* (called the *third-person singular -s*) to the present tense verb.

If the subject *cannot* be replaced by a third-person singular pronoun (as is the case in examples 2 and 3), do *not* add the third-person singular *-s* to the present tense.

Only the verb *be* has past tense forms that change to agree with the subject: *was* is used with first-person singular and third-person singular subjects (*I* ***was*** *in Denver; Aunt Sadie* ***was*** *in Denver*); and *were* is used with all other subjects (*My aunts* ***were*** *in Denver*).

Subordinate clause See dependent clause.

Tense The term *tense* is used in two quite different ways. (1) It can refer to the *time* in which the action of the sentence takes place: present time, past time, and future time. (2) Usually in this book, however, the term is used in a narrower, more technical sense to mean just the *form* of the verb. In this limited sense, the term refers either to the present tense form of a verb (***see*** and ***sees***, for example) or to its past tense form (***saw***). There is no separate future tense form in English; we can talk about future time by using the helping verb *will.*

Tense shifting Tense shifting occurs in a piece of writing when the author shifts from one tense to another—usually from past tense to present tense or vice versa. For example, in the sentence *We* ***ate*** *at the restaurant that* ***is*** *on the pier*, the first verb (*ate*) is in the past tense, while the second verb (*is*) is in the present tense. In this particular sentence, the shifting from past tense to present tense is appropriate; sometimes, however, writers confuse readers by incorrectly shifting tenses when there is no reason to do so.

Transitional term See conjunctive adverb.

Vague pronoun A pronoun must have an antecedent to make its meaning clear. A vague pronoun is one that does not seem to refer to anything or anyone in particular. For example, in the sentence ***They*** *should do something about these* *terrible roads*, the pronoun *they* is a vague pronoun because it could refer to anybody—the highway department, the police, the government.

Verb A verb tells about an action in a sentence (*Alfy* ***sneezed***) or describes the subject of the sentence (*Alfy* ***seemed*** *angry*). Only verbs can change form to show tense. That is, only verbs have present tense and past tense forms. A simple test to see whether a word is a verb is to see whether you can change it into a past tense by adding *-ed* to it.

Voice *Voice* is a technical term in grammar that refers to the relation of the subject of a sentence to the verb. If the subject is the "doer" of the action of the verb, as in the sentence ***Thelma*** *wrecked the car*, then the sentence is said to be in the active voice. However, if the subject is the recipient of the action of the verb, as in the sentence *The* ***car*** *was wrecked by Thelma*, then the sentence is said to be in the passive voice.

Yes-no question Yes-no questions do not ask for answers that involve *when, where, why,* or other information; instead, they must be answered with a "yes" or a "no"; for example: *Can you dance? Am I right? Do you know the answer?* Yes-no questions are particularly useful in identifying sentences (or independent clauses) because only sentences can be turned into yes-no questions. A fragment or a dependent clause cannot be turned into a yes-no question because it is not a complete sentence.

FRAG
FS

UNIT ONE
Sentence Basics

OVERVIEW

Terms That Can Help You Understand Sentence Basics

If you are not familiar with any of the following terms that appear in this unit, look them up in the Guide to Grammar Terminology beginning on page 1. The numbers in parentheses indicate the lessons in which each term appears.

complete sentence (1, 2)
compound sentence (2)
fragment (1)
fused sentence (2)
main clause (1)
subject (1)
subordinate clause (1)
verb (1)
yes-no question (1)

The Nuts and Bolts of Sentence Basics

We have devoted this unit to just two concepts because they provide the foundation for understanding at least half the errors covered in this text.

1. The first—and most important—of these concepts is the notion of a complete sentence. A **complete sentence** can stand alone to express a thought, and it consists of at least one subject and one verb.

subject + verb
EXAMPLE: **Judy fell.**

The opposite of a complete sentence is a **fragment**—a group of words that cannot stand alone (see Lesson 1). Even though some fragments have a subject and a verb, they still cannot stand alone. For example, the underlined words in the following example create a fragment; the word *which* makes it essential to put the entire statement into the preceding sentence.

FRAGMENT: **Celeste found a cat. ✘ Which she took home.**

CORRECTION: **Celeste found a cat, which she took home.**

2. The second major concept of this unit is that of combining one sentence with another. One way to combine sentences is simply to link them using a comma plus *and*, *but*, or *or*.

EXAMPLE: **Judy fell, but she seemed OK.**

Although there are many ways to combine sentences, the writer does not have the option of simply putting sentences together without anything between them. In the preceding example, for instance, you should not omit the word *but* or the comma right before it. Doing so would create an error known as a **fused sentence** (see Lesson 2). Also see Lessons 3 and 4 in Unit Two for more information about combining sentences.

Can You Detect Problems Involving Sentence Basics?

(Corrected sentences appear on page 297.)

Correct all errors in the following paragraphs using the first correction as a model. The number in parentheses at the end of each paragraph indicates how many errors you should find.

One of the highest honors that can be given in the movie industry is an Academy Award. ~~Which~~ [, which] is more commonly known as an Oscar. Winning just one Oscar is a notable feat. A few movies, however, are exceptional they have won several Oscars. Four of the most important Oscars are for best actress, best actor, best director, and best picture. Only a few movies have won even three of these four awards. In 1982, *Gandhi* received Oscars for best actor, best director, and best picture. Two years later, *Amadeus* won the same awards the best actress Oscar went to Sally Field for her role in *Places in the Heart*. In 1988, *Rain Man* captured the same three Oscars. While the best actress award went to Jody Foster for her role in *The Accused*. (3)

Some movies have done even better with the Academy Awards. Back in 1975, *One Flew over the Cuckoo's Nest* won all four of these Oscars. A movie that also helped propel actor Jack Nicholson to fame. The first movie to win all four was *It Happened One Night*. Which won awards back in 1934. (2)

FRAG

LESSON 1
Fragments

Sample Errors

In both examples, fragments have an ✘ *in front* of them.

SAMPLE 1: **I entered my apartment and saw an unexpected guest. ✘ A cat in the middle of my living room.**

SAMPLE 2: **Philip is unhappy. ✘ Because his window was broken last night.**

What's the Problem?

A **fragment** is a group of words that cannot stand alone as a **complete sentence**. That is, a fragment is *not* a **main clause**. (A main clause is a group of words that can be written as a complete sentence.)

Often, the fragment exists because it lacks either a **subject** or a **verb**. In English, both a subject and a verb are needed for a complete sentence. Sample 1 has no verb (the cat isn't *doing* anything).

At other times, the fragment has both a subject and a verb, but the fragment is what we call a **subordinate clause** (as with the statement beginning with *Because* in Sample 2). A subordinate clause cannot stand alone; it depends on something else to be grammatically complete.

What Causes the Problem?

A common reason for making a fragment error is that the fragment is really part of the sentence that comes *right before* the fragment. Writers often sense a "pause" when thinking about how a sentence will sound when it is read aloud. This pause *sometimes* means that a new sentence is coming up.

With a fragment, however, this pause is misleading. *Perhaps* a comma is needed to indicate a pause, but a fragment cannot stand alone as a complete sentence.

Diagnostic Exercise **(Corrected sentences appear on page 297.)**

Correct all errors in the following paragraph using the first correction as a model. The number in parentheses at the end of the paragraph indicates how many errors you should find.

My roommate has an annoying habit, leaving ~~habit. Leaving~~ his dirty dishes on the cabinet. I've asked him to at least put them in the sink. Or rinse them off a little. However, he just ignores me. Perhaps I am a little sensitive, but I wish he would clean up after himself. Because it is really embarrassing when friends visit. Or when my parents drop in. I plan to speak to him very soon about this situation. (3)

Fixing This Problem in Your Writing

Some people detect fragments by reading backward, sentence by sentence. They read each sentence in a normal fashion, but they start at the *end* of the paper. We offer two other tips for identifying a fragment. These work best for sentences that are in statement form. They do not work for sentences that are in the form of a question (such as *Did the governor call?*) or a command (such as *Leave me alone!*).

"I REALIZE" TIP: You can put *I realize* in front of most *complete* sentences. The result should be a meaningful and complete sentence. The statement will not change meaning—except that it claims that you realize something. If you can't put *I realize* in front of the group of words, it is probably a fragment.

The *I Realize* Tip is easy to use, but it may not work if a sentence begins with introductory words (such as *Therefore, I left.*).

YES/NO TIP: Turn the sentence into a **yes-no question**. You can turn a *complete* sentence into a question that can be answered with "yes" or "no." Sometimes, you must add *do, does,* or *did,* but a complete sentence can be turned into a question without adding other words. You *cannot* do so with fragments.

A fragment can be corrected in various ways, but the following strategy will work for most fragments.

CORRECTION STRATEGY: **You might be able to combine the fragment with a nearby sentence, usually with the sentence immediately before it. Avoid inserting a comma between the two word groups unless you know why it should go there.**

SAMPLE 2: **Philip is unhappy. ✗ Because his window was broken last night.**

CORRECTION: **Philip is unhappy because his window was broken last night.**

For Example . . .

If you put *I realize* before a fragment, the resulting statement doesn't make sense:

SAMPLE 1: **I entered my apartment and saw an unexpected guest. ✗ A cat in the middle of my living room.**

TIP APPLIED: **I realize I entered my apartment and saw an unexpected guest. ✗ I realize a cat in the middle of my living room.**

The *Yes/No* Tip shows that the following sentence is *complete*:

COMPLETE SENTENCE: **I entered my apartment and saw an unexpected guest.**

TIP APPLIED: **Did I enter my apartment and see an unexpected guest?**

We added *did* and altered the form of a couple of words, but no major changes were needed. However, the *Yes/No* Tip cannot be applied to the fragment.

TIP APPLIED: **✗ Did a cat in the middle of my living room?**

Now You Try It, 1 **(Corrected sentences appear on page 297.)**

Find the fragments by using the *I Realize* Tip. Write *OK* above each complete sentence and *frag* above each fragment. Correct the fragment by combining it with the complete sentence next to it. *Hint:* In each pair, at least one word group is a complete sentence.

I realize OK I realize because frag

EXAMPLE: **I started a poem but couldn't finish. ~~Because~~ I ran out of ideas.**

1. We heard a noise. A loud, frightful noise.

2. The bull charged. What happened next is too horrible to tell.

3. A river runs through San Antonio. A peaceful, beautiful river.

4. Hearing the hunter approach. Bambi fled.

5. The dam broke. Millions of gallons of water flooded the valley.

Now You Try It, 2 **(Corrected sentences appear on page 297.)**

Find the fragments by using the *Yes/No* Tip. Write *OK* above each complete sentence and *frag* above each fragment. Correct the fragment by combining it with the complete sentence next to it. *Hint:* In each pair, at least one word group is a complete sentence.

Did we give up? ✗ Did having lost all confidence?

OK , having frag

EXAMPLE: **We gave up. ~~Having~~ lost all confidence.**

1. A capital offense is a crime punishable by death. A penalty for only the most serious of crimes.

2. Jan told me she plans to become a parapsychologist. Because she really believes a person can communicate with the spirits.

3. I vividly recall January 12, 1995. The day my parents made a surprise visit while I was in the middle of holding a wild party.

4. Our astronomy class took a field trip to Mount Palomar, California. Where one of the world's largest telescopes is located.

5. You should not go to class because you are sick. I can take notes for you.

FRAG

Now You Try It, 3

Find the fragments by using the *Yes/No* Tip. Write *OK* above each complete sentence and *frag* above each fragment. Correct the fragment by combining it with the complete sentence next to it. *Hint:* In each pair, at least one word group is a complete sentence.

Did we play softball? ✗ Was even though it was raining?

OK frag

even

EXAMPLE: **We played softball, ~~Even~~ though it was raining.**

1. Fluoride is found in most drinking water in the United States. Even though many people believe fluoride is a harmful additive.

2. Great Britain dominated most of the Persian Gulf until the late 1960's. When it agreed to relinquish British power in the area.

3. In the last 100 years, the Philippines have been significantly affected by governments of other countries. Including Spain, Japan, and the United States.

4. My parents frequently go to Reno. Where they lose hundreds of dollars in the casinos.

5. Shelly is not feeling well. Perhaps because she ate six Twinkies.

Editing Practice, 1 **(Corrected sentences appear on page 297.)**

Correct all errors in the following paragraph using the first correction as a model. The number in parentheses at the end of the paragraph indicates how many errors you should find.

, especially

Many cities played an important role in the forming of the United States, ~~Especially~~ Philadelphia. Which has some of the nation's most important historical treasures. Most of them found around Independence Mall. The most famous is Independence Hall. Where the Declaration of Independence was signed. The Liberty Bell was, at one time, located there as well, but it was moved. Because it was not very accessible. (4)

Editing Practice, 2 (Corrected sentences appear on page 298.)

Correct all errors in the following paragraphs using the first correction as a model. The number in parentheses at the end of each paragraph indicates how many errors you should find.

Several of Babe Ruth's baseball records have been broken, by ~~By~~ Roger Maris and Hank Aaron, for example. However, Babe may well be the most famous baseball player of all time. Largely because of his personality as much as his baseball playing. He played with an enthusiasm that excited the fans. (1)

Babe's personality frequently made news. Even when his character got him into trouble. In 1922, his behavior resulted in five suspensions, and in 1925 his drinking and quarreling with management resulted in a $5,000 fine. A huge amount at the time for even well-paid players. He gained even more fame, though, when he turned himself around. Hitting a record sixty home runs in 1927. He had a comeback again in the World Series of 1932. After a September attack of what was thought to be appendicitis, he fought back and played all games in the World Series. In which he batted .333. Even in his retirement, he remained a popular favorite and a spokesperson for the game he loved. (4)

Editing Practice, 3

Correct all errors in the following paragraphs using the first correction as a model. The number in parentheses at the end of each paragraph indicates how many errors you should find.

Our college installed a new piece of artwork, a ~~A~~ statue in front of the library. It is a tribute to the men and women who served during the Vietnam War. A war that greatly divided our country. Part of the cost of the sculpture was paid by donations from alumni. And by a grant from a local company. Which has close connections with our school. (3)

It is the policy of our college to encourage the arts by donating space and money for art exhibits and concerts. Such as dance, theater, and music. Some students would prefer the money to be spent on new buildings. Or on cutting back the cost of tuition. I think most students like to see some funding of art. Even if it means cutting back in a few other areas. (3)

Writing Practice

On your own paper, write a paragraph or two describing a work of art (sculpture, photograph, painting, and so on) that you like or dislike. Use the Proofreading Checklist to make sure there are no fragments.

PROOFREADING CHECKLIST

Using Complete Sentences in Your Writing

- Some people detect fragments by reading backward, sentence by sentence. Read each sentence in a normal fashion, but start at the *end* of your paper.
- See whether *I realize* can be placed before any group of words that you have questions about. If it can't go there, then the words may be a fragment.
- Also see whether the group of words can be turned into a yes-no question. You shouldn't have to make any major additions to do so. If the test fails, you probably have a fragment.
- To correct a fragment, try combining it with the sentence immediately before it or after it (or add whatever words are necessary to make it complete). Double-check your correction with one or both of the tests mentioned above.

THE BOTTOM LINE

I realize you can place *I realize* in front of a complete sentence.

LESSON 2
Fused Sentences

Sample Errors

SAMPLE 1: ✗ **Albert left his umbrella on the bus he dropped his gloves on the sidewalk.**

SAMPLE 2: ✗ **Our exam is next week it will be hard.**

What's the Problem?

A **fused sentence** occurs when two **complete sentences** are put together with *nothing* to separate them—no punctuation and no *and*, *but*, or *or*. In other words, the error occurs when a compound sentence has nothing to show where one idea ends and another begins. A **compound sentence** is a sentence that combines what could be at least two separate sentences.

Sample 1 has nothing to separate *Albert left his umbrella on the bus* from *he dropped his gloves on the sidewalk.* Similarly, Sample 2 needs something between *Our exam is next week* and *it will be hard* in order to separate two complete ideas.

What Causes the Problem?

Writers frequently put two complete ideas in one sentence so that readers will see how closely connected the ideas are. This is a useful tactic because it helps readers see connections, creating a nice "flow" to the writer's style.

A fused sentence often occurs when the writer stresses this flow in the wrong way—by leaving out *too much*. That is, a fused sentence does not indicate where one idea ends and another begins.

There must be something to show where one idea joins with another. Otherwise, readers can easily become confused. The writer should follow certain conventions when combining ideas so that readers can clearly see where one idea stops and another starts.

FS

Diagnostic Exercise **(Corrected sentences appear on page 298.)**

Correct all errors in the following paragraph using the first correction as a model. The number in parentheses at the end of the paragraph indicates how many errors you should find.

My friend Miranda is a junior majoring in government ^, and^ she plans to go to law school. Most law schools do not require applicants to major in certain areas, but she's been told that majoring in government helps prepare students for law. Most law schools do require a very high grade-point average and a good score on the law school examination. Her grades are high she has about a 3.8 GPA at present. Still, law schools have high entrance requirements, and she studies more than anyone else I know. She plans to take the law school examination soon she will be studying hard for it as well. (2)

Fixing This Problem in Your Writing

A fused sentence occurs when there is *nothing* to separate two ideas. Here is one way to tell whether a sentence is fused:

IMAGINARY PERIOD TIP: Locate the "vacant" spot in the sentence—the place where one independent idea ends and the next one begins. This spot is also the place needing punctuation and possibly an *and, but,* or *or.* Mentally place an imaginary period in that spot. If you can create *two complete sentences* by doing so, the original sentence is probably a fused sentence.

SAMPLE 1: ✗ **Albert left his umbrella on the bus he dropped his gloves on the sidewalk.**

TIP APPLIED: **Albert left his umbrella on the bus. He dropped his gloves on the sidewalk.**

Following are two ways to correct a fused sentence.

CORRECTION STRATEGY A: **Place a semicolon where you can put the imaginary period (see page 80 about semicolons). For the semicolon to be correct, it *must* separate what could be two separate sentences, as follows:**

CORRECTION: **Albert left his umbrella on the bus; he dropped his gloves on the sidewalk.**

CORRECTION STRATEGY B: **Put a comma and then either *and*, *but*, or *or* where you put the imaginary period in the fused sentence. Here, for instance, is another way to correct Sample 1:**

CORRECTION: **Albert left his umbrella on the bus, and he dropped his gloves on the sidewalk.**

Another method is to use a real period instead of an imaginary one; however, that approach tends to create choppy sentences.

For Example . . .

The error in Sample 2 can be detected in the same way.

SAMPLE 2: **✗ Our exam is next week it will be hard.**

TIP APPLIED: **Our exam is next week. It will be hard.**

Again, the error can be corrected in either of the ways discussed.

CORRECTION STRATEGY A: **Our exam is next week; it will be hard.**

CORRECTION STRATEGY B: **Our exam is next week, and it will be hard.**

Now You Try It, 1 **(Corrected sentences appear on page 298.)**

Write *OK* if the sentence is not fused. If it is fused, underline each of the two independent ideas to show where the first idea ends and the second idea begins. Then, correct the error.

EXAMPLE: **My friend owns two pigs ^(, and) both are housebroken.**

1. I'm writing a short story and can't decide whether I want to represent laughter as "Ha! ha! ha!" or "Haw-haw!"

2. A pidgin language is not a natural language people invent it when they need to communicate but do not share a common language.

3. Many people thought Lou Gehrig's record of playing in consecutive baseball games would never be broken, but it finally was.

4. I write using a computer I don't know what I'd do without it.

5. It's about time you arrived I was getting very worried!

Now You Try It, 2 **(Corrected sentences appear on page 298.)**

Write *OK* if the sentence is not fused. If it is fused, underline each of the two independent ideas to show where the first idea ends and the second idea begins. Then, correct the error.

EXAMPLE: **The scientific name for okra is *hibiscus esculentus* ^(;) the scientific name for an onion is *allium cepa.***

1. The Miracle Strip is Florida's greatest expanse of beach the sand there is composed of pure white quartz.

2. I have three papers due tomorrow but have already written them.

3. Two of my teachers are male two are female.

4. The coldest place on Earth is the Pole of Cole in Antarctica the annual mean temperature is –72°F.

5. Kimberly told me about her dream it was about her missing sister.

Now You Try It, 3

Combine each pair of sentences. Avoid a fused sentence either by using a semicolon or by using a comma plus *and*, *but*, or *or*.

, but the
EXAMPLE: **Yesterday, Maria and I went to see a movie~~.~~ ~~The~~ movie theater had burned down.**

1. Jill gave me two paintings she made. I put them on my office wall.

2. Although I wasn't hungry, I ate something at the party to be polite. The food was so good that I stuffed myself.

3. A car's thermostat controls the flow of water to the radiator. Most thermostats contain wax intended to melt when the water gets hot.

4. The wax expands when it melts. This expansion opens a valve that lets cooling water come through to the radiator.

5. My thermostat is broken now. I took it apart to find out how it works.

Editing Practice, 1 **(Corrected sentences appear on page 298.)**

Correct all errors in the following paragraph using the first correction as a model. The number in parentheses at the end of the paragraph indicates how many errors you should find.

, and
Sausage is a popular food around the globe it has been around for centuries. Nobody knows for sure who first thought of stuffing ground meat into a casing to form what we now call "sausage." Over 3,500 years ago, the Babylonians made sausage the ancient poet Homer referred to sausage in his classic work *The Odyssey*. Romans were particularly fond of sausages made from ground pork and pine nuts. In fact, the word *sausage* comes from the Latin word *salsus* it is roughly translated as "salty." One Roman ruler thought sausages were so divine that he would not permit the lower classes to eat them. (2)

Editing Practice, 2 **(Corrected sentences appear on page 299.)**

Correct all errors in the following paragraphs using the first correction as a model. The number in parentheses at the end of each paragraph indicates how many errors you should find.

My cousin has never been the overly romantic type, but recently he put on quite a presentation when he proposed to his girlfriend. He did so on her birthday he put the ring inside a toy packet that he placed in a Cap'n Crunch box. It took a bit of effort to get her to open the cereal box and wade through the cereal to the "toy surprise" inside. He carefully timed the proceedings he wanted to be sure that she found the ring during halftime of the Dallas Cowboys game on TV he was also sure to be reclining in his armchair. (3)

When she found the ring, he gallantly hit the mute button for the TV and said that he would like for her to be his wife. The ring, by the way, was not a real wedding ring it was a plastic ring with a tiny boot jingling from it. She took it all in stride because she knew he was just trying to make the event memorable by adding some humor. I suppose she appreciated his humor she never did give him an answer. (2)

Editing Practice, 3

Correct all errors in the following paragraphs using the first correction as a model. The number in parentheses at the end of each paragraph indicates how many errors you should find.

Politeness is not as simple as it may seem; it certainly goes beyond table manners. Some language researchers argue that politeness is a way to show people that we approve of them or that we are not trying to tell them what to do or think. These researchers have studied diverse cultures and found that such politeness is a worldwide phenomenon it is central to the human experience. (1)

Politeness is often subtle it does not have to be an explicit "thank you" or "please." For instance, consider how you ask somebody to close a door you might say, "Will you close the door?" The question is not a demand it is simply a request for information. The listener knows your real point but does not have to feel that he or she is being ordered around. (3)

Writing Practice

On your own paper, write a paragraph or two describing someone's politeness (or rudeness). Vary your sentence structures so that several are compound sentences (sentences combining two complete ideas). Use the Proofreading Checklist to see whether each sentence you wrote is punctuated correctly.

PROOFREADING CHECKLIST

Combining Sentences in Your Writing

- A fused sentence occurs when there is nothing to indicate the spot where two complete sentences are joined. The reader may not be able to tell where the first thought ends and the second one begins.
- See whether you can place a period in the "vacant spot" between the two complete ideas.
- If you can create two complete sentences by placing a period in the vacant spot, the original sentence is likely to be a fused sentence.
- One way to correct the error is to use a semicolon in the vacant spot.
- Another way to correct the error is to use a comma plus *and*, *but*, or *or* in the vacant spot.

THE BOTTOM LINE

If you combine two sentences, use the appropriate punctuation to separate the two ideas; a semicolon is one way to do so.

UNIT ONE
PUTTING IT ALL TOGETHER

To write effective sentences, a person should understand two fundamental concepts: (1) what constitutes a complete sentence and (2) how one complete sentence can be combined with another. Thus, a writer should generally avoid using a fragment because it is not a complete sentence. A writer should also avoid putting together a fused sentence. A fused sentence is created by putting two sentences together with nothing at all to separate them—no comma, no semicolon, and no word to connect the sentences.

Avoiding Fragments

Use at least one of these tips to help you recognize a complete sentence and to avoid fragments.

"I REALIZE" TIP: Put *I realize* in front of what you believe to be a complete sentence. The result should be a meaningful statement that has not changed meaning. If you cannot put *I realize* in front, it is probably a fragment.

YES/NO TIP: See whether you can turn what you believe to be a complete sentence into a yes-no question. You can turn a *complete* sentence into a question that can be answered with "yes" or "no." Sometimes, you must add *do, did,* or *does.* You *cannot* do this with fragments.

COMPLETE SENTENCE: **A white star is a tiny star about the size of Earth.**

TIPS APPLIED: **I realize a white star is a tiny star about the size of Earth.**

Is a white star a tiny star about the size of Earth?

Avoiding Fused Sentences

Sentences can be combined in many ways, but each method requires you to do something to show where one complete idea ends and another begins. A fused sentence provides no such indication.

IMAGINARY PERIOD TIP: Locate the "vacant" spot in the sentence—the place separating two ideas and also the place lacking punctuation and a word like *and, but,* or *or.* Mentally place an imaginary period in that spot. If you can create two complete sentences by doing this, the original sentence is probably a fused sentence.

FUSED SENTENCE: ✗ **Villa-Lobos is a famous Brazilian composer his works were influenced by Brazilian folk songs.**

TIP APPLIED: **Villa-Lobos is a famous Brazilian composer. His works were influenced by Brazilian folk songs.**

Because the sample sentence could easily be separated into two sentences, the original sentence needs something to separate the two ideas, as follows.

CORRECTIONS: **Villa-Lobos is a famous Brazilian composer; his works were influenced by Brazilian folk songs.**

Villa-Lobos is a famous Brazilian composer, and his works were influenced by Brazilian folk songs.

Review

Correct all errors in the following paragraphs using the first correction as a model. The number in parentheses at the end of each paragraph indicates how many errors you should find.

I read an article on washing clothes, ~~After~~ after ruining an expensive sweater by using bleach. I thought I could just toss everything in the washer. Regardless of the color or type of fabric. I learned a valuable lesson I wish it weren't so expensive a lesson, though. (2)

Most items made of heavy cotton can be washed in very hot water it is best if white cotton items are washed by themselves. Lightweight cottons do best in warm water. Unless they are dark colors, which require cold water. (2)

Badly soiled laundry is most likely to be cleansed in very hot water you have to be careful, however, not to use very hot water when the garment label says you shouldn't. The mistake I made with my sweater. (2)

UNIT TWO
Commas

^
,

OVERVIEW

Terms That Can Help You Understand Commas

If you are not familiar with any of the following terms that appear in this unit, look them up in the Guide to Grammar Terminology beginning on page 1. The numbers in parentheses indicate the lessons in which each term appears.

adjective clause (relative clause) (7)
appositive (8)
comma splice (4)
complete sentence (3, 4, 5)
conjunctive adverb (transitional term) (6)
coordinating conjunction (3, 4)
fragment (5)
independent clause (4)
introductory element (5)
noun (7, 8)
pronoun (7, 8)
relative pronoun (7)
run-on sentence (3)

The Nuts and Bolts of Commas

Commas are often the most troubling aspect of formal punctuation; commas serve so many different functions that it's difficult to keep track of when to use (or not use) them. In addition, people do not altogether agree on the "rules" for certain functions of commas (as you will see in Lesson 5).

Here are the most common functions of commas that cause difficulties for writers:

- To separate two independent clauses that are also separated by *and*, *but*, or *or* (see Lessons 3 and 4).

  EXAMPLE: **Malcolm X was a prominent African American, but he was assassinated in 1965.**

- To set off an introductory element (see Lesson 5).

  EXAMPLE: **When the tip of a tornado touches the ground, it can create incredible destruction.**

- To set off transitional words (see Lesson 6).

  EXAMPLE: **My sister, however, was born in New York City.**

▶ To set off nonessential adjective clauses (see Lesson 7).

EXAMPLE: **Albert Einstein, who was born in Germany, fled to the United States because of Nazi persecution.**

▶ To set off nonessential appositives (see Lesson 8).

EXAMPLE: **I was born in Istanbul, the largest city in Turkey.**

Can You Detect Comma Problems?

(Corrected sentences appear on page 299.)

Correct all comma errors in the following paragraphs using the first correction as a model. The number in parentheses at the end of each paragraph indicates how many errors you should find.

Linguists,^ people who formally study language,^ have long noted that children learn their native language in similar ways. Although linguists do not fully understand the reason they do know that children go through similar stages in learning to speak. Children tend for instance to go through a "cooing and laughing" stage, which ends at about twenty weeks of age. When they move into the "vocal play" stage children string together long, steady sounds consisting of a consonant and a vowel and they move from there into a "babbling" stage. When children are almost a year old they tend to move into the "melodic utterance" stage a time when their sounds seem more purposeful and meaningful. (7)

Around this time, children enter the "one word" stage which lasts until they are about eighteen months of age. During this stage, they produce one-word utterances, two common utterances are "Mama" and "Bye-bye." Children move subsequently into the "two word" stage and they string together pairs of the single words they know. These are not just subject-verb sentences (such as "Daddy gone"), they are also composed of structures not having a verb (such as "There Daddy"). At this time, they are learning grammar the system for putting words together in a language. (7)

LESSON 3

Commas Used with And, But, Or

Sample Errors

SAMPLE 1: **✗ Derek finally finished writing his book of poems but his publisher was not satisfied.**

SAMPLE 2: **✗ A moose wandered into town, and scared several kids.**

What's the Problem?

In sentences like the two above, a comma is needed if *and* or *but* separates what could be two separate sentences. According to this general rule, Sample 1 needs a comma immediately before *but.*

On the other hand, avoid using a comma before *and* or *but* if even one part could not stand alone as a separate sentence. For example, Sample 2 uses a comma before *and*, but it shouldn't because *scared several kids* could not possibly be a complete sentence (for information about detecting **complete sentences**, see Lesson 1).

These two rules apply to every **coordinating conjunction**:

and **but** **or** **for** **nor** **so** **yet**

This lesson focuses on the first three coordinating conjunctions because they are by far the most frequently used.

What Causes the Problem?

If you leave out a comma before a coordinating conjunction when it is needed, the resulting sentence is usually considered an error (some people call this a **run-on sentence**). And if you use a comma before a coordinating conjunction when it is not needed, another error results. Thus, part of the problem is that writers are likely to be confused when it seems easy to create an error no matter what they do. Still, you can avoid a problem by checking what comes both *before* and *after* the coordinating conjunction.

Diagnostic Exercise **(Corrected sentences appear on page 299.)**

Correct all errors in the following paragraph using the first correction as a model. The number in parentheses at the end of the paragraph indicates how many errors you should find.

Because Christopher Columbus believed he had reached the East Indies, Native Americans were called *Indians*, and the name is still often used. Actually, there are many types of Native Americans but they are usually referred to collectively. Along the northwest coast, there were the Haida, Modoc, and Kwakiutl tribes and these tribes differed considerably from the tribes of the plains. The northwest tribes subsisted largely on salmon, and built wooden houses and boats. The plains tribes hunted buffalo, and farmed the river valleys. (4)

Fixing This Problem in Your Writing

This tip helps determine whether you can correctly use a comma with *and*, *but*, or *or*.

> IMAGINARY PERIOD TIP: Imagine that there is a period right before *and, but,* or *or.* Can each part that is divided by this period stand alone as a complete sentence? If so, use a comma before the *and, but,* or *or.* If not, you should usually leave the comma out. The resulting sentences should *not* change the meaning of the original sentence.

This tip works because the comma is acting like a weak period; it provides a pause that lets you know when you are moving to a new subject and verb.

If you are not moving to a new subject and verb, leave the comma out. In Sample 1, you can put a period before *but.* Although the second sentence begins with *but*, it is still complete.

SAMPLE 1: ✗ **Derek finally finished writing his book of poems but his publisher was not satisfied.**

TIP APPLIED: **Derek finally finished writing his book of poems.**

TIP APPLIED: **But his publisher was not satisfied.**

Because *each* of these test sentences can stand on its own, Sample 1 needs a comma.

CORRECTION: **Derek finally finished writing his book of poems, but his publisher was not satisfied.**

In sum, if a period can go, use a comma. If a period can't go, don't use a comma.

For Example . . .

Try making two sentences out of Sample 2. The second part is *not* a complete sentence. Thus, it should *not* have a comma before it.

SAMPLE 2: ✗ **A moose wandered into town, and scared several kids.**

TIP APPLIED: **A moose wandered into town.**

TIP APPLIED: ✗ **And scared several kids.**

CORRECTION: **A moose wandered into town and scared several kids.**

This next sentence is correct. Both parts can stand alone, so the comma is required before the coordinating conjunction.

Somebody called me yesterday, but I forget who it was.

TIP APPLIED: **Somebody called me yesterday.**

TIP APPLIED: **But I forget who it was.**

Now You Try It, 1 **(Corrected sentences appear on page 299.)**

Write *OK* above all sentences that correctly use a comma before a coordinating conjunction. Show they are correct by turning each part of the sentence into a complete sentence. If a sentence has an unnecessary comma, correct it.

This paper is torn. But can still be used for scratch paper.

EXAMPLE: **This paper is torn, but can still be used for scratch paper.**

1. Pig iron is refined in a blast furnace, and contains iron along with small amounts of manganese and other minerals.
2. Piero di Cosimo was a Florentine painter, and is remembered for his scenes depicting mythology.
3. Tom decided he would walk to class, but changed his mind when it started raining.
4. You should return this book to the library, or you can renew it by phone.
5. José Rizal was a Philippine patriot who wrote *The Lost Eden* in 1886, and he was exiled in 1887 by the Spanish regime.

Now You Try It, 2 **(Corrected sentences appear on page 300.)**

Write *OK* above all sentences that correctly use a comma before a coordinating conjunction. Show they are correct by turning each part of the sentence into a complete sentence. If a sentence has an unnecessary comma, correct it.

My friend Al wants to buy a car. But can't afford one.

EXAMPLE: **My friend Al wants to buy a car, but can't afford one.**

1. Sitting Bull was a famous Sioux chief, and appeared with Buffalo Bill in his Wild West Show.
2. The Norman Conquest of England took place in 1066, and brought many changes in English life.
3. My father bought an old sword in England, but paid too much.
4. Jan asked me to lend her my notes, and I did.
5. Tony is dropping by my place and I suppose I should clean up a bit.

Now You Try It, 3

Write *OK* above all sentences that correctly use a comma before a coordinating conjunction. Show they are correct by turning each part of the sentence into a complete sentence. If a sentence has an unnecessary comma, correct it.

I may go shopping today. Or put it off until Friday.

EXAMPLE: **I may go shopping today, or put it off until Friday.**

1. Find a lid that will fit this jar, or you will need to find a different jar. [*Hint:* The first part of the sentence has an understood *you* in front of it.]

2. The last sentence is called an imperative sentence, but this one is a regular declarative sentence.

3. My hat doesn't fit well, and keeps falling off when I ride my bike.

4. I downloaded software from the Internet, but am supposed to send $15 to the author of the software.

5. I wrote a check today, and I will put it in the mail tomorrow.

Editing Practice, 1 **(Corrected sentences appear on page 300.)**

Correct all errors in the following paragraphs using the first correction as a model. The number in parentheses at the end of each paragraph indicates how many errors you should find.

Languages use symbols to represent meaning, and various forms of language exist besides speech. Braille is a form of language for people who cannot see and it consists of a sequence of cells. Each cell contains dots that can be variously arranged. Braille is slightly raised so that people can run their fingers across the dots and determine what they represent. (1)

Each particular arrangement means something different. Grade 1 Braille is a system in which the dots represent letters, numbers, punctuation, and some very short words but in Grade 2 Braille the dots represent highly abbreviated forms of words. However, Grade 2 Braille is not a different system; it is simply a form of shorthand based on Grade 1 Braille. (1)

Editing Practice, 2 **(Corrected sentences appear on page 300.)**

Correct all errors in the following paragraphs using the first correction as a model. The number in parentheses at the end of each paragraph indicates how many errors you should find.

Humans appear to be the only animal to use language naturally‸, but there is much about language that we may never know. People have come up with various theories about the origins of language but nobody knows for sure how or why humans learned to speak. According to the "bow-wow" theory, speech began when people imitated the sounds of nature, such as animal sounds. Most languages have a few words (such as "meow") that clearly imitate these sounds but usually these words are relatively rare in a given language. (2)

According to the "pooh-pooh" theory, speech arose when humans made instinctive noises resulting from pain, fear, or other emotions. For instance, a gasp, a sigh, or a cry of fear might have been the primitive beginnings of words used to express these emotions. Again, most languages have words (such as "hey" or "oh") that convey emotional responses but they are so rare in a given language that it is hard to claim they are the root of language itself. (1)

Editing Practice, 3

Correct all errors in the following paragraph using the first correction as a model. The number in parentheses at the end of the paragraph indicates how many errors you should find.

I still have much to learn about using a computer‸, but my computer skills have improved a lot over the last couple of years. I once used the computer as a glorified typewriter, and knew very little about spreadsheets and graphics programs. Most of the time, all I need to do is word processing, but I have also learned a good deal about doing that. For instance, at one time I did not even understand how to use the spell-checking function that comes with my word-

processing program. I did not have anybody who could explain how to use it, or how to use other functions that would have made my life easier. By trial and error, however, I have become fairly proficient with word processing and almost all my writing is done on the computer nowadays. I may be wrong, but I think that my writing has improved as a result. I certainly am able to revise more quickly and more easily than just two years ago. (3)

Writing Practice

On your own paper, write a paragraph or two describing your experiences or attitudes toward computers. Try to include five sentences using a coordinating conjunction and a comma as described in this lesson. Use the Proofreading Checklist to see whether each sentence is punctuated correctly.

PROOFREADING CHECKLIST

Using Commas before And, But, and Or

- See whether what comes *before* the *and*, *but*, or *or* can stand alone as a complete sentence.
- Do the same with what comes *after* those three words.
- If *both* parts can stand alone without changing the meaning of the original, then use a comma before the *and*, *but*, or *or*.
- If even one part cannot stand alone, then do not use a comma.

THE BOTTOM LINE

See whether what comes before *and, but,* or *or* can stand alone, *and* do the same with what comes after *and, but,* or *or.*

LESSON 4

Comma Splices

CS

Sample Errors

SAMPLE 1: ✗ **Henry Roebuck won a card game using the ace of clubs, he later built a castle in the shape of this card.**

SAMPLE 2: ✗ **Ben Franklin did not want the eagle to be the U.S. emblem, he preferred the turkey.**

What's the Problem?

A **comma splice** is an error that occurs when a comma alone is used to join independent clauses. (An **independent clause** is a group of words that can be written as a complete sentence.) In other words, a comma splice is created by using *only* a comma to join what *could be* two complete sentences.

A comma splice is similar to another error, the fused sentence, which has nothing at all separating two independent clauses (see Lesson 2).

In Samples 1 and 2, commas are inappropriately used by themselves to join two complete ideas (two independent clauses). Neither sentence has a **coordinating conjunction** (such as *and*, *but*, or *or*) to help the comma indicate where one of these ideas ends and the next one begins.

What Causes the Problem?

Often, this error occurs because a writer is trying to join two closely related statements. Combining such statements can be an effective strategy because it emphasizes the relationship between two ideas. The trick is to make sure the two statements are linked in a way that helps readers understand what the writer has done. Commas serve so many functions that using *just* a comma to combine sentences does not help readers determine the type of sentence they are reading.

CS

Diagnostic Exercise **(Corrected sentences appear on page 300.)**

Correct all errors in the following paragraph using the first correction as a model. The number in parentheses at the end of the paragraph indicates how many errors you should find.

My roommate and I finally had a garage sale. ~~, it~~ It was something we've talked about all quarter to help us get rid of the junk we accumulated since our sophomore year. As our neighbor reminded me one day, it's not a bad idea to get rid of stuff you haven't touched in a year. We sold more than I expected, the total sales came out to about $200. Yesterday, I managed to spend most of it on car repairs. I took what was left over and bought some junk food as a "reward" for having uncluttered the house. Maybe we will have another garage sale before we graduate, we will probably have bought more junk by then. (2)

Fixing This Problem in Your Writing

Here is a tip that will help you detect a comma splice.

> TWO-SENTENCES TIP: If what comes *before* a comma and what comes *after* it could be *two separate sentences*, there probably is a comma splice.

In Sample 1, for example, everything before the comma could be one sentence, and everything after it could be a second sentence. (For information on detecting a complete sentence, see page 17.) In other words, if you have an independent clause before as well as after the comma, then you need a coordinating conjunction after the comma.

SAMPLE 1: **✗ Henry Roebuck won a card game using the ace of clubs, he later built a castle in the shape of this card.**

TIP APPLIED: **Henry Roebuck won a card game using the ace of clubs. He later built a castle in the shape of this card.**

Following are two methods for correcting a comma splice.

CORRECTION STRATEGY A: **As seen in the following correction of Sample 1, you can add a coordinating conjunction (*and*, *but*, *or*, *so*, *nor*, *yet*) right after the comma.**

CORRECTION: **Henry Roebuck won a card game using the ace of clubs, so he later built a castle in the shape of this card.**

CORRECTION STRATEGY B: **Change the comma to a semicolon. The major function of a semicolon is to divide what could be two separate sentences.**

CORRECTION: **Henry Roebuck won a card game using the ace of clubs; he later built a castle in the shape of this card.**

For Example . . .

Sample 2 can also be separated into two complete sentences, meaning that a comma alone can't be used in the original.

SAMPLE 2: **✗ Ben Franklin did not want the eagle to be the U.S. emblem, he preferred the turkey.**

TIP APPLIED: **Ben Franklin did not want the eagle to be the U.S. emblem. He preferred the turkey.**

Theoretically, both correction strategies could be applied to Sample 2, but we've used a semicolon since no coordinating conjunction really seems to fit the meaning of the sentence.

CORRECTION: **Ben Franklin did not want the eagle to be the U.S. emblem; he preferred the turkey.**

CS

Now You Try It, 1 **(Corrected sentences appear on page 300.)**

Check each sentence for a comma splice by applying the Two-Sentences Tip. If a sentence does not have a comma splice, write *OK* above it. Edit the original sentences that have comma splices to correct the errors.

Susan has a colorful poster on her wall. Her little brother wrote all over it.

EXAMPLE: **Susan has a colorful poster on her wall,** ^but **her little brother wrote all over it.**

1. My history class is on the other side of campus, I have to run to get there on time.
2. In order to buy a new car, John started working on weekends.
3. My computer seems broken, I cannot get it to save this file.
4. My mom just finished *Gone with the Wind*, a book I lent her.
5. The Russian cosmonaut Yuri Gagarin was the first person to orbit Earth, John Glenn was the first American to do so.

Now You Try It, 2 **(Corrected sentences appear on page 301.)**

Check each sentence for a comma splice by applying the Two-Sentences Tip. If a sentence does not have a comma splice, write *OK* above it. Edit the original sentences that have comma splices to correct the errors.

Bill seems a bit confused. I'm not very confident either.

EXAMPLE: **Bill seems a bit confused, I'm not very confident either.**

1. The library does not have a copy of *Doc Savage: The Man of Bronze*, but I have one you can borrow.
2. Some companies like résumés kept to one page, other companies are more flexible about the length of résumés.
3. Because of the rainy weather, the game was postponed.
4. Sharon made us some of her salsa, it was hotter than I expected.
5. In the winter, this lake eventually freezes from one end to the other, but in some places the ice is very thin.

Now You Try It, 3

Combine each pair of sentences by using either a semicolon or a comma followed by *and*, *but*, or *or*.

, but nobody

EXAMPLE: **Class was canceled because of the blizzard. Nobody knows whether there will be class tomorrow.**

1. Mick Taylor originally played lead guitar for the Rolling Stones. Ron Wood took over that position in 1974.

2. My father listens to the Rolling Stones. I prefer to listen to rock music played by people who couldn't be my parents.

3. China has a larger population than any other country. India has the second-largest population.

4. Some smaller countries, such as Nauru, have fewer than ten thousand people. A few have only a couple of thousand people.

5. My brother might enroll at this college. He might get a scholarship to UCLA.

Editing Practice, 1 **(Corrected sentences appear on page 301.)**

Correct all errors in the following paragraph using the first correction as a model. The number in parentheses at the end of the paragraph indicates how many errors you should find.

but

Many satellites and probes have been launched into space, two of the most traveled probes are the two *Voyager* probes. Both left Earth in 1977, both visited Jupiter and Saturn. Both probes use a "slingshot" method of studying the planets, the probes cannot land safely on the planets but use their gravity to pull the probes into a path leading to their next objective. In the late 1990's, the *Voyagers* will be propelled in this fashion completely out of the solar system, beginning a long journey to the stars. Nobody knows when their travels will end, they might travel forever or crash into a star. (3)

Editing Practice, 2 **(Corrected sentences appear on page 301.)**

Correct all errors in the following paragraphs using the first correction as a model. The number in parentheses at the end of each paragraph indicates how many errors you should find.

Congress passes hundreds of bills each year; some greatly affect the lives of all Americans. The Social Security Act of 1935 is one of the most influential acts passed by the U.S. government. The most important part of this act established the old-age pension system, the original tax was a mere 1 percent each on workers and their employers. (1)

The act also created the unemployment insurance system, it provided federal grants to states as well so they could give aid to handicapped people, dependent children, and the elderly poor. The original act, however, excluded a great many people who have since been covered by other bills. For instance, the bill did little or nothing for farm workers, domestic servants, and other low-paid occupations. Franklin D. Roosevelt is largely responsible for the act, he intentionally arranged the bill so that Social Security would depend in part on the paychecks of future workers. In this way, he hoped to discourage politicians from doing away with the system, a strategy that has worked—so far. (2)

Editing Practice, 3

Correct all errors in the following paragraphs using the first correction as a model. The number in parentheses at the end of each paragraph indicates how many errors you should find.

I took a bowling class as an elective; I heard it was a good course. Our teacher helped me find a ball that wasn't too scratched up, the management did not like to invest money in bowling balls. I finally got my equipment, and it was my turn to bowl. I was pretty nervous, the last time I had bowled was after my senior prom in high school. (2)

I tried to remember everything our textbook went over, a lot of material was crammed into fifty pages. My first ball managed to go straight into the gutter. I tried again, this time the ball went for the gutter but curved back inside. To my surprise, the ball managed to hit right in the pocket, all ten pins fell over. It was scored as a spare, the first one I had ever made. I did not make any other spares that game, the next game brought me three strikes. Once I managed to apply what the textbook taught me, I finally became a successful bowler. (4)

Writing Practice

On your own paper, write a paragraph or two describing an early attempt on your part to learn a new sport or game. Have at least three sentences that correctly combine two independent clauses. Use the Proofreading Checklist to see whether each sentence you wrote is punctuated correctly.

PROOFREADING CHECKLIST

Using a Comma to Join Sentences in Your Writing

- See whether what comes *before* the comma could stand alone as a complete, grammatical sentence.
- Do the same with what comes *after* the comma.
- If *each* part can stand alone, *do not use just a comma* to join the two parts.
- You can fix the error by putting an appropriate coordinating conjunction (such as *and*, *but*, *or*) immediately after the comma.
- You can also fix a comma splice by turning the comma into a semicolon (;).

THE BOTTOM LINE

You can't use just a comma between two independent clauses, but you can use a comma plus a coordinating conjunction.

LESSON 5

Commas and Introductory Elements

Sample Errors

SAMPLE 1: ✗ **Running as quickly as her legs could carry her Pam managed to get to the phone in time.**

SAMPLE 2: ✗ **When you called Tom was listening on the phone downstairs.**

What's the Problem?

In formal writing, an **introductory element** usually ends with a comma. This comma is a cue to the reader about where the "heart" of the sentence begins. Sometimes, this comma prevents misreading—even when the introductory element is short, as in Sample 2. If there is no comma, a reader might think that *Tom* is part of the introductory element in that sentence.

The term *introductory element* refers to several structures that can start off a sentence. For example, it can refer to the structures that are underlined in the following sentences:

PREPOSITIONAL PHRASE: **<u>In a few moments</u>, I'll join you.**

ADVERB CLAUSE: **<u>When the settlers first arrived</u>, they were not pleased with the cold weather.**

PARTICIPIAL PHRASE: **<u>Hitting his thumb instead of the nail</u>, Tim let out a string of obscenities.**

There are other types of introductory elements as well, including words like *however* and *therefore* (see, for instance, Lesson 6).

What Causes the Problem?

In part, this problem results from the fact that there are several types of introductory elements. Some almost always require a comma, but the comma is optional for other introductory elements. We will not cover each type of introductory element, but we will offer a relatively simple way to deal with commas and introductory elements.

Diagnostic Exercise **(Corrected sentences appear on page 301.)**

Insert commas after all introductory elements in the following paragraph using the first correction as a model. The number in parentheses at the end of the paragraph indicates how many commas you should add.

Last Monday‸, there was a fire in one of the dorms. According to the newspaper nobody was hurt. When the fire department finally arrived six rooms were engulfed in flames. A friend of mine had her room filled with smoke. However her room suffered no major damage. Tomorrow school officials will tour the dorm and make recommendations. I have heard they plan to move everybody out within the next two weeks. (4)

Fixing This Problem in Your Writing

The first step is to locate introductory elements. Following is a tip to help you identify them.

> DELETION TIP: Almost any sort of introductory element can be deleted without leaving a sentence **fragment**. The remaining word group should be a **complete sentence.**

See Lesson 1 for information about fragments and complete sentences.

In Sample 1, the introductory element can be deleted; the sentence loses some meaning, but it is a complete sentence.

SAMPLE 1: **✗ Running as quickly as her legs could carry her Pam managed to get to the phone in time.**

TIP APPLIED: **~~Running as quickly as her legs could carry her~~ Pam managed to get to the phone in time.**

Not everybody agrees about whether you have to put commas after certain types of introductory elements. Sometimes, you have the option of omitting the comma, but it is rarely wrong to use the comma after an introductory element. Until you can determine the preferences of a particular audience, we recommend this correction strategy:

CORRECTION STRATEGY: **Put a comma after introductory elements of any sort.**

Sample 1 can easily be corrected by inserting a comma after *her.*

CORRECTION: **Running as quickly as her legs could carry her, Pam managed to get to the phone in time.**

For Example . . .

The tip works with Sample 2 as well. We know that *When you called* is an introductory element because it can be deleted. We also know that *Tom* is *not* part of the introductory element because we cannot delete *Tom* and still leave a complete sentence.

SAMPLE 2: **✗ When you called Tom was listening on the phone downstairs.**

TIP APPLIED: **~~When you called~~ Tom was listening on the phone downstairs.**

CORRECTION: **When you called, Tom was listening on the phone downstairs.**

Now You Try It, 1 **(Corrected sentences appear on page 301.)**

If a sentence has an introductory element, place a comma in the appropriate place. Draw a line through the introductory element to show that it can be deleted without leaving a fragment. Write *No intro element* above each sentence that has no introductory element.

EXAMPLE: **~~During our history test~~, somebody fell asleep.**

1. When we got the tests back nobody even thought about sleeping.
2. In France shepherds once carried portable wooden sundials as pocket watches.
3. My roommate and I went shopping but couldn't agree on what to buy for cleaning the apartment.
4. Somebody called for Hanah last night.
5. Each time my brother or sister calls I seem to be out of the house.

Now You Try It, 2 **(Corrected sentences appear on page 302.)**

If a sentence has an introductory element, place a comma in the appropriate place. Draw a line through the introductory element to show that it can be deleted without leaving a fragment. Write *No intro element* above each sentence that has no introductory element.

EXAMPLE: **~~According to a recent study~~, women are far more likely than men to take apart an Oreo cookie so they can first eat the white filling.**

1. In the middle of the night our house was burglarized.
2. My friend was worried when he didn't hear from me for two weeks.
3. Because the roads are slippery from ice and slush classes are canceled.
4. A worn, battered, and ripped coat was sprawled in the mud next to my car.
5. However I picked the coat up and gave it to a friend who likes to mend old clothes.

Now You Try It, 3

Complete each group of words to form a complete sentence having an introductory element. Set off the element with a comma.

EXAMPLE: **During the game**, somebody fell off the bleachers.

1. When my neighbor called to complain about my music

2. On Tuesday

3. Once upon a time

4. Because my feet were cold

5. Noticing a crack in the windshield of his new truck

Editing Practice, 1 **(Corrected sentences appear on page 302.)**

Add a comma after each introductory element in the following paragraphs using the first correction as a model. The number in parentheses at the end of each paragraph indicates how many commas you should add.

Although many people may not be aware of this fact, Pearl Buck was the first American woman to win a Nobel Prize in Literature. After spending years as missionaries in China her parents returned to the United States for a short time in the early 1890's, during which Pearl was born. When she was just three months old Pearl went with her parents to China, where she would spend many years of her life. Her nursemaid would teach her Chinese, and the family lived among the Chinese rather than among American visitors. (2)

During her stay in China there were many racial problems and protests against the Western governments that had controlled China's economy for years. Her most famous novel, *The Good Earth*, would reflect her compassion for the Chinese and their culture. When Pearl Buck died President Nixon said in a tribute that she served as a "human bridge between the civilizations of the East and West." (2)

Editing Practice, 2 **(Corrected sentences appear on page 302.)**

Add a comma after each introductory element in the following paragraphs using the first correction as a model. The number in parentheses at the end of each paragraph indicates how many commas you should add.

In my never-ending pursuit to be physically fit, I bought a weight machine that I could set up in my basement. I carefully compared various brands and referred to several guides and reports on the models available. After examining my options I bought one with a built-in stair-stepping mechanism. (1)

Unfortunately I forgot to compare two things: the height of the weight machine and the height of my basement. When I finally assembled the metal monster I discovered that it needed four more inches than my basement ceiling allowed. I was furious at myself. The thing was such a hassle to transport from the store and then to assemble that I did not want to return it. In desperation I punched a hole through the sheet-rock ceiling. The weight machine fits now, but there is a really ugly hole in my ceiling. (3)

Editing Practice, 3

Add a comma after each introductory element in the following paragraphs using the first correction as a model. The number in parentheses at the end of each paragraph indicates how many commas you should add.

Only a year ago, I had no idea what my major would be. Because I had many interests I couldn't decide whether I should major in history, biology, or math. Even after an academic counselor spoke with me I could not decide. (2)

However I spoke with my roommate about what she was studying. Our discussion really helped because she made me think about what I wanted to be doing for the next thirty years or so. Before we had this talk I tended to just think about the subjects I liked to study—not the sorts of jobs I really wanted.

Admittedly it was a simple idea, but it never hit home until I talked my life over with somebody who was going through the same problem. (3)

Writing Practice

On your own paper, write a paragraph or two explaining what you might major in and what led you to this choice. If you are unsure of a major, pick one possible area and explain why it interests you. Try to use at least five introductory elements. Use the Proofreading Checklist to see whether each introductory element is followed by a comma. Check all sentences, even those which you think don't have an introductory element.

PROOFREADING CHECKLIST

Punctuating Introductory Elements in Your Writing

- In formal writing, an introductory element usually ends with a comma. To determine whether a sentence has an introductory element, see whether you can delete the part of the sentence that you believe is an introductory element.
- If the remaining word group is a fragment, then you probably do not have an introductory element. In this case, you do not need a comma.
- If the result is a complete sentence, then you probably do have an introductory element. Not all introductory elements need commas, but our suggestion is that you go ahead and use a comma right after the introductory element.
- Try to discover the preferences of your readers; some may prefer that writers use as few commas as possible.

THE BOTTOM LINE

If you use an introductory element, it's usually a good idea to set it off with a comma.

LESSON 6

Commas with Transitional Terms

Sample Errors

SAMPLE 1: **In 1972, the Miami Dolphins won all their football games in their regular season. ✗ Furthermore they won all their playoff games.**

SAMPLE 2: **✗ The Hope diamond may be the best-known diamond; the largest diamond however was the Cullinan, which was cut into 106 smaller diamonds.**

What's the Problem?

A **transitional term** (sometimes called a **conjunctive adverb**) offers a useful way to make a connection between separate ideas. Transitional terms usually consist of one word, although occasionally they may consist of two or more words (as with *in fact* and *on the other hand*).

Transitional terms normally do not describe just one word. Instead, they establish some type of relationship between *entire* ideas. Each of the underlined words in Samples 1 and 2 establishes a relationship between two ideas. Unlike other words that establish a relationship between ideas, a transitional term is not essential and can easily be left out without creating an error. However, transitional words are used because they can help create clearer, more coherent groups of sentences. Here are a few more examples of transitional words:

accordingly	**hence**	**subsequently**
also	**instead**	**then**
consequently	**nevertheless**	**therefore**
for example	**similarly**	**thus**

Most handbooks of grammar suggest using commas to set off transitional words. Thus, Samples 1 and 2 could use commas.

Many sentences begin with transitional terms. Thus, transitional terms are sometimes a type of introductory element (see Lesson 5). Transitional terms, however, are not limited to starting off sentences; they can also appear in the middle or at the end of sentences.

What Causes the Problem?

Problems occur with transitional words for at least two reasons. First, they resemble other words (like *and*, *but*, and *because*) that also connect ideas but are punctuated differently (for example, see Lesson 3). Second, not all handbooks or readers agree about how to punctuate transitional words; some suggest always using commas, while others say commas are not essential. Writers can easily be confused by this lack of consistent rules. We suggest using commas because they draw attention to the transitional words that are intended to indicate a relationship between ideas.

Diagnostic Exercise **(Corrected sentences appear on page 302.)**

Add commas to all transitional words in the following paragraph using the first correction as a model. The number in parentheses at the end of the paragraph indicates how many commas you should add.

> **Many places around the globe have universal appeal. They are, however, associated with just one country or another. A twenty-one-member international committee has designated some sites as World Heritage Sites, sites having international value and responsibility. In the United States for example the committee has chosen Yosemite Park and the Statue of Liberty. (2)**

Fixing This Problem in Your Writing

To set off transitional words, you must first recognize them. Look for any word that establishes a relationship between two ideas (such as two sentences). Then, use the following tip to see whether it is a transitional term.

> MOVEMENT TIP: A transitional word can always be moved around in a sentence. Move only the term you are testing—no other word or group of words. If a term that establishes a relationship between ideas can be moved around, it is probably a transitional term.

Hardly any other type of word can so easily be moved around. Other words that can be moved around as easily do not establish a relationship between ideas. For instance, the word *quickly* can be moved around in *I quickly ate lunch*. But because *quickly* does *not* establish a relationship between ideas, it is not a transitional term and does not need commas.

How do you know *where* a transitional term can be moved in a sentence? Unfortunately, it is difficult to offer a rule on this matter. A native speaker of English can usually rely on his or her intuition about what "sounds right," but a non-native speaker may have to consult with a native speaker to learn where a transitional term can be moved.

In Sample 1, *furthermore* could be moved around, and it also establishes a connection between two ideas; thus it is a transitional word.

SAMPLE 1: **✗ Furthermore they won all their playoff games.**

TIP APPLIED: **They won all their playoff games, furthermore.**

Once you identify transitional words, use commas to set them off. Use two commas unless the transitional word comes at the beginning or the end of a sentence (or if the word comes after a semicolon).

CORRECTION: **Furthermore, they won all their playoff games.**

For Example . . .

The Movement Tip works for Sample 2 because *however* can be moved.

SAMPLE 2: **✗ The Hope diamond may be the best-known diamond; the largest diamond however was the Cullinan, which was cut into 106 smaller diamonds.**

TIP APPLIED: **The Hope diamond may be the best-known diamond; however, the largest diamond was the Cullinan, which was cut into 106 smaller diamonds.**

CORRECTION: **The Hope diamond may be the best-known diamond; the largest diamond, however, was the Cullinan, which was cut into 106 smaller diamonds.**

But try the Movement Tip with *but*. You could move it *if* you moved other words, but it fails the movement test because it alone can't be moved.

EXAMPLE: **But I want a diamond that's even bigger!**

TIP APPLIED: **✗ I, but, want a diamond that's even bigger!**

Since *but* is not mobile, it cannot be a transitional word and does not need a comma right after it.

Now You Try It, 1 **(Corrected sentences appear on page 302.)**

Write *None* above any sentence that has no transitional words. If there is such a word, set it off with one or more commas. Then, prove it is a transitional word by applying the Movement Tip.

, *indeed,*

EXAMPLE: **Bill said he might be late. Indeed, he was four hours late.**

1. Tecumseh led an attempt to drive the whites from Indian territory. His forces however were defeated by General Harrison.

2. Little is known about the Pilgrims' *Mayflower*; we do know however that it weighed about 180 tons.

3. English is the predominant language in the United States, but over three hundred languages are spoken within its borders.

4. The oldest known weapon is a broken spear found in Great Britain; it is estimated to have been made around 200,000 B.C.

5. Mozart wrote many musical works. In fact it takes 180 CD's to hold all work known to be his.

Now You Try It, 2 **(Corrected sentences appear on page 302.)**

Write *None* above any sentence that has no transitional words. If there is such a word, set it off with one or more commas. Then, prove it is a transitional word by applying the Movement Tip.

, *also*

EXAMPLE: **Our computers are down. Also, the phones are out of order.**

1. Sean Connery is remembered most for his James Bond movies. However he won an Oscar for a different role in *The Untouchables.*

2. Some people consider Scotland part of England, but both are part of the United Kingdom.

3. The top position in Britain's army is field marshal. The top position in its navy in contrast is admiral of the fleet.

4. Corpus Christi is the name of a city in Texas, and it is the name of a university in Oxford, England.

5. Some countries' names come from unexpected sources. *Brazil* for example comes from *brasila*—the Portuguese name for a tree.

Now You Try It, 3

Write a follow-up sentence for each of the following sentences and use a transitional word set off by commas in your follow-up sentence.

> EXAMPLE: **I rarely go out and watch movies.** *Nonetheless, I am going to do so tonight.*

1. My parents prefer that I major in a business-related field.

2. The English translation of the unofficial national anthem of Japan is "His Majesty's Reign."

3. Women's and men's clothes are measured in very different ways.

4. Finger spelling is a way to spell out letters to people who are deaf.

5. My grandfather insists that he be buried with his hearing aid.

Editing Practice, 1 **(Corrected sentences appear on page 303.)**

Use commas to set off all transitional words in the following paragraphs using the first correction as a model. The number in parentheses at the end of each paragraph indicates how many commas you should add.

My friend Collett is moving to Oakland, California. Consequently, she wants to fix up her house and sell it. Because she's a good friend, I volunteered to help. A realtor advised her to repaint the living room because this area makes a big impression on potential home buyers. A kitchen similarly draws much interest, and hers needs work done on the cabinets. (2)

The biggest task was working on the cabinets. We began therefore with taking them apart. Then we replaced the old knobs with ceramic ones. Two of the cabinet doors had bad cracks. We decided therefore to put putty in the cracks and see whether it would hide the problem. The rollers on the drawers were badly worn, so we replaced them as well. We painted everything but the countertop and made plans for painting the living room. (5)

Editing Practice, 2 **(Corrected sentences appear on page 303.)**

Use commas to set off all transitional words in the following paragraphs using the first correction as a model. The number in parentheses at the end of each paragraph indicates how many commas you should add.

Americans are often proud of their history; nonetheless, there are some unpleasant episodes. One troubling aspect of U.S. history is the many attempts to kill presidents or presidential candidates. The assassinations of Lincoln and the Kennedy brothers are the most famous; there have been however many other assassinations and attempts. In 1881, Charles Guiteau shot President Garfield, who died later. Likewise President McKinley was shot in 1901 and died of his wounds later. Two men tried to shoot their way into a house where President Truman was staying, but their plot failed when one was killed by a guard. (3)

Political fanaticism has led to many assassination attempts. Others in contrast seem to have been the result of pure insanity. John Schrank for example tried to assassinate Theodore Roosevelt as the president was leaving a hotel. Schrank's sanity was questionable; he said McKinley's ghost told him to kill Roosevelt. (4)

Editing Practice, 3

Use commas to set off all transitional words in the following paragraphs using the first correction as a model. The number in parentheses at the end of each paragraph indicates how many commas you should add.

Empanadas are considered a South American meat pie. Some historians argue, though, that empanadas originated in the Middle East centuries ago and were introduced to the Western Hemisphere by conquistadors in the fifteenth century. Although empanadas have similar origins, they take different forms. In

Central America for example corn is used, while wheat is the primary ingredient in Spain and Portugal. (2)

Empanadas are filled with a meat or fish such as pork, chicken, sardines, or ground beef. Some people however prefer vegetable filling. Also spices are key ingredients. Seasonings include for example paprika, chili powder, and black pepper. Many people in addition use garlic, cumin, and white pepper. The final step in making an empanada is either baking or frying it until brown. (7)

Writing Practice

On your own paper write a paragraph or two describing one of your favorite foods or meals. Try to use four transitional words. Use the Proofreading Checklist to make sure that transitional words are set off by commas.

PROOFREADING CHECKLIST

Using Commas with Transitional Words in Your Writing

- To identify transitional words, look for words that establish a clear connection with another idea (often, with another sentence).
- As a double-check, see whether you can move the transitional word around in the sentence.
- If this word can be moved, it is probably a transitional word, and the safe approach is to set it off with commas unless doing so makes the sentence sound bizarre and unnatural.

THE BOTTOM LINE

Transitional words do not always have to be set off by commas. *However*, the safe approach is to do so unless the commas seem unnatural and forced.

LESSON 7

Commas and Adjective Clauses

Sample Errors

SAMPLE 1: **✗ I want to go to Chicago where I was born.**

SAMPLE 2: **✗ There is the man, who owes me a dollar.**

What's the Problem?

An **adjective clause** (sometimes called a **relative clause**) is a group of words that work together to describe a person, place, or thing. More specifically, an adjective clause usually begins with a **relative pronoun**.

RELATIVE PRONOUNS: **who, whom, whose, which, that, when, where**

People often assume these relative pronouns indicate a need for commas, but the real issue is the *entire* adjective clause. Sometimes these clauses require commas. At other times, it's a mistake to set them off with commas.

Basically, adjective clauses are *set off* with commas when they are nonessential, and *not set off* when they contain essential information.

What Causes the Problem?

Writers cannot always settle punctuation decisions simply by looking for a rule in a grammar textbook. Sometimes, writers must interpret rules on the basis of the specific piece of writing.

Indeed, one reason why this particular comma error occurs is that a sentence may be grammatically correct with *or* without commas, but the meaning changes according to whether or not commas are used. Compare, for instance, these two statements.

VERSION 1: **All my classmates who went to the midnight show were late for class.**

VERSION 2: **All my classmates, who went to the midnight show, were late for class.**

In Version 1, the writer is referring *only* to those classmates who went to the show. In Version 2, however, the commas indicate that readers do not need the clause *who went to the midnight show* to identify the classmates. In other words, the commas in Version 2 indicate that *all* the classmates went to the midnight show and were late for class.

Diagnostic Exercise **(Corrected sentences appear on page 303.)**

Correct all errors in the following paragraph using the first correction as a model. The number in parentheses at the end of the paragraph indicates how many commas you should add or delete.

It was strange going back to my high school reunion^, which was held last summer. Monica, who was my best friend as a senior, didn't recognize me. I guess she didn't expect to see me bald. I also saw a friend, whom I've stayed in touch with over the phone but haven't actually seen in ages. He told me he moved to northern California, where he got married and bought a house. Since I now live in Oregon, we agreed to visit. After the reunion was over, I had a snack with him and Monica who finally became used to my new hair. (2)

Fixing This Problem in Your Writing

First, find the noun or pronoun being described by the adjective clause. Usually, this word will be right before the relative pronoun. Here are two tips to help you decide whether an adjective clause needs a comma before (and perhaps after) it. We suggest using both tips.

> SPECIFIC OR GENERAL TIP: If the noun or pronoun being described by the clause is specific, a comma is usually needed. If the noun or pronoun is general, a comma is probably not needed.

Consider this sentence:

> **My writing instructor, whose daughter lives near me, drives through my neighborhood often.**

The tip tells us that *my writing instructor* is so specific that the audience will know which person the sentence is describing. Thus, commas are required.

CLARITY TIP: If the sentence will be clear to readers if you leave out the adjective clause, *use* a comma. But if readers will be confused about which person, place, or thing you are referring to, *do not use* a comma.

A comma used with an adjective clause signals your readers and lets them know that they don't really need the information being set off. It's a way of showing them how to read and interpret your sentences.

Now consider this sentence:

We saw the police officer who gave you a ticket.

Even though *the police officer* seems specific, your readers are not likely to know *which* officer you are referring to. Because the *who* clause is needed for clarity, commas are not used to set it off. Of course, much depends on the sentences that come before the one in question. If previous sentences had already referred to this police officer, you probably would not need the *who* clause in this sentence, meaning that you would, indeed, set it off with commas. The bottom line is that you need to decide whether the readers know which person, place, or thing the adjective clause is modifying.

For Example . . .

Consider the Specific or General Tip. In Sample 1, *Chicago* is so specific that readers won't need the *where* clause to identify this place. Therefore, the error can be fixed by adding the comma before this nonessential clause.

SAMPLE 1: **✗ I want to go to Chicago where I was born.**

CORRECTION: **I want to go to Chicago, where I was born.**

Consider Sample 2 in terms of the Specific or General Tip. Although *the man* seems specific because of *the*, the noun *man* is still very general.

See whether the Clarity Tip helps. Can readers identify *the man* without the *who* clause? Based on this sentence alone, it seems the *who* clause is needed so that readers will know which man is being described. Since the *who* clause is necessary, it shouldn't be set off by a comma.

SAMPLE 2: **✗ There is the man, who owes me a dollar.**

CORRECTION: **There is the man who owes me a dollar.**

Now You Try It, 1 **(Corrected sentences appear on page 303.)**

Use the Specific or General Tip to determine whether these sentences are punctuated correctly. First, underline the word or words described by the adjective clause. Next, write either *general* or *specific* above it. Finally, either write *OK* above the sentence or make any changes (add or delete commas).

specific

Example: **I borrowed a quarter from my dad, who always seems to have one in his pocket.**

1. Anna is reading *The Ginger Man*, which was written by J. P. Donleavy.
2. My professor asked us to write about someone whom we admire.
3. She wanted to go to a place, where she could be alone.
4. This neighborhood cafe, which was established in 1919, is one of my favorite places to drink coffee.
5. My parents were married in the Middle East country of Yemen, where the wedding feast often lasts twenty-one days.

Now You Try It, 2 **(Corrected sentences appear on page 303.)**

Use the Clarity Tip to determine whether the following adjective clauses require commas. First, underline the word or words described by the adjective clause. Next, explain why the sentence would be either clear or unclear without the adjective clause. Finally, write *OK* above the sentence, or make any changes (add or delete commas).

The adjective clause is needed to identify *the* guy.

EXAMPLE: **Cindy asked whether I knew the guy, who bumped into her.**

1. My roommate is from New York City, which is also my hometown.
2. The person whose books are all over the floor should pick them up.
3. My mother who graduated from my school plans to attend homecoming.
4. Meet me at the place where you and I first met.
5. I read the book that you recommended, but I didn't like it.

Now You Try It, 3

Use each of the following groups of words as an adjective clause. Refer to this lesson's tips to be sure that you used the appropriate punctuation.

EXAMPLE: Ms. Tange likes these shoes, ^ **which I borrowed from you.**

1. whose house is next to mine

2. that you lent me

3. whom I have always admired

4. who helped me study for the test

5. where you took me for my birthday

Editing Practice, 1 **(Corrected sentences appear on page 304.)**

Correct all errors in the following paragraphs using the first correction as a model. The number in parentheses at the end of each paragraph indicates how many commas you should add or delete.

I went to high school in San Bernardino, which is not far from Los Angeles. It's been ten years since I graduated from high school, and I've rarely been back to my hometown since attending San Diego State University which is fairly far away. But I recently spent a week back at my hometown and was surprised at the changes at my high school. (1)

For one thing, my favorite teacher who taught world history is now the principal, and the principal, who was there when I attended, is now the school superintendent. About half the teachers whom I had classes with have left entirely, and several of the ones who are still there are considering retirement. I found the new cafeteria which is twice as big as the one I remember, and the classroom where I once took three English classes is now a detention hall. I can't help but wonder how many more changes will occur before I visit again. (5)

Editing Practice, 2 **(Corrected sentences appear on page 304.)**

Correct all errors in the following paragraph using the first correction as a model. The number in parentheses at the end of the paragraph indicates how many commas you should add or delete.

I am presently rooming with Harold Lee,‸ who is very practical when it comes to buying gifts. We couldn't afford to spend much for Christmas gifts, so we decided to prepare seasonings and can some vegetables. We first made some spicy Cajun seasoning which was the easiest part of our gift-giving adventure. Then, we made a relish that was primarily composed of tomatoes, onion, and cabbage. The tomatoes which we bought at the local market had to be completely green. The jars had to be carefully sterilized, and the directions confused us. Luckily, we received expert advice from my mom whom I called in desperation. Once we understood the process better, we went on to asparagus which has always been a personal favorite. I'm not sure we really saved much time or money, but the experience was fun. (5)

Editing Practice, 3

Correct all errors in the following paragraphs using the first correction as a model. The number in parentheses at the end of each paragraph indicates how many commas you should add or delete.

Ethics,‸ which is basically the study of goodness,‸ is a complex subject because there are diverse systems of ethics. Utilitarianism is an ethical system, which argues that ethical behavior results when we consider what does the most good for the most people. People who believe in such a stance think of the needs of the community rather than their own needs. (1)

Another ethical system which is called the ethic of care maintains that caring for one another's needs and our own needs is all-important. This approach to ethics is often associated with Carol Gilligan who wrote *In a Different Voice*.

The ethic of care stresses that people are unique and that we cannot devise a list of moral codes. This system is just one alternative to utilitarianism which has fallen out of favor. (4)

Writing Practice

On your own paper, write a paragraph or two explaining your thoughts about ethical behavior and the people who have influenced your thinking. Try to use at least five adjective clauses. Use the Proofreading Checklist to see whether each sentence you wrote is punctuated correctly.

PROOFREADING CHECKLIST

Punctuating Adjective Clauses in Your Writing

- Find the word that the adjective clause is describing. This word should refer to a person, place, or thing, and it is usually placed in front of the adjective clause.
- Is this word general or specific? If it is general, then a comma is usually unnecessary. If the word is specific, a comma is usually needed.
- Double-check your decision. Consider the information you've given readers about the word described by the adjective clause. Do they need the adjective clause to identify the person, place, or thing being described? If your answer is yes, a comma is usually unnecessary. If your answer is no, a comma is usually needed.
- If the two tips conflict, there may be no straightforward right or wrong answer. We suggest leaning toward the second tip, since it focuses on your readers' needs.

THE BOTTOM LINE

Commas are used to set off a nonessential adjective clause, *which is a clause that is not necessary to identify the person, place, or thing being described.*

Lesson 8
Commas with Appositives

Sample Errors

SAMPLE 1: ✗ **Shakespeare's play, *Hamlet*, has been made into a film several times.**

SAMPLE 2: ✗ **Senator Cook a Republican voted for the bill.**

What's the Problem?

An **appositive** is a noun or pronoun that renames another noun or pronoun. An appositive almost always comes immediately after the word being renamed. Some appositives supply crucial information for the "meat" of the sentence; readers would be confused without the appositive. These **essential appositives** should *not* be set off with commas. Other appositives are more like "gravy"—they offer supplemental information or additional detail. Because these appositives aren't necessary, commas set them off.

What Causes the Problem?

Appositives are not always easy to identify, and then—once they are identified—the writer still has to decide whether or not they supply essential information. Often, this second decision isn't a simple matter; the writer has to figure out how much the readers already know about the person, place, or thing renamed. Commas are, nonetheless, important. They serve as a signpost to readers, letting them know that the appositive is not essential.

Diagnostic Exercise (Corrected sentences appear on page 304.)

Correct all errors in the following paragraph using the first correction as a model. The number in parentheses at the end of the paragraph indicates how many commas you should add or delete.

Joseph McCarthy,^ a senator in the 1940's and 1950's,^ led an extreme movement to guard America against communism, a form of government much feared in the United States at that time. The term, *McCarthyism*, now refers to hysterical investigation of the opponents of an institution or government. (2)

Fixing This Problem in Your Writing

You first need to be able to detect an appositive. Knowing it is a noun or a pronoun renaming a previous noun or pronoun helps, but here is a tip that can serve as a double-check.

> SWITCHING TIP: An appositive can be recognized because it can be switched with the word it renames. The resulting sentence should be grammatical and coherent.

At this point, don't worry about commas; just see whether the words can be switched. The Switching Tip confirms that there is an appositive in Sample 1.

SAMPLE 1: **✗ Shakespeare's play, *Hamlet*, has been made into a film several times.**

TIP APPLIED: ***Hamlet*, Shakespeare's play, has been made into a film several times.**

Once you have detected an appositive, you can determine whether it needs to be set off by commas. Put commas around an appositive *unless* it provides readers with essential information for identifying the word it renames. In other words, an essential appositive isn't set off by commas. In Sample 1, the original appositive appears to be necessary, since it tells us *which* Shakespearean play is being described. Thus, the appositive should *not* have commas.

CORRECTION: **Shakespeare's play *Hamlet* has been made into a film several times.**

For Example . . .

The Switching Tip confirms that there is an appositive in Sample 2.

SAMPLE 2: **✗ Senator Cook a Republican voted for the bill.**

TIP APPLIED: **A Republican, Senator Cook, voted for the bill.**

Next, cover up the original appositive (*a Republican*) to determine whether the information it provides is essential for identifying the words it renames (*Senator Cook*). Readers probably would not be confused, so the appositive requires commas. True, readers would not know that Cook is a Republican, but they still would know whom you are talking about.

CORRECTION: **Senator Cook, a Republican, voted for the bill.**

Now You Try It, 1 **(Corrected sentences appear on page 304.)**

Use the Switching Tip to locate all appositives. Rewrite each sentence by flip-flopping the appositive with the word renamed. Then, either correct the sentence by adding or deleting commas *or* write *OK* above the sentence.

My physics professor is from the capital of Thailand, Bangkok.

EXAMPLE: **My physics professor is from Bangkok, the capital of Thailand.**

1. Admiral Chester Nimitz the World War II commander of the U.S. Pacific Fleet has an aircraft carrier named after him.

2. Six thousand people were killed by a hurricane in Galveston a port in Texas.

3. An emperor penguin *aptenodytes forsteri* can remain under water for fifteen minutes.

4. Richard a guy in my geology class fell asleep during the lecture.

5. My friend Monica taught me everything I know about grammar. [*Hint:* Assume that the writer has other friends besides Monica.]

Now You Try It, 2 **(Corrected sentences appear on page 304.)**

Use the Switching Tip to locate all appositives. Rewrite each sentence by flip-flopping the appositive with the word renamed. Then, either correct the sentence by adding or deleting commas *or* write *OK* above the sentence.

While walking, I met a guy in my math class, Ike Lee.

EXAMPLE: **While walking, I met Ike Lee, a guy in my math class.**

1. My grandparents recall "Black Thursday" the stock-market crash of 1929.

2. The bookstore finally received shipments of the novels *Pride and Prejudice* and *Tess of the d'Urbervilles.*

3. My roommate said I should read the book he just finished, *Alive!*

4. One of my friends Pauline wrote this poem.

5. Victoria Woodhull and Tennessee Cook two sisters were the first female stockbrokers in New York.

Now You Try It, 3

Rewrite each sentence by adding an appositive and any commas that might be needed. Check to see whether you created an appositive by using the Switching Tip.

I asked Myra, *one of my former roommates*, to help me study.

EXAMPLE: **I asked one of my former roommates ^, Myra,^ to help me study.**

1. The boxer took a hard right from his opponent.

2. Arnold flew into a rage when he saw Alvin.

3. Walking out of the mall, the security officer saw two people waving their arms wildly.

4. The history teacher asked Martie to lead a group discussion.

5. My friend bought a recording by my favorite singer.

Editing Practice, 1 **(Corrected sentences appear on page 304.)**

Correct all errors in the following paragraph using the first correction as a model. The number in parentheses at the end of the paragraph indicates how many commas you should add or delete.

Gary^,^ my nephew^,^ called and suggested we throw a surprise birthday party for my mother, who just turned sixty-five. I'm not much for birthday parties, but I agreed to help. We asked my friend Sharon to assist. Sharon an interior-design major has an excellent eye for decorating, so she took charge of turning my living room, a very plain room, into a more festive place for the occasion. My mother, who has a notorious sweet tooth, is particularly fond of chocolate, so we ordered an enormous cake made of dark chocolate. Gary asked my oldest sister Stephanie to arrange to bring my mom to my house tomorrow. Everything is just about finished, and thirty-five people plan to attend the party. (4)

Editing Practice, 2 **(Corrected sentences appear on page 305.)**

Correct all errors in the following paragraphs using the first correction as a model. The number in parentheses at the end of each paragraph indicates how many commas you should either add or delete.

World War II, one of the best-known wars of all time, was followed a few years later by a conflict that still is not well understood. The Korean War, a conflict between the United Nations and North Korea, was never officially a war. Harry Truman the U.S. president at the time of the conflict never asked Congress to declare war, and the U.S. troops fought as part of the United Nations forces. The conflict was therefore called a "police action." (2)

This war caused many problems for the United States, possibly because its status and purpose were not clear. General Douglas MacArthur the commander of the UN forces was removed from office for insubordination to President Truman the commander in chief. After the landings at Inchon a major turning point the North Koreans were pushed back. Neither side completely achieved its goals, and a truce was signed in 1953. (5)

Editing Practice, 3

Correct all errors in the following paragraphs using the first correction as a model. The number in parentheses at the end of each paragraph indicates how many commas you should either add or delete.

The Mason-Dixon line, a famous boundary line, was laid out in the 1760's by surveyors Charles Mason and Jeremiah Dixon. It separated Pennsylvania and Maryland two regions having unclear boundaries at the time. However, it become symbolic of something else, the political divisions between North and South. (1)

Until the Civil War ended, the Mason-Dixon line was a distinct border between slaveholding states and free states. It's from this line that we get the

name, *Dixie*, to designate the South and the Confederacy. Although Maryland is south of the boundary, it never seceded from the Union and is not considered part of the South. Today, the Mason-Dixon line, a boundary rarely designated on a map, seems to be gradually fading from use. With more and more people moving from one part of the country to another, it is becoming harder to find sharp regional divisions. (2)

Writing Practice

Consider boundaries in your hometown. On your own paper, write a paragraph or two explaining boundaries that are either on a map or that people consider significant (like track crossings or neighborhood boundaries). Try to use at least three appositives. Use the Proofreading Checklist to correct any punctuation errors in the sentences you write.

PROOFREADING CHECKLIST

Punctuating Appositives in Your Writing

- To help you decide whether a word or group of words is an appositive, see if you can switch it with the word being renamed. If the test sentence is grammatically complete and coherent, there is, indeed, an appositive.
- Cover up the appositive and ask, "Would readers be confused if the appositive were deleted?"
- If readers would be confused, do not put commas around the appositive, since it is essential.
- If readers would not be confused, set off the appositive with commas.

THE BOTTOM LINE

An appositive, *a word that renames another word,* is set off by commas unless the appositive is essential.

UNIT TWO
PUTTING IT ALL TOGETHER

Commas serve a variety of specific functions, but generally their purpose is to indicate a pause intended to help readers separate one concept from another. Be careful that you do not use a comma simply because you think there is a pause; also be aware of the formal guidelines for using commas.

Following is an overview of how the comma *can* be used along with the tips we have offered.

Commas Used With *And, But, Or*

Use a comma with *and, but,* or *or* to separate one independent clause from another (see Lesson 3).

Theresa asked me to visit her, but she lives too far away.

IMAGINARY PERIOD TIP: Imagine a period right before *and, but,* or *or.* Can each part divided by this period stand alone as a complete sentence? If so, use a comma before the *and, but,* or *or.*

Avoiding Comma Splices

A comma alone is not enough punctuation to separate one independent clause from another (see Lesson 4).

TWO-SENTENCES TIP: If what comes *before* a comma and what comes *after* it could be *two separate sentences,* there probably is a comma splice.

CORRECTION STRATEGY A: **Add *and*, *but*, or *or* right after the comma.**

CORRECTION STRATEGY B: **Change the comma to a semicolon.**

COMMA SPLICE: **✗ My paper is late, it won't be penalized.**

CORRECTION A: **My paper is late, but it won't be penalized.**

CORRECTION B: **My paper is late; it won't be penalized.**

Commas and Introductory Elements

Use a comma pause to show readers where the introduction ends and where the major part of the sentence really begins (see Lesson 5). Introductory elements do not always require a comma, but the safest approach is to use one.

introductory element
While Dr. Clark was lecturing, the fire alarm went off.

DELETION TIP: Almost any introductory element can be deleted without creating an error.

Commas with Transitional Words

Purpose of the comma pause: To call attention to a term that connects one complete idea to another (see Lesson 6).

Dana couldn't make it to class. Therefore, I took notes for him.

MOVEMENT TIP: A transitional word can always be moved around in a sentence.

Commas with Adjective Clauses

Purpose of the comma pause: To show readers that the adjective clause is not essential to identifying the person, place, or thing that the clause describes (see Lesson 7). If the sentence will be *clear* to readers if you leave out the adjective clause, *use* a comma.

word described — adjective clause
I received a call from Jan, whom I met at the beach last week.

SPECIFIC OR GENERAL TIP: If the word being described by the clause is specific, a comma is usually needed. If the word is general, a comma is probably not needed.

Commas with Appositives

Purpose of the comma pause: To separate nonessential appositives from the words they rename (see Lesson 8). Put commas around an appositive *unless* readers would be confused if the appositive were omitted.

nonessential appositive
Jean, <u>my neighbor</u>, invited me for Thanksgiving dinner.

SWITCHING TIP: An appositive can be recognized because it can be flip-flopped with the word it renames. The resulting sentence should be coherent.

Review

Correct all errors in the following paragraphs using the first correction as a model. The number in parentheses at the end of each paragraph indicates how many errors you should find.

Americans may place too much emphasis on being thin; too many people are obsessed with the idea. On the other hand too many Americans are overweight, and need to consider how their eating habits can lead to serious health risks. (2)

Although many people connect being overweight with food liquids play a role in losing or gaining weight. For instance a person who eats salty foods will tend to retain fluids, which add to a person's body weight even if not in the form of fat. Salt the most common form of sodium has that effect on the body. Although dieticians are not in complete agreement about the effects of drinking water there is evidence that drinking eight or so glasses of water each day will help flush waste fluids out of the body. However it is clearly a good idea to cut back on one certain liquid alcohol. Alcohol adds extra calories, a six-ounce glass of white wine has 120 calories. While offering plenty of calories alcohol offers almost no vitamins or nutrients. In addition alcohol stimulates most people's appetite, and lowers their willpower. Some evidence indicates that alcohol decreases the body's ability to burn fat but more research is needed to confirm that possibility. (12)

UNIT THREE
Other Punctuation and Capitalization

; ’ ^ “ ” : CAP

OVERVIEW

Terms That Can Help You Understand Punctuation and Capitalization

If you are not familiar with any of the following terms that appear in this unit, look them up in the Guide to Grammar Terminology beginning on page 1. The numbers in parentheses indicate the lessons in which each term appears.

complete sentence (9, 15)
contraction (10, 12)
direct quotation (13)
paraphrase (13)
plural (12)
possessive apostrophe (11, 12)
proper adjective (16)
proper noun (16)

The Nuts and Bolts of Punctuation and Capitalization

This section describes the functions of punctuation that most commonly cause writers difficulties (except for commas, which are covered in Unit Two).

Semicolons almost always separate one group of words that could stand alone from another group of words that also could stand alone (see Lesson 9).

EXAMPLE: **Roses are red; violets are blue.**

Apostrophes have the following three functions:

- To indicate letters have been left out, as in *I'll* for *I will* (see Lesson 10).
- To indicate possession, as in *Bill's cat* (see Lesson 11).
- To indicate plurality with numbers, letters, and abbreviations, as in *1970's* (see Lesson 12).

Quotation marks have the following two common functions:

- To show that the writer is repeating somebody word for word (see Lesson 13).

  EXAMPLE: **H. L. Mencken once wrote, "Puritanism is the haunting fear that someone, somewhere, may be happy."**

- To set off titles of written works that are considered part of a larger work.

  EXAMPLE: **Have you read the poem "Paul Revere's Ride"?**

Colons set off explanatory or illustrative words, such as some—but not all—lists of words (see Lesson 15).

EXAMPLE: **Paint the room in these colors: brown, tan, and white.**

One important function of capitalization is to indicate proper nouns and proper adjectives (see Lesson 16).

EXAMPLE: **Our guest speaker, Professor Janet Williams from the University of Chicago, will speak about Hispanic literature.**

Can You Detect Punctuation and Capitalization Problems?

(Corrected sentences appear on page 305.)

Correct all errors in the following paragraph using the first correction as a model. The number in parentheses at the end of the paragraph indicates how many errors you should find.

Because my ~~History~~ [history] class ends at 11:30 and my Math class begins at noon, I have little time to eat lunch. I can still hear my Mother saying, "You need a nutritious lunch", so I try to eat something quick that is still filling and at least somewhat healthy, such as: vegetable soup, roll's, and fruit juice. Luckily, several vendors' on campus sell healthy food; and specialize in ethnic food for the most part. (7)

LESSON 9

Semicolons

Sample Errors

SAMPLE 1: **✗ Sam brought almost everything; drinks, cake, and crackers.**

SAMPLE 2: **✗ He forgot; however, to bring glasses.**

;

What's the Problem?

The main use of a semicolon (;) is to separate two groups of words in a sentence when *each* group could stand *alone* as a **complete sentence**. Although each group of words could stand alone, the ideas are so closely related that the writer puts them into one sentence instead of two. A problem occurs, however, when one of the word groups that are separated by the semicolon *cannot* stand alone as a complete sentence.

What Causes the Problem?

People often confuse the semicolon with the colon (:), as in Sample 1. And some people mistakenly believe that a semicolon *always* goes before words like *however* and *therefore*, as in Sample 2 (also, see Lesson 8). The semicolon provides a strong pause; however, it cannot be used simply because the writer feels a pause is needed.

Diagnostic Exercise **(Corrected sentences appear on page 305.)**

Correct all errors in the following paragraph using the first correction as a model. The number in parentheses at the end of the paragraph indicates how many errors you should find.

In the earlier part of this century;, pulp magazines were extremely popular. They were composed of cheap paper (pulp) and contained various types of stories; adventure, detective stories, romance tales, and western stories. One successful pulp publisher was Street & Smith; this firm sold millions of magazines. Most issues; however, have been destroyed or lost. (2)

Fixing This Problem in Your Writing

This tip can help you determine whether you used a semicolon correctly.

> IMAGINARY PERIOD TIP: *First,* imagine that the semicolon is a period. *Second,* see whether what comes before this imaginary period could be a complete sentence. *Third,* see whether what comes after the imaginary period could also be a complete sentence. If *both* parts could stand alone without changing their original meanings, then the semicolon is correctly used.

In other words, if a period can be used, so can the semicolon. If this test fails, you probably have an error (see Lesson 1 about recognizing a complete sentence). Following are two ways to fix it.

CORRECTION STRATEGY A: **Use something other than a semicolon.**

People sometimes mistakenly use semicolons when other punctuation is needed. Sample 1, for example, really needs a colon (see Lesson 15).

SAMPLE 1: **✗ Sam brought almost everything; drinks, cake, and crackers.**

CORRECTION: **Sam brought almost everything: drinks, cake, and crackers.**

CORRECTION STRATEGY B: **Change the sentence structure or wording.**

What happens when you have no idea which punctuation is needed in place of a semicolon? As a last resort, rewrite the sentence so that you have something you know how to punctuate. For Sample 2, we moved *however* to the front simply because we know we don't have to worry about any sort of punctuation going *before* the first word in a sentence. That may not be the most courageous approach, but it works for now.

For Example . . .

In Sample 2, what comes before the semicolon can stand on its own. However, what comes after it cannot. Therefore, the original sentence has a semicolon error.

SAMPLE 2: **✗ He forgot; however, to bring glasses.**

CORRECTION: **However, he forgot to bring glasses.**

Now You Try It, 1 **(Corrected sentences appear on page 305.)**

Underline the part of the sentence before the semicolon and the part after the semicolon. If either part can stand alone as a complete sentence, write *OK* above it. If either part cannot stand alone as a complete sentence, mark an *X* above it. If there is a semicolon error in the original sentence, correct the error.

OK ✘

EXAMPLE: **Aaron wanted to borrow my book; , a book that I myself borrowed from someone.**

;

1. On Friday, there will be a test; one that will be hard.
2. Delaware's nickname is the First State; it was first to ratify the Constitution.
3. My neighbor's car is far too loud; I think it needs a new muffler.
4. Sylvia and I went to the same high school; Pine Tree High School.
5. Macbeth was the king of Scotland in the eleventh century; Shakespeare wrote a play about Macbeth's reign.

Now You Try It, 2 **(Corrected sentences appear on page 305.)**

Underline the part of the sentence before the semicolon and the part after the semicolon. If either part can stand alone as a complete sentence, write *OK* above it. If either part cannot stand alone as a complete sentence, mark an *X* above it. If there is a semicolon error in the original sentence, correct the error.

OK ✘

EXAMPLE: **Arizona has an appropriate choice for its state bird; , the cactus wren.**

1. My car wouldn't start this morning; because the battery was dead.
2. When I was in elementary school, I had a set of forty-eight crayons in a box that had a built-in sharpener; it was my most-prized possession.
3. For dessert Amy had a parfait; a dessert made of ice cream, fruit, and syrup.
4. A plutocracy is a government composed of the wealthy; some countries have governments that resemble a plutocracy.
5. Last Friday, our meteorology class traveled to a weather observatory; which was located 20 miles from the college.

Now You Try It, 3

Finish each sentence by adding a semicolon followed by another statement.

EXAMPLE: **Allan's sister called for him**; *however, he was not around.*

1. This class is not as hard as I thought it would be

2. The tabloid claimed a comet would crash into Earth this year

3. I wanted to watch the football game

4. It will be numbingly cold today

5. We have a paper due this Friday

;

Editing Practice, 1 **(Corrected sentences appear on page 306.)**

Correct all errors in the following paragraphs using the first correction as a model. The number in parentheses at the end of each paragraph indicates how many errors you should find.

Langston Hughes is one of the best-known African American poets, ; his reputation having begun in 1915, when he was thirteen. At that time, he was elected poet of his graduating class; an unusual selection not merely because he was one of only two African American students in his class but because he had never written any poems. Hughes explained that nobody else in the class had written any poetry either. His classmates elected him; however, because they assumed that poetry requires rhythm and that he must have rhythm because of his ethnicity. (2)

Even though such reasoning had an element of stereotyping, Hughes was inspired; and wrote a graduation poem that the teachers and students enthusiastically received. He went on to publish many types of writing; poems, plays, short stories, children's books, histories, and song lyrics, just to name a few. (2)

Editing Practice, 2 **(Corrected sentences appear on page 306.)**

Correct all errors in the following paragraphs using the first correction as a model. The number in parentheses at the end of each paragraph indicates how many errors you should find.

Some science projects can take time. Others~~;~~, however, are relatively easy. A terrarium is a small environment that is built for living plants and animals; it is not terribly difficult to make. It can be built out of containers such as; a large glass jug, a plastic container, or even a glass baking pan covered with plastic wrap. A particularly good container; however, is an aquarium, even if it has minor cracks or holes. (2)

The bottom of the container must be lined with a shallow layer of pebbles; this layer allows for good drainage. A couple of inches of a sand and soil mixture go on top of the pebbles. The terrarium then needs a small dish of water placed into the soil; so that the rim of the dish is level with the top of the soil. Then a variety of plants and minerals can be added, including; ferns, moss, rotting bark, and a few rocks. The terrarium must be covered with glass or plastic; and placed out of direct sunlight. You can also put lizards, toads, or other small animals into the environment; just give them the appropriate food. (3)

Editing Practice, 3

Correct all errors in the following paragraphs using the first correction as a model. The number in parentheses at the end of each paragraph indicates how many errors you should find.

Our football team won most of its games last year~~;~~, all except one. The one loss was a 21 to 7 bowl game. Before that game; we were ranked fourth in the nation; our opponent was ranked fifth. Needless to say, it was a big game. We were well prepared; however, the other team was even better prepared. (1)

Unfortunately, we dropped to number 10 in the nation after the big loss; that was the lowest ranking we had all year. This year, the preseason polls put us in the top twenty; we are ranked by one poll as seventeenth and by another as twentieth. Most people I have talked to; however, think we have a chance to end up in the top five. Some are even saying; that we might compete for the national championship. We'll wait and see; I don't want to get my hopes up. (2)

;

Writing Practice

On your own paper, write a paragraph or two describing a sports team you like or dislike (or perhaps a paragraph about why you *don't* have a favorite team). Try to use three semicolons. Use the Proofreading Checklist to correct any semicolon errors in the sentences you wrote.

PROOFREADING CHECKLIST

Avoiding Semicolon Errors in Your Writing

- Each time you use a semicolon, see whether what comes *before* it could stand alone as a complete, grammatical sentence.
- Do the same with what comes *after* the semicolon.
- If *both* parts can stand alone without changing the meaning of the original sentence, then the semicolon should be *correct*.
- If even one part cannot stand alone, then you may have an error.
- Correct a semicolon error in one of two ways: (a) delete the semicolon and—if necessary—add the correct punctuation, or (b) reword the sentence so you know how to punctuate it.

THE BOTTOM LINE

See whether what comes before a semicolon could stand alone; do the same with what comes after the semicolon.

LESSON 10

Apostrophes in Contractions

Sample Errors

SAMPLE 1: ✗ **Pacifism is the belief that warfare isnt justified.**

SAMPLE 2: ✗ **The ethics committee announced that its no longer supporting the senator's decision to remain in office.**

What's the Problem?

Contractions are shortened forms of words, and—for better or worse—they add an informal tone to writing, as well as some conciseness. Many readers prefer that writers not use contractions in formal writing, so one way to avoid contraction errors is simply to avoid using contractions. However, many writers want to use contractions, so here we describe how they can be correctly "assembled."

An error occurs when a contraction lacks an apostrophe or when the apostrophe is in the wrong place. We focus on the first situation, since it is by far the more frequent error. An apostrophe offers a cue to readers, letting them know that you are using a contraction (and letting them know you fully realize the word is a contraction).

Sample 1 has a contraction error because *isnt* ("is not") lacks an apostrophe between the *n* and the *t*. Similarly, Sample 2 requires an apostrophe to show that *its* stands for "it is."

What Causes the Problem?

Contractions are especially common in speech. In fact, many writers use contractions to lend a relaxed, natural tone such as that found in conversations. Thus, it is easy to overlook the apostrophe, since we do not worry about it in speech. Additionally, some contractions are used so often that we forget that they are, indeed, just contractions.

And then there is the confusion between the contraction *it's* ("it is") and the possessive *its* (as in *The fish ate its neighbor*). Many writers—even the most experienced ones—often confuse these two words.

Diagnostic Exercise **(Corrected sentences appear on page 306.)**

Correct all errors in the following paragraph using the first correction as a model. The number in parentheses at the end of the paragraph indicates how many errors you should find.

The student government announced today the election results for representation in the student senate. Almost half the students ~~didnt~~ didn't vote at all, and there werent many candidates running. I'm not sure why, but apathy was widespread. My guess is that many students dont think the senators have much real power, or perhaps the candidates' qualifications and goals were unclear. Its clear that students aren't enthusiastic about our student government, so perhaps we should consider large-scale changes to the system. (3)

Fixing This Problem in Your Writing

For writers who have a habit of overlooking a contraction, here is a proofreading tip.

CONTRACTION TIP: Reread and see whether you can "expand" any one word by filling in missing letters (or numbers, as in *the class of '97*). If so, you probably have a contraction, which needs an apostrophe wherever letters or numbers are missing.

For instance, note how the following words can all be expanded and how the apostrophe replaces the missing letters:

they're = they are didn't = did not '97 = 1997 let's = let us

The Contraction Tip almost always works, but notice that *won't* is an irregular contraction in which *will not* becomes *won't*.

The most troublesome contraction is *it's* ("it is"). The contraction *it's* is often confused with *its*—which deals with possession and is not a contraction. To help you determine whether you are using the contraction *it's*, we offer the *It's* Tip.

"IT'S" TIP: Look at the apostrophe in *it's* and think of it as the little dot above the letter *i*—the letter that just happens to be the one the apostrophe stands for in *it's.*

In other words, if you see *it's* you should be able to imagine *it is* as well. If *it is* fits into the sentence, your choice of *it's* is correct. If you use *its*, the fact that there is no apostrophe should remind you there is no little dot and, thus, no contraction. The word *its* should always refer to possession (as in *a dog bit its tail*).

’ V

For Example . . .

In Samples 1 and 2, we can easily expand the words *isnt* and *its* to *is not* and *it is.* Thus, they are contractions, and we can either write them out completely or put the apostrophe in the right place.

SAMPLE 1: ✗ **Pacifism is the belief that warfare isnt justified.**

CONTRACTION TIP APPLIED: **Pacifism is the belief that warfare is not justified.**

CORRECTION: **Pacifism is the belief that warfare isn't justified.**

SAMPLE 2: ✗ **The ethics committee announced that its no longer supporting the senator's decision to remain in office.**

CONTRACTION TIP APPLIED: **The ethics committee announced that it is no longer supporting the senator's decision to remain in office.**

CORRECTION: **The ethics committee announced that it's no longer supporting the senator's decision to remain in office.**

Try the *It's* Tip to see whether the following is correctly punctuated:

It's about time the bell rang.

The apostrophe in *it's* should make you think of the dot above the letter *i*—the missing letter. Indeed, you could replace *It's* with *It is*, so the sentence is correct.

Now You Try It, 1 **(Corrected sentences appear on page 306.)**

If a sentence does not have a contraction error, write *OK* above it. If there is an error, cross it out. Then, write out the full form of the word or words to show that the original is a contraction. In addition, supply the correct form of the contraction.

do not
don't

EXAMPLE: **Forget what I said; we ~~dont~~ ^ need your help after all.**

1. Although a friend told me that Mark Twain wrote the poem "Trees," isnt Joyce Kilmer the actual author?

2. Its a fine time for you to leave me, Lucille.

3. I wouldnt do that if I were you.

4. Because it's raining, we wont be going for a walk today.

5. "Its feeding time for the baby," said Tom.

Now You Try It, 2 **(Corrected sentences appear on page 306.)**

If a sentence does not have a contraction error, write *OK* above it. If there is an error, cross it out. Then, write out the full form of the word or words to show that the original is a contraction. In addition, supply the correct form of the contraction.

is not
isn't

EXAMPLE: **The skull ~~isnt~~ ^ just a single bone; it is composed of some twenty-two separate bones.**

1. Didnt Fran manage to break her femur while playing soccer?

2. The United States produces more than its share of carbon dioxide emissions from energy use.

3. My biology class cant meet today because the room was flooded.

4. Havent I met you somewhere before?

5. Lets meet at the study hall around noon.

Now You Try It, 3

If a sentence does not have an *it's/its* error, write *OK* above it. If there is an error, correct it. Refer to the *It's* Tip to help you decide whether there is an error.

EXAMPLE: **~~Its~~ It's too late to turn back now.**

1. A hurricane loses most of it's force when it reaches land.
2. King George's War was a European war lasting from 1744 to 1748, but its impact was felt in New England in the form of minor raids.
3. It's not cold enough to be wearing such a heavy jacket as yours!
4. Your horse has it's leg caught in some barbed wire.
5. When its five o'clock, please turn off the stove.

Editing Practice, 1 **(Corrected sentences appear on page 307.)**

Correct all errors in the following paragraphs using the first correction as a model. The number in parentheses at the end of each paragraph indicates how many errors you should find.

People ~~dont~~ don't think often about where their favorite foods come from, but the subject can be interesting. For instance, there isnt much evidence that waffles originated in Belgium. The waffle seems so popular that many countries claim its origin is with them. The Scots say that the waffle resulted accidentally when Sir Giles Whimple sat on a fresh oatcake while wearing a suit of chain mail. (1)

In France, waffles go back to at least the fifteenth century. Street vendors would sell them in front of churches during religious festivals. Theyd cook waffles with shapes reflecting religious themes to attract the attention of the celebrators. In modern Mexico, waffles are topped with cinnamon and sugar. In tropical countries, theyll often be topped with exotic fruits, while northern countries use whipped cream. For whatever reason, though, *Belgian waffle* has come to be a worldwide term referring to thick waffles. (2)

Editing Practice, 2 **(Corrected sentences appear on page 307.)**

Correct all errors in the following paragraphs using the first correction as a model. The number in parentheses at the end of each paragraph indicates how many errors you should find.

Many holidays are celebrated around the globe, but ~~theyre~~ they're often celebrated in diverse ways. For example, Christmas is celebrated in many countries, but each culture has it's own Christmas traditions. In France, for example, the Noel celebration begins right after December 6 (the feast day of St. Nicholas) and doesnt end until January 6. Many French have a grand meal that isnt served until after midnight mass on Christmas Eve. (3)

In Brazil, Christmas isnt simply a product of one culture; it represents a blend of Portuguese, African, and indigenous Indian cultures. On Christmas Eve, for instance, a traditional dinner includes a stuffing thats made out of a potato-like root from the indigenous Indians' diet. On December 31, many Brazilians go to the beach to celebrate the festival of a religious group that reflects both Roman Catholic and African beliefs. (2)

Editing Practice, 3

Correct all errors in the following paragraphs using the first correction as a model. The number in parentheses at the end of each paragraph indicates how many errors you should find.

Margaret Mead's book, *Coming of Age in Samoa*, is an observer's account of life in Samoa, and ~~its~~ it's standard reading in many anthropology courses. In 1928, this book revolutionized the field of anthropology. Mead didnt stress the effects of biological factors on people's behavior. Rather, she emphasized the effects of social conventions and culture. (1)

Her findings arent the only revolutionary aspect of the book; her methods were also new. Although many social scientists assume that observers should be detached from what theyre studying, Mead argued that its impossible to understand people and their culture fully unless observers have an insider's perspective. Accordingly, she tried to integrate herself into a Samoan community as much as possible. Her approach has its drawbacks but is generally well respected and often used today. (3)

Writing Practice

On your own paper, write a paragraph or two explaining an experience you had among a group of people who seemed quite different from you. Try to use at least three contractions. Use the Proofreading Checklist to correct any contraction errors in your writing.

PROOFREADING CHECKLIST

Using Contractions in Your Writing

- Proofread your words to see whether any one word can be "expanded" into two words. If so, it is probably a contraction.
- Be sure each contraction has an apostrophe positioned over the place where the missing letters (or numbers) are located. Alternatively, you might do away with the contraction entirely, using the expanded form (especially in formal writing).
- The contraction *it's* and the possessive pronoun *its* are often confused. Think about the dot above the letter *i* when you see the apostrophe in *it's*. This signal should remind you that *it's* can stand *only* for *it is*.

THE BOTTOM LINE

If you use a contraction, *it'll* need an apostrophe.

LESSON 11

Apostrophes Showing Possession

Sample Errors

SAMPLE 1: **✗ The quarterbacks pass was incomplete.**

SAMPLE 2: **✗ Todays high temperature was 94°.**

What's the Problem?

Normally, writers show that somebody possesses (or owns) something else by adding an apostrophe and an *s* to a word (as with the "'s" in *Sue's shirt*). If you leave out this apostrophe, there is a possession error.

Put the apostrophe before the *s* if the owner is singular (as in *this man's car*). If it is plural, you usually add just the apostrophe (as in *the three guys' cars*). If the plural form of the word does not end in *s*, add an apostrophe and *then* an *s* to indicate possession (as in *two women's jobs*).

What Causes the Problem?

In speech, people do not use the apostrophe to indicate possession, so it is easy to omit it in writing. Still, it is important to use an apostrophe when showing that something belongs to something else. The vast majority of apostrophes are used for showing possession and contractions. (See Lesson 10 for information about contractions.)

Diagnostic Exercise **(Corrected sentences appear on page 307.)**

Correct all errors in the following paragraph using the first correction as a model. The number in parentheses at the end of the paragraph indicates how many errors you should find.

Two of my close friends were born in Mexico. Paul ~~Morales~~ [Morales's] fathers employer relocated to Arizona when Paul was six. Juanita Lopez moved to the United States recently; Juanitas goal is to learn more about this country. (2)

Fixing This Problem in Your Writing

Here is one way to tell whether you need an apostrophe to show possession.

> "OF" TIP: See whether you can reword the sentence by using the word *of* to show that something belongs to somebody or something else. You'll need to flip-flop some of the words and to separate them by *of*. If you can make this change without affecting the meaning, the original sentence involves possession; you should keep the apostrophe.

For instance, we could easily reword Sample 1 like this:

SAMPLE 1: **✗ The quarterbacks pass was incomplete.**

TIP APPLIED: **The pass <u>of</u> the quarterback was incomplete.**

All we did was flip-flop part of the sentence and insert *of*. The test sentence means the same thing as the original, so the original involves possession and requires an apostrophe. Following is a corrected version of Sample 1.

CORRECTION: **The quarterback's pass was incomplete.**

Caution: Two possessive words that do not require an apostrophe are *its* (as in *The mouse ate its food*) and *whose* (as in *I saw someone whose hat was afire*). See Lesson 10 for information about using *its* instead of *it's*.

For Example . . .

We can reword and correct Sample 2 in the same way.

SAMPLE 2: **✗ Todays high temperature was 94°.**

TIP APPLIED: **The high temperature <u>of</u> today was 94°.**

CORRECTION: **Today's high temperature was 94°.**

But we *cannot* reword a sentence in this way unless there is possession. Does *astronauts* in this next sentence need an apostrophe?

The two astronauts repaired the satellite.

We cannot reword this sentence using *of*—without drastically changing its meaning. Thus, the sentence *does not* need an apostrophe to indicate possession.

Now You Try It, 1 **(Corrected sentences appear on page 307.)**

Each sentence has at least one omitted apostrophe. Correct the error or errors, and show that an apostrophe is needed by rewriting the sentence using *of.*

I found the credit card of my father in my wallet.

father's
EXAMPLE: **I found my ~~fathers~~ ^ credit card in my wallet.**

1. In my communications class, we analyzed the presidents speech.

2. Margaret talked to the manager about the salespersons attitude.

3. Tonys favorite meal is ham and lima beans. [*Hint:* Sometimes *the* has to be added in the test sentence.]

4. I strongly recommend going to this repair shop; my best friends father owns it.

5. Paula managed to get three movie stars autographs.

Now You Try It, 2 **(Corrected sentences appear on page 307.)**

Each sentence has at least one omitted apostrophe. Correct the error or errors, and show that an apostrophe is needed by rewriting the sentence using *of.*

The house of Hank was sold for $80,000.

Hank's
EXAMPLE: **~~Hanks~~ ^ house was sold for $80,000.**

1. Bobs illness lasted almost three weeks.

2. Steve Martins place of birth is Waco, Texas; however, he doesn't have a Southern accent.

3. Turkeys population is about the same as that of Iran.

4. Many people would be surprised to know that Canadas total land area is one of the largest in the world.

5. I heard that tomorrows weather will be awful, but let's go to the beach anyway.

Now You Try It, 3

For each pair of words, write a sentence so that you use an apostrophe to show that the first word "possesses" the second word.

EXAMPLE: **teacher** **hobby**

My teacher's hobby seems to be grading papers.

1. Doris home
2. horse leg
3. historian book
4. somebody belief
5. today weather

Editing Practice, 1 **(Corrected sentences appear on page 307.)**

Correct all errors in the following paragraphs using the first correction as a model. The number in parentheses at the end of each paragraph indicates how many errors you should find.

Jack London's best-known work may be *The Call of the Wild*, the story of one dogs adventures in Alaska. However, London was a prolific writer, having published some forty-three books and countless short stories. In fact, this famous writers goal was to produce a thousand words a day—a goal he usually achieved. (2)

London also held a variety of jobs during his lifetime. At the age of fifteen, he was an oyster pirate in San Francisco Bay, stealing private landowners' oysters and selling them in the citys saloons. Ironically, he then became one of the California Fish Patrols deputies. When just seventeen, he signed on as a sailor for a seal-hunting schooner. These adventures with the sea were the basis for another of Londons widely read books, *The Sea-Wolf*. (3)

Editing Practice, 2 **(Corrected sentences appear on page 308.)**

Correct all errors in the following paragraphs using the first correction as a model. The number in parentheses at the end of each paragraph indicates how many errors you should find.

Abraham Lincoln may be one of America’s most widely recognized presidents, but Lincolns chances as the Republicans presidential candidate in 1860 were considered very slim at the time. He was scarcely known at all. (2)

Lincolns debates with Stephen Douglas gained Lincoln some attention, but some historians believe it was the Cooper Union Speech that propelled Lincoln to the candidacy. When giving this speech, Lincoln was actually in William Sewards home territory. Seward was the leading candidate at the time for the Republican nomination, but Lincoln’s speech gained the attention of the voters and delegates. In this speech, Lincoln challenged many peoples belief that the Constitution and its framers intended to preserve slavery. This was a controversial stance, yet Lincoln’s courageous stance was one shared by many voters. (3)

Editing Practice, 3

Correct all errors in the following paragraphs using the first correction as a model. The number in parentheses at the end of each paragraph indicates how many errors you should find.

I bought a motorcycle earlier this summer, even though my mom’s warning was not to get one because bikes can be dangerous. I took a motorcycle safety course and learned a lot. I learned, for example, that the riders vision should not be impaired by using mirrors that are too small to see what’s coming up from behind. Also, the goggles and helmet should have openings that are large and unobstructed. The passengers view should be unobstructed as well, even though he or she isn’t driving. (2)

Sometimes, the advice is not so clear-cut. Many people suggest that motorcycles shouldn't travel down the center of their side of the road, since that is where oil collects. Other peoples advice is to drive down the center because car drivers see you better there in their rear-view mirrors. That way, you can avoid being in the cars blind spot. (2)

Writing Practice

On your own paper, write a paragraph or two describing some good (or bad) advice you've received. Try to include at least four instances of possession. Use the Proofreading Checklist to see whether each sentence is punctuated correctly in terms of apostrophes.

PROOFREADING CHECKLIST

Showing Possession in Your Writing

- Look for instances when something seems to belong to somebody or something. This possession will take the form of a person, place, or thing's coming immediately after another person, place, or thing.
- See whether the sentence can be reworded using *of* to show that something belongs to something else (flip-flop the words and separate them by using *of*).
- If this test works, you probably need an apostrophe in the original sentence to indicate possession.
- Put the apostrophe before the *s* if the person, place, or thing is singular (as in *this guy's car*). If it is plural, you usually add just the apostrophe (as in *the three guys' cars*). However, if the plural form of the word does not end in *s*, add an apostrophe and then an *s* to indicate possession (as in *three women's books*).

THE BOTTOM LINE

One of the apostrophe's functions is to indicate possession.

LESSON 12

Unnecessary Apostrophes

Sample Errors

SAMPLE 1: ✗ **Your sentence has three comma's.**

SAMPLE 2: ✗ **Some state's do not have a state income tax.**

SAMPLE 3: ✗ **Two Adams' were elected president.**

What's the Problem?

The apostrophe (') is commonly used to show **possession** (see Lesson 11) or to show that letters have been left out of a word to form a **contraction** (see Lesson 10). For almost all words, it is incorrect to use an apostrophe to indicate *plurality*. That is, rarely will an apostrophe be used to show that there is more than one of something (as seen in Samples 1 and 2).

Many people add an apostrophe and an *s* to form the plural of a last name, but this is *not* one of those rare occasions when an apostrophe is used to show plurality. For instance, the plural of the name *Kennedy* is *Kennedys*, and the plural of the name *Nixon* is *Nixons*. If a last name ends in the letter *s*, the plural is formed by adding *es*; the plural of *Adams* is *Adamses* (See Sample 3).

What Causes the Problem?

One reason apostrophe errors occur is that people associate apostrophes with adding an *s*. However, there are two reasons to add an *s*, and only one of these involves an apostrophe.

The first reason to add an *s* is to indicate that there is more than one of something (as in *five books*). The second reason is to show that something belongs to something else (as in *Bob's car*). *Only* in the second situation should you add an apostrophe with the *s*. An error occurs when you confuse these two situations and add an apostrophe each time an *s* is added to a word.

Only very rarely should you use an apostrophe to show that there is more than one of something. One occasion is when both an apostrophe and an *s* are added to abbreviations, numbers, or letters, as in *Three students earned A's on the last test*. Except for this rare situation, avoid using an apostrophe to show that there is more than one of something.

Diagnostic Exercise (Corrected sentences appear on page 308.)

Correct all errors in the following paragraph using the first correction as a model. The number in parentheses at the end of the paragraph indicates how many errors you should find.

Some old ~~friend's~~ friends of mine stopped by my apartment for coffee. My roommate's coffee pot was broken, so I made them some instant coffee. I'm not good at making coffee, but everybody had two cup's apiece. The coffee was pretty old, yet nobody seemed to care. We talked about our schedule's for next semester, and we all decided we should try to leave some time open for getting together every now and then. (2)

Fixing This Problem in Your Writing

Suppose you use an apostrophe and you want to see whether you should leave it out. Here are three tips you can use.

> "OF" TIP: See whether you can reword the sentence by using the word *of* to show that something belongs to somebody or something else. You'll need to flip-flop some of the words and to separate them by *of*. If you can make this change without affecting the meaning, the original sentence involves possession; you should keep the apostrophe.

For example, we can reword the following sentence by using *of*. Thus, it involves possession and requires the apostrophe.

EXAMPLE: **The mascot's costume is torn.**

TIP APPLIED: **The costume <u>of</u> the mascot is torn.**

See Lesson 11 for more information about the use of the apostrophe to show possession.

> CONTRACTION TIP: Reread and see whether you can "expand" any one word by filling in missing letters (or numbers, as in *the class of '97*). If so, you probably have a contraction, which needs an apostrophe wherever letters or numbers are missing.

See Lesson 10 for more information about using the apostrophe in contractions.

SPECIAL-WORD TIP: Use the apostrophe to indicate plurality *only* with numbers, letters, or abbreviations. (Some readers consider this use of the apostrophe to be optional.)

1920's four *s*'s two VCR's some perfect 10's

For Example . . .

SAMPLE 1: ✗ **Your sentence has three comma's.**

SAMPLE 2: ✗ **Some state's do not have a state income tax.**

SAMPLE 3: ✗ **Two Adams' were elected president.**

None of the samples involves possession because there is no way to reword any of them using *of.* Does the apostrophe in *comma's* or *state's* or *Adams'* take the place of letters? No. Do any of these words resemble the abbreviations, letters, or numbers listed under the *Special-Words* Tip? No. Since these sentences fail all three checks, delete the apostrophes.

SAMPLE 1, CORRECTED: **Your sentence has three commas.**

SAMPLE 2, CORRECTED: **Some states do not have a state income tax.**

SAMPLE 3, CORRECTED: **Two Adamses were elected president.**

In this next sentence, the Contraction Tip indicates *I've* is, indeed, a contraction, so the apostrophe is OK. However, *apostrophe's* cannot be reworded by using *of* (the *Of* Tip), and clearly, it isn't a number, letter, or abbreviation.

ORIGINAL: ✗ **<u>I've</u> used seven <u>apostrophe's</u> already.**

CONTRACTION TIP APPLIED: **<u>I have</u> used . . . .**

CORRECTION: **I've used seven apostrophes already.**

Now You Try It, 1 **(Corrected sentences appear on page 308.)**

Refer to the three tips to label each correct apostrophe as "contraction," "possession," or "special word." If there is an error, make the necessary change by deleting the apostrophe.

possession leaves

EXAMPLE: **My neighbor's trees shed ~~leave's~~ ^ all over my front yard.**

1. Three strange-looking guy's are standing outside the door.
2. Gary ate *two* pizza's last night!
3. My history teacher's remarks offended half the class.
4. I'm not going to class today.
5. Judy's letter was lost in the mail, but it wasn't terribly important.

Now You Try It, 2 **(Corrected sentences appear on page 308.)**

Refer to the three tips to label each correct apostrophe as "contraction," "possession," or "special word." If there is an error, make the necessary change by deleting the apostrophe.

eggs

EXAMPLE: **Tim ate three ~~egg's~~ ^ for lunch.**

1. Rock Island is one of Rhode Island's most popular beach resorts.
2. My roommate's home is Huntsville, Alabama; strangely enough, my home is Huntsville, Texas.
3. In the United States, the 1860's were dominated by civil war, and the 1960's were marked by civil unrest.
4. Janet owns three CD player's, and she has a huge collection of CD's.
5. Do you want to ask the Flores' to give us a ride to Paul's party this weekend?

Now You Try It, 3

Write sentences that use the apostrophe in the way described. Sentences 4 and 5 should use two apostrophes, in the order given.

EXAMPLE: **possessive apostrophe plus contraction apostrophe**
My cat's tail doesn't seem short enough.

1. Special-word apostrophe
2. Possessive apostrophe
3. Contraction apostrophe
4. Contraction apostrophe plus contraction apostrophe
5. Possessive apostrophe plus contraction apostrophe

Editing Practice, 1 **(Corrected sentences appear on page 308.)**

Correct all errors in the following paragraphs using the first correction as a model. The number in parentheses at the end of each paragraph indicates how many errors you should find.

My nephew's birthday was a few ~~day's~~ days ago, and I wasn't sure what to get him. Jimmy just turned four, and he likes all kind's of games and toys. However, I wanted to give him something that would stand out. (1)

The toy store's I visited, however, carried the usual stuff: monster toys, superhero dolls, assorted airplanes and cars, and hundreds of computer game's. I wasn't terribly inspired, so I decided to look at some of my old toys from the late 1970's. They were all broken. However, I went through my mother's attic and found three old military-type action figure's from the 1960's. Unlike today's tiny toy figures, these were about 10 inches high and had movable arms and legs. They were also in good condition. I gave them to Jimmy, and I'm hoping he'll pass them along in decent shape to some other family members. (3)

Editing Practice, 2 **(Corrected sentences appear on page 308.)**

Correct all errors in the following paragraphs using the first correction as a model. The number in parentheses at the end of each paragraph indicates how many errors you should find.

Edith Wharton was one of the best-known ~~novelist's~~ novelists of the early 1900's, but much of her fame in the late 1990's results from movie version's of her books *Ethan Frome* and *The Age of Innocence*. Many of Wharton's stories focus on the wealth and elegance of high society. (1)

Undoubtedly, her settings and themes were influenced by her parents' lifestyle. Not only were the Wharton's well off financially, but their ancestry also could be traced back to prestigious New Yorker's. Her childhood was spent among the well-to-do socialite's of New York City, Rhode Island, and various parts of Europe. Despite her upbringing, Wharton's stories often presented satiric portrait's of the rich that questioned their extravagant lifestyles. (4)

Editing Practice, 3

Correct all errors in the following paragraphs using the first correction as a model. The number in parentheses at the end of each paragraph indicates how many errors you should find.

The term *sexual revolution* refers to the shift in how people, especially ~~American's~~ Americans, view sexual behavior. Starting in the 1960's, the sexual revolution called for a less conservative view of sex. Sex outside marriage wasn't seen as always wrong, nor did partners necessarily need to love one another to have a sexual relationship. The use of birth control pill's fostered the revolution; they offered an inexpensive, generally reliable way of preventing pregnancy's. (2)

One of the effect's of the sexual revolution is that there are fewer restriction's on nudity in magazines and movies. Another effect is found in fashion; with the introduction of the miniskirt, clothe's became skimpier and more provocative. People's views on nudity (or near nudity) differ, but society in general has become accustomed to scantily clad models and actresses. The sexual revolution has slowed considerably, largely because of the spread of AIDS. However, society's views on sex may never return to what they were before the sexual revolution. (3)

Writing Practice

On your own paper, write a paragraph or two explaining a movement or historical event that has affected you. Try to use at least four apostrophes. Use the Proofreading Checklist to see whether each sentence you write is punctuated correctly.

PROOFREADING CHECKLIST

Using Apostrophes in Your Writing

- Check each apostrophe and see whether it is called for by considering these three reasons for having an apostrophe:
  1. **Possession.** An apostrophe can be used to indicate that something belongs to something else (as in *today's temperature* or *the teacher's book*). You can usually reword such possession by using *of* (as in *temperature of today* or *the book of the teacher*).
  2. **Contraction.** An apostrophe takes the place of missing letters or numbers (as in *We're ready* or *the class of '99*).
  3. **Special Word.** An apostrophe indicates plurality *only* for numbers, letters, or abbreviations (as in *X's and O's*).
- If the apostrophe does not seem to fit one of these three situations, it is probably unnecessary.

THE BOTTOM LINE

Writers often add unnecessary apostrophes to plural words, but only numbers, letters, or abbreviations use apostrophes to form plurals.

LESSON 13

Quotation Marks with Direct Quotations and Paraphrases

Sample Errors

SAMPLE 1: **✗ In 1854, Chief Joseph of the Nez Perce tribe met with white leaders and said every part of this soil is sacred to my people.**

SAMPLE 2: **✗ Iva said that "it was cold now in her part of the world."**

What's the Problem?

A primary function of quotation marks (" ") is to indicate *exactly* what a person has said or written—a **direct quotation**.

An alternative to quoting someone exactly is to use a **paraphrase** (or indirect quotation), which means putting most or all of somebody else's words in your own words. A paraphrase does not need quotation marks because a paraphrase *substantially* changes the words and the sentence structure of the original material. By paraphrasing, you signal your readers that you are presenting your interpretation of someone else's idea. If you change only a word or two and do not use quotation marks, you may be accused of plagiarism because you are falsely taking credit for the source's writing style. Try to rewrite the original idea in your own words so that readers could compare the original wording with your rewording and see that you are expressing the same thing but in different words or with a different sentence structure. A paraphrase should not change the meaning of the source. Both direct quotations and paraphrases should give credit to the source of the ideas you are using.

Often, you can't look at one sentence and tell whether quotation marks are needed; you have to know exactly what the original passage says to see whether it is being quoted word for word. Still, the two sample sentences seem to have errors. An error occurs if a direct quotation lacks quotation marks (Sample 1) or if a paraphrase has quotation marks around paraphrased material (Sample 2).

Keep in mind that quotation marks have other functions besides indicating a direct quotation. As seen in several places in this lesson, for instance, quotation marks are used around titles of songs, poems, short stories, and other brief works.

What Causes the Problem?

Quotation marks are an aspect of writing that we don't have in speech. Thus, writers are forced to consider something that they normally don't associate with the familiar task of quoting people. Another reason for errors is that people often think they can avoid quotation marks by changing a word or two of the original.

Diagnostic Exercise **(Corrected sentences appear on page 309.)**

Correct all errors in the following paragraph using the first correction as a model. The number in parentheses at the end of the paragraph indicates how many errors you should find.

My history teacher, Dr. Norris, said that we would spend the next class meeting discussing John F. Kennedy's 1963 inaugural address. Kennedy began by saying, ~~we~~ *"We* observe today not a victory of party but a celebration of freedom. . . ." Dr. Norris said that "he listened to this speech as a boy and recalled parts of it." He remembers Kennedy saying that Americans should consider what they could do for their nation—not vice versa. (1)

Fixing This Problem in Your Writing

If you wish to paraphrase, cover up the original sentence and begin writing (and rewriting) your own interpretation, going back to the original when you're done to make sure your paraphrase means about the same thing. Also, keep in mind that both a direct quotation and a paraphrase should indicate whose ideas or words you are using.

Here is one convention widely used to signal an indirect quotation:

> "THAT" TIP: Use *that* to begin a paraphrase but do not use *that* to begin a direct quotation. Although it is not absolutely essential to use *that* before a paraphrase, inserting *that* will never change the meaning of a paraphrase. Inserting *that* before a direct quotation might change the meaning.

Often, such use of *that* comes naturally, but the tip helps you remember when to use and not use quotation marks. Make sure that you don't use quotation marks when paraphrasing and that you do use them when directly quoting. In Sample 1, there is no *that* and inserting one seems to change the meaning of the sentence.

SAMPLE 1: **✗ In 1854, Chief Joseph of the Nez Perce tribe met with white leaders and said every part of this soil is sacred to my people.**

TIP APPLIED: **✗ In 1854, Chief Joseph of the Nez Perce tribe met with white leaders and said <u>that</u> every part of this soil is sacred to my people.**

“ ”

The *that* version suddenly changes *my* to refer to the writer, not to Chief Joseph. Since *that* doesn't work, there must be a direct quotation needing quotation marks. You also need to add a comma before the quote and to capitalize its first word (see Lesson 14 about using quotation marks combined with commas and other punctuation).

SAMPLE 1, CORRECTED: **In 1854, Chief Joseph of the Nez Perce tribe met with white leaders and said, "Every part of this soil is sacred to my people."**

For Example . . .

Sample 2 has a *that* before quoted material, suggesting it is really a paraphrase. Also, why would Iva use the word *her* to refer to herself? She probably wouldn't, so there is reason to believe that the material in quotation marks is not really a direct quotation.

SAMPLE 2: **✗ Iva said <u>that</u> "it was cold now in <u>her</u> part of the world."**

We can't be positive unless we see *exactly* what Iva said. A writer should be able to track down the original material, so we've provided Iva's original statement. Sample 2 has the same meaning as the original statement, but the wording is much different. Therefore, Sample 2 is, indeed, a paraphrase and should *not* have quotation marks.

ORIGINAL STATEMENT: **Where I live, it's very cold now.**

SAMPLE 2, CORRECTED: **Iva said that it was cold now in her part of the world.**

Now You Try It, 1 (Corrected sentences appear on page 309)

First, use each of the following statements as a direct quotation in a sentence of your own (additional information is in brackets). Second, turn the direct quotation into a paraphrase starting with *that*. Be sure to use quotation marks with direct quotations but not with paraphrases.

Thomas Paine believed that circumstances in his day tested people's convictions.

Thomas Paine once wrote, "These "

EXAMPLE: **~~These~~ are the times that try men's souls. [Thomas Paine, writing about the need to fight the British in 1776]**

“ ”

1. Success is counted sweetest by those who ne'er succeed. [Emily Dickinson, in a poem entitled "Success"]

2. Fish and visitors stink in three days. [Proverb recorded by Benjamin Franklin]

3. Any woman who chooses to behave like a full human being should be warned that the armies of the status quo will treat her as something of a dirty joke; that's their natural and first weapon. [Feminist Gloria Steinem, speaking at Yale University]

4. Oppressed people cannot remain oppressed forever. [Martin Luther King, Jr., explaining why he was in Alabama protesting discrimination]

5. I realize that patriotism is not enough; I must have no hatred or bitterness towards anyone. [Last words of Edith Cavell before being executed by the Germans in 1915]

Now You Try It, 2 **(Corrected sentences appear on page 309.)**

First, use each of the following statements as a direct quotation in a sentence of your own (additional information is in brackets). Second, turn the direct quotation into a paraphrase starting with *that*. Be sure to use quotation marks with direct quotations but not with paraphrases.

EXAMPLE: The poet Robert Frost once remarked, "The ~~The~~ **brain is a wonderful organ. It starts working the moment you get up and does not stop until you get into the office."** **[Poet Robert Frost]**

" "

1. The reason I'm going ahead with this attempt now is because I just cannot wait any longer to impress you. [Letter from John Hinckley to actress Jodie Foster the day he shot President Reagan]

2. It is well that war is so terrible—we should grow too fond of it. [General Robert E. Lee, speaking to General James Longstreet as they watched a Civil War battle]

3. Not a creature was stirring, not even a mouse. [Clement Clarke Moore, in his Christmas poem "A Visit from St. Nicholas"]

4. When I'm good, I'm very good, but when I'm bad, I'm better. [Actress Mae West in the movie *I'm No Angel*]

5. I see one-third of a nation ill-housed, ill-clad, ill-nourished. [President Franklin Roosevelt, referring to the Great Depression]

Now You Try It, 3

Find five interesting statements from a newspaper, book, song, or other source. On a separate sheet of paper, use each statement as a direct quotation in a sentence of your own. Be sure to use the comma and quotation marks. Finally, turn the direct quotation into a paraphrase starting with *that.* In both the direct quotation and paraphrase, indicate the source of the statement.

EXAMPLE: **I know it's only rock 'n' roll, but I like it. [From a song by the rock group the Rolling Stones]**

As the Rolling Stones once proclaimed, "I know it's only rock 'n' roll, but I like it."

The Rolling Stones once defended their music by saying that they knew it was merely rock 'n' roll but they liked it anyway.

Editing Practice, 1 **(Corrected sentences appear on page 310.)**

Correct all errors in the following paragraphs using the first correction as a model. The number in parentheses at the end of each paragraph indicates how many errors you should find.

Many Americans have spoken or written of the need for the United States to provide fair treatment to women. In 1850, for instance, Sojourner Truth, a former slave, said of the feminist cause,‸"If the first woman God ever made was strong enough to turn the world upside down all alone, these women together ought to be able turn it back and get it right side up again!‸" A few years later, Lucy Stone said that From the first years to which my memory stretches, I have been a disappointed woman. She went on to explain that education, the professions, and religion were often closed to her and other women. (1)

The women's movement became increasingly active after the Civil War. After being arrested for leading the fight for women's right to vote, Susan B. Anthony said, "It was we, the people—not we, the white male citizens, nor we, the male citizens—but we the whole people who formed this Union." She went on to argue that "she and all women should be allowed to vote based on the amendments made to the Constitution as a result of the Civil War." (1)

Editing Practice, 2 **(Corrected sentences appear on page 310.)**

(Corrected sentences appear on page 310.)

Correct all errors in the following paragraphs using the first correction as a model. The number in parentheses at the end of each paragraph indicates how many errors you should find.

The music of the 1960's often reflected a belief that change should—and would—occur if people were willing to act and to work together. Some popular songs of that period became theme songs of the civil rights movement. For example, "We Shall Overcome," which was an African American spiritual song of the nineteenth century, became an anthem of the protest marchers. One key statement is repeated over and over in the song: We shall overcome. That is the best-known line, but the civil rights workers singing this song also said that they were unafraid. (1)

"O Freedom" was another African American spiritual that became a protest song of the 1960's. This song proclaims before I'd be a slave, I'd be buried in my grave. As popular hits, protest songs conveyed important messages. (2)

Editing Practice, 3

Correct all errors in the following paragraphs using the first correction as a model. The number in parentheses at the end of each paragraph indicates how many errors you should find.

My brother Pete once said that he wouldn't give up any of his bad habits. He lately had a disagreement with his fiancée, Lynn, who doesn't smoke and wants to avoid the health risks of secondhand smoke. She once said that "she wouldn't allow smoking at their home once they were married." Today, though, she said, "Pete can smoke as long as he does so on the back porch, where I rarely go." Later, she told me that she preferred he not smoke at all but that she knew when they got engaged that he was a heavy smoker. (2)

I think they're coming to an agreement. Pete said I will soon be sharing a home with Lynn and will have to compromise. He read an article that confirmed that "researchers have found that nonsmokers are at risk if they inhale smoke of people smoking around them." (4)

Writing Practice

Write a paragraph or two explaining a disagreement you had with someone. Try to use at least two direct quotations and two paraphrases. Use the Proofreading Checklist to correct any errors in the sentences you write.

" "

PROOFREADING CHECKLIST

Distinguishing Direct Quotations and Paraphrases in Your Writing

- When you want to use your own words to express something that somebody else has said or written (a paraphrase), read the original material carefully. Then, put the original aside, and write your own interpretation. As a proofreading check, go back to make sure the meaning of your paraphrase is the same as the meaning of the original statement.
- When you quote someone word for word (a direct quotation), the quoted material should have quotation marks around it. Do not use quotation marks around a paraphrase.
- If you can use *that* before the material you want to quote, the material is likely a paraphrase. A direct quotation should not be preceded by *that*.
- Finally, remember that both a direct quotation and a paraphrase should indicate whose ideas or words you are using.

THE BOTTOM LINE

As we said earlier in this lesson, "Make sure that you don't use quotation marks when paraphrasing and that you do use them when directly quoting."

LESSON 14

Quotation Marks with Other Punctuation

Sample Errors

SAMPLE 1: **✗ Edgar Allan Poe wrote “The Raven”, “Annabel Lee”, and “The Bells”.**

SAMPLE 2: **✗ Rosa asked, “Do you want to play tennis”?**

What's the Problem?

Periods and commas go *inside* the closing quotation marks—no matter whether the quotation marks are used for a quoted statement or the name of a brief work. Colons (:) and semicolons (;) go *outside* the closing quotation mark—no matter what the quotation marks are used for.

Question marks and exclamation points can go either inside or outside, depending on how they are used. They go inside if the material inside the quotation marks is a question or an exclamation. For instance, the material inside quotation marks in Sample 2 is a question, so the question mark belongs inside the closing quotation mark.

What Causes the Problem?

The misplacement of various punctuation marks when they are used with quotation marks is a problem that occurs in writing but not in speaking. Spoken English offers no clues about correct placement. Another reason for this error is that there is no compelling logical reason to put punctuation marks either inside or outside the closing quotation mark. (In fact, the rule varies, depending on which English-speaking country you're writing in.) Adding to the problem is that placement of question marks and exclamation marks depends on the meaning of the entire sentence.

Nonetheless, this sort of punctuation is one of those relatively minor issues to which the writer should pay attention. For some readers, sentences like Samples 1 and 2 jump out and make them pay attention to something that shouldn't be worth noticing at all. Thus, these errors may distract readers from the writer's important points.

Diagnostic Exercise **(Corrected sentences appear on page 310.)**

Correct all errors in the following paragraph using the first correction as a model. The number in parentheses at the end of the paragraph indicates how many errors you should find.

Yesterday, my literature teacher asked, "Who can name three poems written by African ~~Americans"?~~ Americans?" **I was able to come up with "Incident," which was written by Countee Cullen. Herman, the guy who sits next to me, named Langston Hughes's "Harlem". I started to bring up "Letter from Birmingham Jail;" however, I quickly recalled that was an *essay* by Martin Luther King, Jr. Then, somebody in the back row mentioned Hughes's "Same in Blues", and somebody else remembered Richard Wright's "Between the World and Me". Our teacher seemed glad that it didn't take very long for us to answer. I don't know about any of the other students, but in my high school English classes we studied quite a few African American poets. (4)**

Fixing This Problem in Your Writing

For better or worse, you simply need to memorize the rules stated earlier. In particular, remember that periods and commas go inside the closing quotation mark as long as there is nothing else between them. Thus, Sample 1 needs commas inside the quotation marks following the first two titles and a period inside the quotation mark following the last title.

SAMPLE 1: ✘ **Edgar Allan Poe wrote "The Raven", "Annabel Lee", and "The Bells".**

CORRECTION: **Edgar Allan Poe wrote "The Raven," "Annabel Lee," and "The Bells."**

What about question marks and exclamation points?

> MOVEMENT TIP: Take whatever is inside the quotation marks out of the sentence and out of quotation marks. Now what sort of punctuation would you use?

If you use a question mark or an exclamation point, this same punctuation belongs *inside* the closing quotation mark in the original sentence. Otherwise, put the question mark or exclamation point *outside*.

For Example . . .

Sample 2 has an error because we would use a question mark if the group of words were taken out of quotation marks.

SAMPLE 2: **✘ Rosa asked, "Do you want to play tennis"?**

TIP APPLIED: **Do you want to play tennis?**

CORRECTION: **Rosa asked, "Do you want to play tennis?"**

Because the quoted material is a question, the question mark belongs with the quoted material—*inside* the quotation mark.

Here are some correct examples and test sentences that show that the originals are, indeed, correct:

CORRECT: **My literature teacher asked, "Who can name three poems written by African Americans?"**

TIP APPLIED: **Who can name three poems written by African Americans?**

CORRECT: **Wendy yelled, "Look out!"**

TIP APPLIED: **Look out!**

CORRECT: **Who said, "Can we leave early?"**

TIP APPLIED: **Can we leave early?**

In all three examples, a question mark or exclamation point is needed in the test sentences. Thus, the punctuation goes *inside* the quotation mark. Notice that the tip holds true even for the third example, in which both the whole sentence and the quoted material are questions. Only one closing punctuation mark (a period, question mark, or exclamation point) should appear after the last word in a sentence.

Now You Try It, 1 **(Corrected sentences appear on page 310.)**

For each sentence, take the material that is inside the quotation marks out of the quotation marks. If the test material requires a question mark or an exclamation point, then the original sentence needs that same punctuation *inside* the closing quotation mark. Write *OK* if the sentence is correct, and correct any sentence that has punctuation errors.

Letter from Birmingham Jail ?

EXAMPLE: **Who wrote "Letter from Birmingham Jail?"**

1. Bill asked, "Will we get our papers back this week"?
2. The title of my paper is "Is Surrogate Motherhood Worthwhile?"
3. The platoon leader yelled at the top of her lungs, "Move it!" [*Hint:* When punctuating the test sentence, keep in mind that the material was yelled.]
4. The title of the next chapter is "Who Runs the Stock Market"?
5. Darlene responded, "Why do you ask"?

"?"

""?

Now You Try It, 2 **(Corrected sentences appear on page 311.)**

For each sentence, take the material that is inside the quotation marks out of the quotation marks. If the test material requires a question mark or an exclamation point, then the original sentence needs that same punctuation *inside* the closing quotation mark. Write *OK* if the sentence is correct, and correct any sentence that has punctuation errors.

alliteration ?

EXAMPLE: **Can you tell me the meaning of the word "alliteration?"**

1. Did you hear somebody say, "The store is closing?"
2. Didn't W. H. Auden write "The Unknown Citizen"?
3. Who wrote the song entitled, "Are You Lonesome Tonight?"
4. A strange man yelled at the taxi driver, "Follow that cab"!
5. Will you tell me who asked, "Can you play a harmonica?"

Now You Try It, 3

Use each of the following quotations at the very end of a sentence. Keep each inside quotation marks. A note in brackets will help you identify the nature of each item.

I have never heard anyone sing

EXAMPLE: ^**"Brother, Can You Spare a Dime?" [song popular during the Great Depression]**

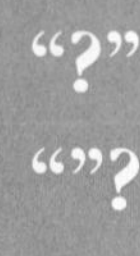

1. "Anchors Aweigh" [theme song of the U.S. Navy]

2. "Look out for that train!" [warning shouted at somebody]

3. "Blowin' in the Wind" [protest song from the 1960's, written by Bob Dylan]

4. "Are you sick?" [question to somebody]

5. "Which Side Are You On?" [song popular with many union members around the middle of this century]

Editing Practice, 1 **(Corrected sentences appear on page 311.)**

Correct all errors in the following paragraph using the first correction as a model. The number in parentheses at the end of the paragraph indicates how many errors you should find.

Have you ever heard the song "Dixie?" ^? Most Americans have heard this song but have not considered its usefulness as a source of information about the Civil War. Other songs of that time, for instance, the spirituals sung by slaves, offer a personal look at their lives and hardships. In "Go Down, Moses", the lyrics refer to attempts by Moses to free his people from slavery, yet the song is also a poignant cry for the freedom of African Americans. In contrast to this melancholy spiritual is "Dixie." This battle hymn of the Confederacy, with its upbeat tempo, is a celebration of the South. Other songs, such as "The Bonnie Blue Flag", were even more explicit about loyalty to the Confederacy, but the one most remembered today is "Dixie". (3)

Editing Practice, 2 **(Corrected sentences appear on page 311.)**

Correct all errors in the following paragraph using the first correction as a model. The number in parentheses at the end of the paragraph indicates how many errors you should find.

Many conflicts have given rise to what might be called “war songs.”~~.~~ Each war, it seems, becomes the subject of popular music. World War I, for example, had its protest songs, such as “I Didn’t Raise My Boy to Be a Soldier”. This song captured many Americans’ desire to stay out of the war. Once the United States entered the war, though, many songs served to rally the troops and the general public. One of the most famous is “Over There”. All good American parents and “sweethearts,” according to this song, should be proud and eager to send their loved one to fight in the war. George M. Cohan received a Congressional Medal of Honor for composing this immensely popular song. In “Oh, How I Hate to Get Up in the Morning”, however, the singer is less enthusiastic about fighting in the trenches, taking a lighthearted view of military life but still celebrating victory. (3)

“?”
“”?

Editing Practice, 3

Correct all errors in the following paragraphs using the first correction as a model. The number in parentheses at the end of each paragraph indicates how many errors you should find.

My literature class read an essay entitled “What If Shakespeare Had a Sister?”~~?~~ It deals with obstacles that female authors have encountered. During the discussion, Paul asked, “Are women writers still discriminated against”? It depends on what one means by “discrimination,” but I imagine women certainly have a harder time if they want to write certain types of material, such as sports stories. However, a male author might have a harder time publishing the so-called “love story”. We still haven’t gotten past all our biases. (2)

We also read Kate Chopin's "The Storm." Our professor asked, "Do you see any similarity between this story and the essay"? Somebody answered, "Both deal with the treatment of women in our society, but the story seems a bit more optimistic." I admit the story didn't seem so hopeful to me, but then we discussed how it suggests that women have the same rights to passion and romance as men do. For tomorrow, we're reading "The Girls in Their Summer Dresses", which also deals with how men and women approach romance. (2)

"?"
""?

Writing Practice

On your own paper, write six sentences so that each one has quotation marks plus another form of punctuation. Try to vary the type of punctuation that occurs with the quotation marks. Use the Proofreading Checklist to see whether each sentence you write is punctuated correctly.

PROOFREADING CHECKLIST

Using Quotation Marks with Other Punctuation in Your Writing

- Periods and commas always go *inside* the quotation marks.
- Colons and semicolons always go *outside* the quotation marks.
- Regarding a question mark or an exclamation point, try this test: Take the material that is inside the quotation marks out of the sentence. If the material would then be punctuated with a question mark or an exclamation point, the original sentence needs a question mark or exclamation point *inside* the closing quotation mark.

THE BOTTOM LINE

As advised, "Periods and commas go *inside* quotation marks."

LESSON 15

Colons

Sample Errors

SAMPLE 1: ✘ **Sarah bought: milk, bread, and crackers.**

SAMPLE 2: ✘ **For the trip, be sure to bring such items as: books, clothes, and lots of money.**

:

What's the Problem?

A colon has several functions, such as introducing a quotation. One common but often misunderstood function of the colon is to introduce *certain types* of lists. A colon introduces lists that are not needed for the sentence to be grammatically complete. In the following example, the colon is used correctly because the sentence would be complete even if you left out the list.

At the football game, I met three friends: José, Tyrone, and Mark.

A colon *cannot* introduce a list *if* the list is needed for the sentence to be complete. In Samples 1 and 2, the lists are necessary. Therefore, these lists should not be introduced by a colon.

In some ways, a colon is similar to "end punctuation" (to a period or question mark, for instance). A colon—just like a period—is usually used only at the end of a grammatically complete set of words.

What Causes the Problem?

One use of the colon is to introduce certain types of lists, but many people overgeneralize this use and mistakenly put a colon before any sort of list. The only type of list to be introduced by a colon is a list that is "expendable." It is expendable because it is grammatically unnecessary.

Diagnostic Exercise **(Corrected sentences appear on page 311.)**

Correct all errors in the following paragraph using the first correction as a model. The number in parentheses at the end of the paragraph indicates how many errors you should find.

My roommate, who is shopping for a new car, looked at several types, including: Fords, Nissans, and Mazdas. She knew which features she wanted, like: automatic transmission, cruise control, and leather seats. However, she quickly discovered that such features were not within her budget. To get the best deal for her money, I suggested that she consult sources such as: her mechanic or *Consumer Reports* magazine. She did some research, but she seemed disappointed because there was no clear choice. She finally narrowed her choices to: a Ford truck and a Nissan sedan. She hasn't gotten much further than that. (3)

Fixing This Problem in Your Writing

Here is a tip that can help you see whether a colon is *incorrectly* used to introduce a list.

> IMAGINARY PERIOD TIP: Imagine that you used a period instead of the colon. If what comes *before* this period could stand alone as a complete sentence, the colon should be correct. Otherwise, there is probably an error.

Why does this tip work? It shows whether or not the list is a necessary part of the sentence. If the list is necessary, it should *not* be separated from the rest of the sentence by a colon. For instance, the colon in Sample 1 fails the test because *Sarah bought* is not a complete sentence (see Lessons 1 and 2 about recognizing complete sentences).

SAMPLE 1: **✗ Sarah bought: milk, bread, and crackers.**

TIP APPLIED: **✗ Sarah bought.**

To correct this sentence, simply leave out the colon.

SAMPLE 1, CORRECTED: **Sarah bought milk, bread, and crackers.**

The next example is more difficult because *the following* is a powerful signal letting readers know that more information is about to be presented. Despite this expectation, what comes before the colon could stand alone as a grammatically complete sentence. Thus, the original sentence is, indeed, correct.

EXAMPLE: **We require the following: paper, pens, a stapler, and a hot tub.**

TIP APPLIED: **We require the following.**

:

For Example . . .

In Sample 2, what comes before the colon could *not* stand alone as a complete sentence.

SAMPLE 2: **✗ For the trip, be sure to bring such items as: books, clothes, and lots of money.**

TIP APPLIED: **✗ For the trip, be sure to bring such items as.**

SAMPLE 2, CORRECTED: **For the trip, be sure to bring such items as books, clothes, and lots of money.**

The test sentence proves that the list is necessary. Thus, the original sentence should not have a colon.

Following, however, are two correct examples in which colons are truly needed. In the test sentences, what comes before the periods could stand alone, so the colons are necessary.

CORRECT: **I'm taking two science courses: Physics 101 and Biology 210.**

TIP APPLIED: **I'm taking two science courses.**

CORRECT: **My roommate, who is shopping for a new car, looked at several types: Fords, Nissans, and Mazdas.**

TIP APPLIED: **My roommate, who is shopping for a new car, looked at several types.**

Now You Try It, 1 **(Corrected sentences appear on page 311.)**

Determine whether the colon is correct by applying the Imaginary Period Tip. If the colon is used incorrectly, put an *X* above it. Write *OK* above colons that are used correctly.

EXAMPLE: **To mend these pants, I will need: scissors, thread, a needle, and a little gratitude.**

1. Farmers in this area grow: wheat, corn, and alfalfa.

2. Kamilah and Steve saved enough money to travel throughout: England, France, and Belgium.

3. This summer, the college will not offer many courses I need, such as: English 100 and Speech 201.

4. You will need to buy: a textbook, gloves, and a dissecting kit.

5. Some famous actors who changed their names are: Jane Wyman, Raquel Welch, and Rudolph Valentino.

Now You Try It, 2 **(Corrected sentences appear on page 312.)**

Determine whether the colon is correct by applying the Imaginary Period Tip. If the colon is used incorrectly, put an *X* over it. Write *OK* above colons that are used correctly.

EXAMPLE: **The subjects I like to read about are: Asian history, computers, and motorcycles.**

1. During the Renaissance, Greek and Latin were used to form such new words for scientific concepts as: *gravity, paradox, chronology,* and *atmosphere.*

2. Native Americans added various new words to English: *totem, tomahawk, hickory, raccoon,* and many others.

3. Many languages have contributed to English, including: French, Latin, Persian, and German.

4. New words arise from many other sources: Valley Girls, the drug culture, popular music, and the computer industry.

5. Some slang words that are still used include: *cool, dork,* and *geek.*

Now You Try It, 3

Finish each sentence by giving a list and deciding whether to use a colon before the list.

EXAMPLE: **For this dish, we need three primary ingredients**: *ground beef, onions, and cheese.*

1. Three of my favorite movies are
2. I don't like
3. There are two things I would like my spouse to remember about me
4. Here are two requirements for my "perfect" boss
5. I would encourage people to take the following classes

:

Editing Practice, 1 **(Corrected sentences appear on page 312.)**

Correct all errors in the following paragraph using the first correction as a model. The number in parentheses at the end of the paragraph indicates how many errors you should find.

In the past, my English teachers discussed various types of writing, including: poetry, drama, and short stories. In my present English class, the teacher discussed the writing we'll do this semester. She discussed three other types of writing that my previous teachers had not covered: expressive essays, arguments, and informative papers. She mentioned that there are many ways a writer can develop an essay, such as using: narration, comparison and contrast, and definition. For her class, we are required to write: six long papers, three fairly short papers, and several in-class paragraphs. Some of these assignments will allow us to pick our own topics, but a few will not. She has already mentioned that we will write about the following: educational reform, male-female relationships, and discrimination. The class seems challenging, but I'm looking forward to it. Next semester, I am looking forward to taking: a technical writing class or a creative writing class. (3)

Editing Practice, 2 **(Corrected sentences appear on page 312.)**

Correct all errors in the following paragraphs using the first correction as a model. The number in parentheses at the end of each paragraph indicates how many errors you should find.

Many people try to get rid of "tummy" fat so they'll feel better about: their appearance, their self-image, and even their relationships with significant others. However, fat has also been linked to health risks such as: heart disease, high blood pressure, and strokes. The most dangerous type of abdominal fat can't even be seen; it's the fat around vital organs like: the intestines and liver. (2)

Two factors that determine how much fat a person has are: gender and habits. Almost all males have more lean tissue per pound than do females, and lean tissue helps burn fat. Thus, females typically have to exercise more to rid themselves of fat. Several bad habits can lead to more fat: smoking, drinking, and partying. Although some people say these habits help them deal with stress, such habits also have been correlated with larger waist-to-hip ratios. (1)

Editing Practice, 3

Correct all errors in the following paragraphs using the first correction as a model. The number in parentheses at the end of each paragraph indicates how many errors you should find.

The Wizard of Oz may seem terribly old-fashioned, but it's still one of my favorite movies. Even though some people consider it just a kids' movie, most adults know: Dorothy, the Wicked Witch, the Tin Man, the Scarecrow, the Cowardly Lion, and the Wizard (and Toto too!). I'm not sure why the movie has become such a classic. Maybe its popularity has something to do with: the colorful characters, the enduring theme of "going home again," and the way in which several scenes are memorable. (1)

Two scenes in particular are etched in my memory: the first appearance of the Wicked Witch and her final scene, when she melted into oblivion. I bet most Americans don't even need these scenes described to them. A couple of other favorite parts are: the discovery of the Cowardly Lion in the dark forest and the farewell scene in which Dorothy clicks her ruby slippers. Next week, this movie will be on TV for the umpteenth time, but I will be watching it yet again! (1)

Writing Practice

On your own paper, write ten sentences that use a colon to introduce a list.

> EXAMPLE: *I signed up for three classes: History 201, English 101, and Psychology 205.*

Use the Proofreading Checklist to see whether each sentence you write is punctuated correctly.

PROOFREADING CHECKLIST

Using Colons with Lists in Your Writing

- Each time you use a colon to introduce a list, see whether what comes *before* the colon could stand alone as a complete, grammatical sentence.
- If that part of the sentence *cannot* stand alone, you do *not* need the colon.
- If it *can* stand alone, then using the colon should be *correct.*

THE BOTTOM LINE

When using a colon to introduce a list, remember these two steps: (1) imagine using a period instead of the colon and (2) see whether what comes before this imaginary period would be a complete sentence.

LESSON 16
Capitalization

CAP

Sample Errors

SAMPLE 1: **✗ My english teacher said that we would read stories by Faulkner and other writers from the south.**

SAMPLE 2: **✗ Did your Math classes in High School cover calculus?**

What's the Problem?

Some words (**proper nouns** and **proper adjectives**) should be capitalized to show they are the "official" names or nicknames of specific persons, places, things, or events. Additionally, many words are capitalized because they are derived from official names. In Sample 1, *English* must be capitalized because it is derived from the name of a country (England). Also, *South* should be capitalized since people widely recognize it as the name of a specific area.

More general words are not capitalized. In Sample 2, *math* should *not* be capitalized because it is a general term for a type of class; *high school* also is a general term and is *not* the name of a specific school. Compare these two terms with *Calculus I* and *Lewis and Clark High School.*

What Causes the Problem?

Capitalization rules are not an issue when people are speaking, so the rules can be difficult to learn. Compounding the problem is that capitalization "rules" are not consistent. For instance, some dictionaries and authorities say that *baroque period* isn't capitalized, while *Renaissance* is capitalized because it is supposedly a more specific reference. Also, many words are capitalized depending on how they are used (compare *My <u>uncle</u> is here* with *I saw <u>Uncle</u> Brett there*).

Although capitalization errors can easily occur, it is important to avoid them. Frequently, capitalization errors—like spelling errors—jump out and distract readers from what the writer is saying. On occasion, errors in capitalization can confuse readers by sending the wrong message about whether a word is the specific name of somebody (or something) or whether the word is just a general description.

This lesson focuses on major capitalization issues about which handbooks tend to agree. If you wish to use a word not covered in this lesson, consult a current dictionary.

Diagnostic Exercise **(Corrected sentences appear on page 312.)**

Correct all errors in the following paragraph using the first correction as a model. The number in parentheses at the end of the paragraph indicates how many errors you should find.

community college

My sister is attending a ~~Community College~~ ^ in Kansas City, and we've been comparing our courses. Her spanish class is much different from mine because hers includes discussion of hispanic and latino cultures. Her teacher, professor Gonzales, believes students are more interested in learning a language when they appreciate the culture connected with that language. (4)

CAP

Fixing This Problem in Your Writing

Concerning capitalization, try to consult the handbook, style guide, or dictionary suggested by your teacher or readers. When such a resource isn't available or suggested, use the following capitalization tips.

> PERSON TIP: Capitalize a person's title or family term (like *Mother, Uncle,* or *Senator*) when it is followed by a name (like *Randy* or *Johnson*) *or* when you could use a name instead of the title or family term.

In these four sentences, a name could take the place of the family terms and titles. Thus, they are correctly capitalized.

Are you ready, Senator?

I called Mother last night.

Was Governor Wilson re-elected?

Wasn't that Officer Bean?

However, the same words are not capitalized in the next four examples because they do not take the place of family terms or a person's title.

We need a new senator.

Is your mother really sick?

The governor of Iowa is here.

The officer gave me a ticket.

GROUP TIP: Capitalize a term accepted by a group of people as describing their culture, nationality, religion, ethnic background, or language (as with *Latino*, *German*, *Muslim*, *Asian*, and *Yiddish*).

SCHOOL TIP: Capitalize the name of a specific school or course (such as *Kilgore Community College* or *Math 101*). Don't capitalize a more general term. You can usually place *a*, *some*, or a possessive term (such as *my*) in front of general terms.

CAP

I took Chemistry 101 at Kansas City Community College.

I studied (some) chemistry in (my) high school.

PLACE TIP: Capitalize any name that you'd find on a map or that is widely recognized as a *distinct* place or region. Thus, not only would names of cities be capitalized, but so would places such as *Rocky Mountains*, *Pacific Ocean*, *Middle East*, *Dixie*, *Cape Cod*, *Oak Street*, and *the West*. Don't capitalize directions (*Go north*) or general locations (*I live in northern Iowa*).

For Example . . .

In regard to Sample 1, the Group Tip indicates that *English* is capitalized. Even though here it refers to a subject someone teaches, *English* is the name of a group of people and the name of a language. Also, the Place Tip reminds us to capitalize *South*.

SAMPLE 1, CORRECTED: **My English teacher said that we would read stories by Faulkner and other writers from the South.**

In Sample 2, the School Tip indicates that *math* is not capitalized; note how a possessive term (*your*) comes right before it. Nor should *high school* be capitalized; *your* could also be placed in front of it.

SAMPLE 2, CORRECTED: **Did your math classes in high school cover calculus?**

Finally, the titles in the next sentence shouldn't be capitalized. They aren't used with names, nor could they be replaced by names (see the Person Tip).

✗ **My Aunt is President of the downtown bank.**

Now You Try It, 1 **(Corrected sentences appear on page 312.)**

If the underlined word is correct in terms of capitalization, write *OK* over it. Correct any error, and write a brief explanation of why the word should or shouldn't be capitalized by referring to the four tips.

General OK OK

EXAMPLE: **Yes, ~~general~~, your uncle called today from Boston.**

Person Tip: "General" is a title that could be replaced by a name.

1. My Mother has a job teaching computer science in east Chicago.
2. Theodore Roosevelt was once governor of New York.
3. Much of the southwestern United States was once Mexican soil.
4. Students write in almost every class at this University, even in Physical Education courses.
5. Tenskwatawa was a native american leader who encouraged his people to give up alcohol along with european clothing and tools.

CAP

Now You Try It, 2 **(Corrected sentences appear on page 313.)**

If the underlined word is correct in terms of capitalization, write *OK* over it. Correct any error, and write a brief explanation of why the word should or shouldn't be capitalized by referring to the four tips.

geology

EXAMPLE: **I have to take my ~~Geology~~ class again.**

School Tip: The term geology is not the name of a specific class (the word "my" in front indicates a general term).

1. The school colors at the High School I attended are blue and gold.
2. A nuclear weapon is a general term for various types of weapons relying on a nuclear reaction for their explosive power.
3. Did you say that aunt Mia is arriving today?
4. The rhone river and the rhine river both rise out of the Alps of Switzerland.
5. My Father thinks we can meet with the Pope during our visit to Rome.

Now You Try It, 3

Write an original sentence that has at least one word that is capitalized and which reflects the tip that is listed.

EXAMPLE: **Person Tip:** *We listened to the debate between Representative Biggs and Governor Garner.*

1. Person Tip:
2. Place Tip:
3. School Tip:
4. Group Tip:
5. School Tip:

CAP

Editing Practice, 1 **(Corrected sentences appear on page 313.)**

Correct all errors in the following paragraphs using the first correction as a model. The number in parentheses at the end of each paragraph indicates how many errors you should find.

Mary, also called ~~molly~~ *Molly*, Dewson was a pioneer in encouraging women to be active in Politics and the Federal Government. In the 1928 presidential campaign, she worked for candidate Al Smith and helped mobilize female supporters. Smith never became president, but Dewson did not abandon her Feminist efforts. (4)

In 1930, Dewson continued to mobilize women to campaign for Franklin Roosevelt's successful bid for governor of New York. Later, she worked for his Presidential campaigns. Perhaps her greatest accomplishment, though, was becoming Head of the Democratic Party's efforts to recruit women for Government jobs. She also worked with Democrats in training women to serve in election campaigns. Though she died in 1962, her legacy lives on, and millions of men as well as women have been affected positively by her efforts to involve women in the Democratic process. (4)

Editing Practice, 2 **(Corrected sentences appear on page 313.)**

Correct all errors in the following paragraphs using the first correction as a model. The number in parentheses at the end of each paragraph indicates how many errors you should find.

Last week, the ~~University~~ ^university I'm attending announced that all history majors would be guaranteed that they could receive a degree in History in no more than four years. As a Sophomore planning to be a history major, I was interested in this announcement and looked into it. (2)

I spoke with an advisor, professor Hearns, about the guarantee. She said the College would do its part in regularly offering courses that are most in demand. In particular, she said that each semester the department would offer several sections of American history I and cultural history of Asia. (5)

Editing Practice, 3

Correct all errors in the following paragraphs using the first correction as a model. The number in parentheses at the end of each paragraph indicates how many errors you should find.

One reason why ~~english~~ ^English is a complex and often confusing language is that it is heavily based on many languages and cultures. The english language did not even exist when Julius Caesar invaded britain in 55 B.C. However, the Celts who lived there had an impact on what later became english. Later, the germanic tribes that sailed across the North sea settled in Britain and passed along their farming vocabulary (such as *ox*, *swine*, and *sheep*). (5)

Another influence was Christianity, for pope Gregory the great sent monks who added many religious words to English, including *angel*, *mass*, and *shrine*. Still later, the Vikings sailed from scandinavia to raid Britain and brought more words, especially many beginning with *sk* (such as *sky* and *skin*). When the normans conquered England in 1066, their language influenced English. For

some time, there were three competing languages in England: latin for the church, french for the rulers, and english for the commoners. Eventually, though, the english absorbed the other two, especially the french language. (9)

Writing Practice

On your own paper, write a paragraph discussing a school or government election. Use at least four different words that should be capitalized (not counting words at the beginning of sentences). Use the Proofreading Checklist to correct any capitalization errors in the sentences you wrote.

PROOFREADING CHECKLIST

Using Capitals in Your Writing

- Proofread references to individuals (the Person Tip). Capitalize a professional title or a family term only if (1) it is immediately followed by a name *or* (2) you could use a name in place of the title or family term.
- Proofread references to groups (the Group Tip). Capitalize any term that a group of people accept as describing their culture, nationality, religion, ethnic background, or language.
- Proofread references to schools, courses, and subjects (the School Tip). Capitalize *only* the actual names. You can put *a*, *some*, or a possessive term (like *my*) in front of a general term, but you cannot put them in front of the specific name of a school or course.
- Proofread references to places (the Place Tip), and capitalize any name found on a map or recognized as a distinct area. Do not capitalize general directions or ordinary geographic descriptions.

THE BOTTOM LINE

According to rules for formal *English*, words that are "official" names, titles, or nicknames are capitalized.

UNIT THREE
PUTTING IT ALL TOGETHER

Punctuation marks form an important part of written English, and each mark has specific purposes. Following is a summary of the tips we have offered.

Semicolons

IMAGINARY PERIOD TIP: Imagine the semicolon is a period. If what comes before this imaginary period and what comes after it could *both* be complete sentences, the semicolon is correctly used (see Lesson 9).

A light bulb consists of a filament of tungsten wire; the filament reaches a temperature of about 4,500°F.

Apostrophes

Apply the following tips to see if you are using one of the three basic functions of the apostrophe.

CONTRACTION TIP: See whether you can replace an apostrophe with letters that have been left out (see Lessons 10 and 12).

I'll **don't** **the summer of '96** **can't** **haven't**

"OF" TIP: Reword the sentence by using *of* to show that something belongs to something else. If you can make this change without affecting the meaning, the original sentence involves possession, so an apostrophe is needed (see Lessons 11 and 12).

mayor's car **teacher's pen** **children's parents**

"SPECIAL-WORD" TIP: Use the apostrophe to indicate plurality *only* with numbers, letters, or abbreviations (see Lesson 12).

1990's two t's six IBM's several 9's

Quotation Marks

Use quotation marks for direct quotations. Don't use quotation marks when you paraphrase.

> "THAT" TIP: Use *that* to begin a paraphrase but *not* a direct quotation. Inserting *that* before a paraphrase will not change the meaning, but inserting *that* before a direct quotation might change the meaning (see Lesson 13).

President Coolidge supposedly claimed that America's business is business itself.

Periods and commas go inside the closing quotation marks. Semicolons and colons go outside. Question marks and exclamation points go inside or outside, depending on the meaning of a sentence.

> MOVEMENT TIP: Take whatever is inside the quotation marks out of the sentence and out of quotation marks. What sort of punctuation would you use? If you'd use a question mark or an exclamation point, use that same punctuation inside the quotation marks in the original (see Lesson 14).

Who said, "All is fair in love and war"?

Colons

> IMAGINARY PERIOD TIP: Imagine you used a period instead of the colon to introduce a list. If what comes *before* this imaginary period could stand alone as a complete sentence, the colon should be correct (see Lesson 15).

could stand alone

The color on a TV is actually made up of only three basic colors: red, blue, and green.

Capitalization

Four tips can help you recognize proper nouns, which require capitalization (see Lesson 16).

PERSON TIP: Capitalize a family term or title when it is followed by a name or used as a name in place of the family term or title *(My father, Chief Harriston, Mother Jones).*

GROUP TIP: Capitalize a term accepted by a group of people as describing their culture, nationality, religion, or ethnic background *(Russian, Hispanic, Irish, Hindu, American, Anglo).*

SCHOOL TIP: Capitalize the name of a specific school or course. Don't capitalize a more general term. You can usually place *a, some,* or a possessive such as *my* in front of general terms *(physics, Physics 101).*

PLACE TIP: Capitalize any name that you'd find on a map or that is widely recognized as a *distinct* place or region. Don't capitalize directions or general locations *(California, western Kansas, North Dakota).*

Review

Correct all errors in the following paragraph using the first correction as a model. The number in parentheses at the end of the paragraph indicates how many errors you should find.

My ~~Roommate~~ roommate ^ Troy invited me to visit his hometown, College Station, Texas. Ive never been to the south, much less Texas. Coincidentally, I had just finished reading a poem, "Blue Field," for my literature class, it was about a small Texas town. Troy said that "We would have to drive east for twelve hours to reach College Station; which is in the Central part of the state." The city is really just a college town, but its also associated with: cotton, retail, and cattle. (8)

UNIT FOUR
Subject-Verb Agreement

S/V AGR

OVERVIEW

Terms That Can Help You Understand Subject-Verb Agreement

If you are not familiar with any of the following terms that appear in this unit, look them up in the Guide to Grammar Terminology beginning on page 1. The numbers in parentheses indicate the lessons in which each term appears.

helping verb (Overview)
main verb (Overview)
past tense (Overview)
personal pronoun (Overview)
present tense (Overview, 17, 18, 19)
subject (Overview, 17, 18, 19)
subject-verb agreement (Overview, 17, 18, 19)
tense (Overview, 17, 18, 19)
verb (Overview, 17, 18, 19)

The Nuts and Bolts of Verb Tense

Every **clause** must contain at least one **subject** and one **verb**. Under certain conditions, speakers and writers must add an *-s* to the verb to make it "agree" with the subject. Unfortunately, these conditions can seem complicated. Following is the basic rule, and we'll get to the "fine print" later:

BASIC RULE OF SUBJECT-VERB AGREEMENT: Add the *-s* to the **present tense** form of the verb *if* the subject is one of these three **personal pronouns**—*he, she, it*—*or if* the subject can be replaced by one of these personal pronouns.

For example, the *-s* is used in the following sentence because the verb *detest* is in the present tense and the subject is the pronoun *she*: *She detests liver.* We would also use the *-s* in the following sentences because the subject *my roommate* can be replaced by the pronouns *he* or *she*: *My roommate detests liver; He detests liver; She detests liver.*

The pronouns *he, she,* and *it* are in what is called the "third-person singular" form. Thus, the subjects that require verbs to use the *-s* are called *third-person singular subjects.*

Now, here is some of that "fine print" we mentioned about subject-verb agreement.

- If there are multiple verbs in a single verb construction (that is, if there are **helping verbs**), only the *first* verb in the string can agree with the subject. For example, in the sentence *My dog has been chasing squirrels again,* only the first (helping) verb—*has*—agrees with the subject *dog.* The remaining two verbs—*been* and *chasing*—cannot change forms to agree with the subject.
- Certain important present tense helping verbs never use the *-s*: *can, may, must, shall,* and *will.* For example, we cannot write ✘ *He musts go.*
- Two of the most common verbs have irregular present tense forms when the *-s* is added: the *-s* form of the verb *be* is *is* (not ✘ "*bes*") and the *-s* form of the verb *have* is *has* (not ✘ "*haves*").
- The verb *be* is unique in that its **past tense** forms must also agree with the subject. For example, when the subject requires an *-s*, the past tense form of *be* is *was*, not *were*: *My roommate was fixing dinner in the kitchen.*

S/V AGR

The first step in dealing with subject-verb agreement errors is finding the verb that will agree with the subject. Here is a tip that may help:

PAST TENSE TIP: To find the word that must agree with the subject, change the sentence into the past tense. The word that adds the *-ed* to show past tense is the verb that agrees with the subject.

This tip works because the verb that agrees with the subject is the only word that can also be used with the past tense *-ed*. For example, in the sentence *The investigating officers report the findings to the commission*, the only word that can be changed into a past tense form is *report*: *The investigating officers reported the findings to the commission.* Therefore, *report* is a verb that *must* agree with the subject. If the subject is in the third-person singular form, then we must add an *-s* to the present tense verb; for example, *The investigating officer reports the findings to the commission.*

Although the subject-verb agreement rule can be tricky, it is not all *that* difficult. So, why is it so difficult for many writers and speakers to eliminate subject-verb agreement errors? The answer seems to lie in complexity. When sentences get long or complex, people lose track of the actual subject and tend to make the verb agree with a word that is not the subject. Research shows us that the vast majority of such errors are most likely to occur in three quite-different situations. Because these three situations *are* so different, we will cover each one in a separate lesson, as follows:

▶ *Lost Subject:* Lesson 17
When the subject phrase is long or complicated, people may forget what the subject is and may make the verb agree with a nearby word rather than with the more distant, actual subject.

EXAMPLE: **✗ The cost of all the repairs that we needed <u>were</u> more than we could afford.**

The verb *were* should be *was* to agree with *cost*, not with the nearby noun *repairs*.

▶ *There Is/There Was*: Lesson 18
When the verbs *is* or *was* follow the word *there* (meaning "there exists"), the subject is moved to a position *following* the verb. Instead of making the verb agree with the following, actual subject, people may make the verb agree with the preceding word, *there,* as though it were the subject.

EXAMPLE: **✗ There <u>is</u> usually some leftovers in the refrigerator.**

The verb *is* should be *are*, to agree with *leftovers*.

▶ *Compound Subject*: Lesson 19
When two different subjects are made into a **compound** joined by the word *and*, the compound subject is nearly always plural. However, sometimes writers may think of the two subjects as making a single, collective unit. The writers then mistakenly use a singular verb to agree with the supposedly singular subject.

EXAMPLE: **✗ Good planning and careful follow-through <u>is</u> the key to success.**

The verb *is* should be *are*, to agree with the compound subject *planning and follow-through*.

Can You Detect Problems in Subject-Verb Agreement?

(Corrected sentences appear on page 313.)

Correct all errors in the following paragraphs using the first correction as a model. The number in parentheses at the end of each paragraph indicates how many errors you should find.

When I was in high school, my family enjoyed camping, so nearly every school vacation, we would go camping. We soon realized that there ~~is~~ *are* three completely different kinds of campers. We called them the "nature lovers," the "homeboys," and the "bikers." The people whom we called "nature lovers" enjoy setting up camp in small, isolated sites where there is often no toilet facilities. Of course, the food and water is a constant concern, especially when all supplies have to be carried in. "Nature lovers" always try to have a minimal impact on the area that they have camped in. For example, their trash and garbage is always taken out. (3)

The "homeboys" are people who want to go to the mountains, beach, or desert without ever actually leaving home. They buy a mobile home—an entire apartment complete with living room, kitchen, and bathroom—that have been mounted on wheels. There is some mobile homes that even come equipped with satellite dishes so that the "homeboys" will not miss any TV programs while they are in the wilderness. (2)

The "bikers" are people who see the wilderness only as a huge empty parking lot. All they want to do is race their bikes and make as much noise as possible. The fragile ecology and unspoiled beauty means nothing to them. The problem with the bikers and all their machines are that they often do extensive damage to the surprisingly delicate plant life of the desert. They also make enough noise to drive the rest of us back to the quiet city. (2)

LESSON 17

Agreement Involving Verbs with a Lost Subject

Sample Errors

SAMPLE 1: **✗ Matt told us that his beach house, one of the cottages on Ocean Street near the boardwalk, were not damaged by the hurricane.**

SAMPLE 2: **✗ The advantages of this entertainment system is that it is compact and that it is less expensive than what you would pay if you bought the cassette recorder, CD player, and radio separately.**

What's the Problem?

The problem in a lost subject error is that the verb agrees with a word that is not the actual subject—usually with a noun that is closer to the verb than the actual subject is. In Sample 1, *were* is **plural** to agree with *cottages,* but the real subject is *house,* which is **singular** and should have a singular verb. Sample 2 has the opposite error, a singular verb, *is,* which agrees with *system,* but should be plural to agree with *advantages.*

Every time you use a present tense verb (or the past tense of *be*), you must consciously check the sentence again to find the subject and make sure that the verb properly agrees with it. If the subject is singular, the verb must also be singular; if the subject is plural, the verb must be plural, too.

What Causes the Problem?

When the subject phrase is long or complicated, writers tend to lose track of the actual subject at the beginning of the sentence. Instead, they make the verb agree with the noun or pronoun nearest to the verb that could make sense as a subject rather than with the more distant, actual subject at the beginning of the sentence.

Diagnostic Exercise **(Corrected sentences appear on page 314.)**

Underline and correct all errors involving lost-subject agreement using the first correction as a model. The number in parentheses at the end of the paragraph indicates how many errors you should find.

The beginning of the first public schools in the United States ~~date~~ *dates* from the early 1800's. The pressure to create public schools open to children of working-class parents were a direct result of the union movements in large cities. In response, state legislatures gave communities the legal right to levy local property taxes to pay for free schools open to the public. By the middle of the nineteenth century, control of school policies and curriculum were in the hands of the state government. As school populations outgrew one-room schoolhouses, the design of school buildings on the East Coast were completely changed to accommodate separate rooms for children of different ages. Before this time, all children in a schoolhouse, regardless of age, was taught together in the same room by the same teacher. (4)

S/V AGR

Fixing This Problem in Your Writing

In English, the subject of a sentence is usually the *first noun* or *pronoun* in the sentence (excluding, of course, introductory adverb elements, which are not part of the beginning of the sentence). The following tip will help you find the subject.

> FIRST-WORD TIP: When you check your verbs for subject-verb agreement, jump clear back to the beginning of the sentence and find the *first* word that makes sense as the subject. In nearly all cases, that first word will be the subject.

Here is how jumping to the beginning of the sentence and taking the first word that makes sense would have correctly identified the subject in the first sample sentence:

SAMPLE 1: ✘ **Matt told us that his beach house, one of the cottages on Ocean Street near the boardwalk, were not damaged by the hurricane.**

Even though *Matt* is the first word in the sentence, *Matt* is not a possible subject because you would not say *Matt was not damaged by the hurricane.* The first possible word that makes sense as the subject of *were not damaged by the hurricane* is *house* in the phrase *beach house.* This subject is singular, so the verb should also be singular.

TIP APPLIED: **Matt told us that his <u>beach house</u>, one of the cottages on Ocean Street near the boardwalk, <u>was</u> not damaged by the hurricane.**

For Example . . .

Now apply the *First-Word* Tip to Sample 2.

SAMPLE 2: ✘ **The advantages of this entertainment system is that it is compact and that it is less expensive than what you would pay if you bought the cassette recorder, CD player, and radio separately.**

The first word that makes sense as the subject of *is* is *advantages.*

TIP APPLIED: **The <u>advantages</u> of this entertainment system <u>are</u> that it is compact and that it is less expensive than what you would pay if you bought the cassette recorder, CD player, and radio separately.**

Now You Try It, 1 **(Corrected sentences appear on page 314.)**

In the following sentences, the dictionary form of the verb is in **boldface** type. Jump to the beginning of the sentence, and find the first word that makes sense as the subject. Underline this subject, and then make the verb agree with it.

EXAMPLE: **The identity of the suspects in the recent robberies**
has
~~have~~ ^ not been released to the press.

1. In our recent games, the margin of our losses **have** been agonizingly small.

2. Our response to the accusations made by our opponents clearly **show** that they have misunderstood the facts of the case.

3. In the opinion of the committee, the type of programs shown during the hours that children usually watch television **be** clearly inappropriate.

4. The reasons for the collapse of the settlement agreement between the union and company management **remain** unclear to outside observers.

5. The time for cooking roasts in ovens **depend** on the type of meat.

S/V AGR

Now You Try It, 2 **(Corrected sentences appear on page 314.)**

In the following sentences, the dictionary form of the verb is in **boldface** type. Jump to the beginning of the sentence, and find the first word that makes sense as the subject. Underline this subject, and then make the verb agree with it.

EXAMPLE: **We bought the children some games on our last trip that**
were
~~be~~ ^ made by hand from the most beautiful hardwood.

1. Disagreements about the interpretation of the agreement **have** led to considerable unpleasantness among the parties involved.

2. The social aspects of developing of the country's resources **be** often overlooked.

3. It always seems to be the case that the simplest solutions to a complex problem **seem** the most difficult to discover.

4. A group of incredibly noisy children playing outside my windows **delight** in keeping me from doing my homework.

5. Speculation about the nominees for the various Oscars **dominate** today's news.

Now You Try It, 3

Make up a sentence using the first word as the subject and the second word (in **boldface** type) as the verb that must agree with the subject. In addition, add modifiers after the subject so that there are at least five words between the subject and the verb. Keep the verb in the present tense.

EXAMPLE: **diplomats appear** The diplomats at Archduke Ferdinand's gala New Year's Eve ball appear to be enjoying themselves flirting with the Grand Duchess.

1. lawyer **have**

2. reports **suggest**

3. owners **deserve**

4. complaint **justify**

5. comparisons **be**

S/V AGR

Editing Practice, 1 **(Corrected sentences appear on page 314.)**

Correct all errors in the following paragraphs using the first correction as a model. The number in parentheses at the end of each paragraph indicates how many errors you should find.

The house cat is one of the oldest domesticated animals. Researchers who study the history of the cat ~~believes~~ ^believe that the ancestor of all of today's domestic cats were a species of small wildcats found in Africa and Europe. The first group of people to bring cats into human habitations were in Africa. (2)

However, the first actual domestication of cats as residents with humans was carried out by the Egyptians, who tamed cats to hunt rats and mice in grain storehouses. The pet cats of an important official or government officer was sacred. When one of these sacred cats were killed by a servant, even accidentally, the servant would be severely punished, possibly even put to death. (2)

Editing Practice, 2 **(Corrected sentences appear on page 314.)**

Correct all errors in the following paragraph using the first correction as a model. The number in parentheses at the end of the paragraph indicates how many errors you should find.

One of the largest families of vertebrate animals ~~are~~ *is* the family of reptiles. Reptiles include alligators, crocodiles, lizards, snakes, and turtles. They share the feature of being cold-blooded. Reptiles are among the oldest families of animals on earth. Reptiles played a key role in bringing animal life out of the oceans and onto land through the evolution of eggs. Reptiles evolved from amphibians, the first creatures to come onto land. The great evolutionary advantage of reptiles were their eggs. Reptile eggs, with their leathery membrane or hard shell, has a great advantage: the embryo is encased in its own self-contained sack of fluid. The ability of reptiles to reproduce away from bodies of water give reptiles an enormous advantage over amphibians and explain why reptiles were able to expand into all the dry areas of the world. (4)

Editing Practice, 3

Correct all errors in the following paragraph using the first correction as a model. The number in parentheses at the end of the paragraph indicates how many errors you should find.

Reptiles, during the entire period of the Mesozoic Era (from 225 million to 65 million years ago), ~~was~~ *were* the dominant life form on land. Since they had no competition from other families of animals, reptiles were free to occupy every possible ecological niche, with the result that the family of reptiles were able to diversify with almost unimaginable variety. The feature that today characterizes reptiles are their being cold-blooded. We think of cold-blooded animals as sluggish and primitive; however, that idea may be just our mammal bias in favor of being warm-blooded. The major part of the calories that we consume every day

are burned in merely keeping our warm-blooded metabolism fueled. A cold-blooded animal, whose need for calories is only a fraction of what equivalent-weight warm-blooded animals need, survive easily in environments that could not sustain warm-blooded animals. Many scientists now believe that a type of dinosaurs, the most famous ancient branch of the reptile family, were actually warm-blooded. And a family of reptiles closely related to the dinosaurs were the direct ancestors of birds, which, of course, are all warm-blooded. (6)

Writing Practice

On your own paper, write a paragraph or two about a camping trip you remember. What good things, bad things, or funny things make you remember it? Use the Proofreading Checklist to guide you in drawing an arrow from each verb to its subject. Then, check to see that you do not have any lost-subject errors.

PROOFREADING CHECKLIST

Eliminating Lost-Subject Errors from Your Writing

- Whenever the subject and verb are not side by side, you need to check for lost subjects.
- Jump back to the beginning of the sentence to find the first word that could serve as the subject.
- If that word does not make sense as the subject, continue reading from the beginning of the sentence until you find the word that must be the subject.

THE BOTTOM LINE

Subjects that are not next to their verb still *determine* whether the verb is singular or plural. Jump back to the beginning of the sentence to find the subject.

LESSON 18

Agreement Involving There Is *and* There Was

Sample Errors

SAMPLE 1: ✗ **There is a million stories in every big city.**

SAMPLE 2: ✗ **There was dozens of books piled on the couch.**

What's the Problem?

S/V AGR

English, like most languages, has a special construction to point out the existence of something. In English, we use *there* plus some form of the verb *be* (or a similar verb like *seem* or *appear*) for this purpose. For example, you might want to call a waiter's attention to a dead fly floating in your soup by saying, "Waiter! *There is* a fly in my soup!" In this construction, the subject *follows* the verb. A problem occurs when the subject is plural but the verb is singular.

What Causes the Problem?

This type of construction creates a problem with subject-verb agreement because the subject is not in its normal position. We create sentences of this type by moving the subject to *follow* the verb and filling the vacant subject position with *there*. In conversation, we tend to use the singular form of the verb *be*, as though the verb were agreeing with the empty word *there*.

Diagnostic Exercise **(Corrected sentences appear on page 315.)**

Correct all errors in the following paragraph using the first correction as a model. The number in parentheses at the end of the paragraph indicates how many errors you should find.

Each year there ~~is~~ *are* many new movies coming out of Hollywood. Each is designed for a certain segment of the moviegoing audience. There is car-crash films aimed at males under thirty. There is heart-warming romantic comedies for women over twenty. There is even the dreadful "slasher" movies for an audience that it is better not to think about. (3)

Fixing the Problem in Your Own Writing

The following tip shows that the *there* in a "there exists" sentence is an empty word used as a placeholder for the real subject.

> "THERE" DELETION TIP: Rearrange the word order of the sentence to eliminate *there*. If this paraphrase is grammatical, then the original sentence contains an "existential there" construction.

This paraphrase has the additional advantage of helping identify the real subject of the sentence. You may even decide that the paraphrase results in a livelier sentence than the *there is/there was* construction of the original version.

Once you know that a sentence contains a *there is/there was* construction, then you have to make sure that the verb agrees with the actual subject, not with the place-holder word *there*.

S/V AGR

> BEHIND-THE-VERB TIP: In *there is/there was* sentences, the subject is the first word after the verb that makes sense as a subject.

For Example . . .

Here is how you can use the *There* Deletion Tip to identify the sample sentences as containing the *there is/there was* construction:

SAMPLE 1: ✗ **There is a million stories in every big city.**

TIP APPLIED: **A million stories are in every big city.**

SAMPLE 2: ✗ **There was dozens of books piled on the couch.**

TIP APPLIED: **Dozens of books were piled on the couch.**

Now you can use the Behind-the-Verb Tip to find the correct subject and make the verb agree with the real subject:

SAMPLE 1: ✗ **There <u>is</u> a million stories in every big city.**

TIP APPLIED: **There <u>are</u> a million <u>stories</u> in every big city.**

SAMPLE 2: ✗ **There <u>was</u> dozens of books piled on the couch.**

TIP APPLIED: **There <u>were</u> <u>dozens</u> of books piled on the couch.**

Now You Try It, 1 **(Corrected sentences appear on page 315.)**

Underline the first word or words following the verb that make sense as a subject. If there is an error in subject-verb agreement, write the correct form of the verb above the incorrect verb.

EXAMPLE: **There ~~was~~ *were* usually some special <u>presents</u> hidden under the Christmas tree.**

1. There was many errands that still needed to be taken care of.
2. Unfortunately, there is still some bugs in the new program.
3. There is always a thousand things to do!
4. We discovered that there was a special tool that we could use.
5. Carl Sagan is fond of pointing out that there is billions of stars.

Now You Try It, 2 **(Corrected sentences appear on page 315.)**

Underline the first word or words following the verb that make sense as a subject. If there is an error in subject-verb agreement, write the correct form of the verb above the incorrect verb.

EXAMPLE: **We discovered that there ~~was~~ *were* a downed <u>power pole</u> and an uprooted <u>tree</u> blocking the road.**

1. We were all upset about what had happened, but there wasn't many things we could do about it.
2. There has been a lot of discussion about the problems we will face when we renovate our house.
3. There is a couple of openings down at the plant.
4. If you look back at the story carefully, there is plenty of hints that tell us what is going to happen at the end.
5. There is a museum and a gallery that we would like to visit when we go to Philadelphia next month.

Now You Try It, 3

Rewrite the following sentences as *there is/there are* sentences.

EXAMPLE: **Trains are coming into the station now.**

There are trains coming into the station now.

1. Some kittens in the barn are just opening their eyes.

2. Some cups and saucers that we can use are in the kitchen.

3. A terrible strain of flu is going around.

4. An old flashlight and some batteries were in the cabin.

5. Some books that you might like are on the bottom shelf.

Editing Practice, 1 **(Corrected sentences appear on page 315.)**

Correct all errors in the following paragraphs using the first correction as a model. The number in parentheses at the end of each paragraph indicates how many errors you should find.

There ~~is~~ ^are two countries in the Iberian Peninsula: Spain and Portugal. Portugal occupies most of the western coast, while Spain covers the rest of the peninsula. There is three basic regions in the peninsula: coastal plains on the west, south, and east; a long strip of mountains across the northern part; and a huge, dry plateau that covers most of the central area. (1)

Although the coastal plains account for only a tiny portion of the land mass of the peninsula, there is a high percentage of the population in that region. Along the coast, there is both a mild climate and fertile soil. In addition, there is many rivers that flow into the plains from the mountains in the interior of the country. These rivers provide irrigation water for the fields and orchards in the coastal plains. Especially along the southern coast, there is thousands of acres of orange and lemon orchards. (3)

Editing Practice, 2 **(Corrected sentences appear on page 315.)**

Correct all errors in the following paragraphs using the first correction as a model. The number in parentheses at the end of each paragraph indicates how many errors you should find.

The largest distinctive geographical feature in the United States and Canada is the Rocky Mountains. In the lower forty-eight states, there ~~is~~ ^ *are* eight states that contain a portion of the Rockies: Idaho, Montana, Wyoming, Nevada, Utah, Colorado, New Mexico, and Arizona. There is even branches of the mountains that extend north through two Canadian provinces and into Alaska. There is rich veins of minerals, especially gold, silver, copper, lead, and zinc, in the region. Nowadays, however, there is greater riches in liquid mining: petroleum and natural gas. (3)

The great natural beauty of the Rocky Mountains has made them very popular. There is many National Parks throughout the region; two of the best known are Yellowstone and Glacier National Parks. There is many winter sports, especially downhill and cross-country skiing, that have made the Rocky Mountains as important as the Alps as a winter tourist destination. (2)

Editing Practice, 3

Correct all errors in the following paragraphs using the first correction as a model. The number in parentheses at the end of each paragraph indicates how many errors you should find.

There ~~is~~ ^ *are* two north-south physical <u>divisions</u> that have affected the country in many ways. Going from east to west, there is the Rocky Mountains, and then there is the Cascades. The crest of the Rocky Mountains literally divides the North American continent in half, since it forms the continental watershed; rain falling on the western slopes of the crest flows into the Pacific, and rain falling on the eastern slopes flows into the Atlantic. There is other consequences of

S/V AGR

these great mountain chains as well. Both mountain chains block the prevailing moist weather from the west, creating gigantic rain shadows on their eastern slopes that turn much of western North America into near deserts. (3)

Then there is the problems of transportation created by the mountains. Until the railroads passed through the mountains in the 1870's, it was often easier to travel from the East Coast to California by sailing around the tip of South America than to cross the two great mountain chains. Even today, there is only a few east-west routes that pass through the mountains. (2)

Writing Practice

Using the Editing Practice essays in this lesson as your model, write a paragraph or two that describes the geography, climate, or scenic attractions of a place that you are familiar with. Try to use as many examples of the *there is/there was* construction as you can. Then, use the Proofreading Checklist to show that all uses of *there is/there was* are correct.

PROOFREADING CHECKLIST

Avoiding There Is/There Was *Errors in Your Writing*

- Whenever you use *there*, check to see whether the sentence contains a *there is/there was* construction by paraphrasing the sentence to eliminate the *there*.
- The subject in this kind of sentence will always be the first word or words after the verb that make sense as the subject.
- Make the verb agree with this subject.

THE BOTTOM LINE

There is often a subject *after* the verb in a *there is* or *there was* construction.

LESSON 19

Agreement Involving Compound Subjects

Sample Errors

SAMPLE 1: ✗ **The pencils and some paper <u>is</u> on the desk.**

SAMPLE 2: ✗ **Our genetic endowment and our personal experience <u>makes</u> us who we are.**

What's the Problem?

When two (or more) subjects are joined by *and*, they are called a **compound subject**. When using compound subjects, writers have a tendency to use a singular verb, one with an added third-person-singular *-s*, even though compound subjects are normally plural. Thus, the third-person-singular *-s* is incorrect. Use the plural form of the verb, which has no added third-person-singular *-s*. (Note that the verb *be* has an irregular plural form *are*.)

S/V AGR

What Causes the Problem?

Compound subjects are usually plural. Certain compound subjects, however, create a problem because writers may incorrectly think of them as being a single collective unit. Consider this example:

✗ **<u>Good planning</u> and <u>follow-through</u> is the key to success.**

The writer of this sentence probably thought that the two subjects (*planning* and *follow-through*) should be taken together as a singular, collective unit and, therefore, that the verb *is* should also be singular to agree with it. Although this argument has a certain logic to it, the usual grammatical convention is that compound subjects are plural and must have plural verbs.

Contributing to compound-subject errors is the fact that a number of compounds (especially ones referring to food) are fixed phrases that people use with singular verbs. Some examples are *macaroni and cheese*, *bacon and eggs*, and *salt and pepper*. A different kind of exception to the general rule is found in the plural titles of books, which are treated as singular: *<u>The Prince and the Pauper</u>* ***is*** *one of Mark Twain's most enjoyable books.*

Diagnostic Exercise **(Corrected sentences appear on page 316.)**

Correct all errors in the following paragraph using the first correction as a model. The number in parentheses at the end of the paragraph indicates how many errors you should find.

I work in a busy law office. Even though we now have voice mail, answering the phone and writing down messages ~~takes~~ take up a lot of my time. I am also responsible for maintaining the law library, although most of the time I do nothing more glamorous than shelving. The law books and reference material is always left scattered around the library, and some of the lawyers even leave their dirty coffee cups on the tables. I used to have a relatively comfortable working area, but the new computer terminal and modem has now taken up most of my personal space; that's progress, I guess. Despite all the stress, meeting the needs of clients and keeping track of all the information required in a modern law office makes it a fascinating, if demanding, job. (3)

Fixing This Problem in Your Writing

Whenever the subject contains *and*, check to see whether the *and* has joined two subjects together to create a compound subject. If so, then the subject is plural, and you must also use a plural verb—unless the compound is a recognized fixed phrase like *macaroni and cheese* that is accepted as being singular.

Following is a tip to help you identify compound subjects.

> "THEY" TIP: Whenever *and* is used in the subject part of a sentence, see whether you can replace the entire subject portion with the pronoun *they*. If you can, then the subject is a compound, and the verb must be made plural to agree with *they*.

This rule applies *only* to *and*. It does not apply when the subject parts are joined by *or*. When subjects are joined by *or*, the rules are completely different: the verb agrees only with the *nearest* subject, which may be either singular or plural.

The following three sentences are all correct, but only the last one has a compound subject:

Either the instructor or the students were mistaken about the date of the final exam.

Either the students or the instructor was mistaken about the date of the final exam.

The students and the instructor were mistaken about the date of the final exam.

For Example . . .

Here is how replacing the compound subject with *they* identifies the right form of the verb in the two sample sentences.

SAMPLE 1: ✗ **The pencils and some paper is on the desk.**

TIP APPLIED: ✗ **The pencils and some paper is on the desk.** (*They* written above *The pencils and some paper*)

Since we know that the substitution of *they* for *the pencils and some paper* makes sense, we know that the sentence contains a compound subject. When *they* is the subject, it is easy to tell that the verb must be plural: *They are on the desk.* Thus, the sentence with the compound must also be plural:

CORRECTION: **The pencils and some paper are on the desk.**

SAMPLE 2: ✗ **Our genetic endowment and our personal experience makes us who we are.**

TIP APPLIED: ✗ **Our genetic endowment and our personal experience makes us who we are.** (*They* written above *Our genetic endowment and our personal experience*)

Since we know that the substitution of *they* for *our genetic endowment and our personal experience* makes sense, we know that the sentence contains a compound subject. When *they* is the subject, it is easy to tell that the verb must be plural: *They make us who we are.* Thus, the sentence with the compound must also be plural:

CORRECTION: **Our genetic endowment and our personal experience make us who we are.**

S/V AGR

Now You Try It, 1 **(Corrected sentences appear on page 316.)**

Underline the compound subjects in the following sentences. If there is an error in subject-verb agreement, make the necessary correction.

EXAMPLE: **Green <u>vegetables</u> and fresh <u>fruit</u> ~~is~~ ^are^ the basis of a good diet.**

1. In Monopoly, four railroads and both utilities is too much to pay for the Boardwalk.

2. A lock and the key that goes with it is given to everyone who uses the lockers.

3. When there is a storm, the thunder and lightning scares my dog.

4. The debits and credits always adds up to zero.

5. Lunch and dinner is not included as part of the package.

Now You Try It, 2 **(Corrected sentences appear on page 316.)**

Underline the compound subjects in the following sentences. If there is an error in subject-verb agreement, make the necessary correction.

EXAMPLE: **<u>Linen</u> and <u>cotton</u> ~~is~~ ^are^ made from plants.**

1. What we see and what we hear gives us our picture of the world.

2. In a poker hand, aces and eights is called a "dead man's hand."

3. The sun and the nine planets composes our solar system.

4. His great natural dignity and his consideration for others was something that his friends and relatives would never forget.

5. The plants and the animals found in this region is adapted to the extreme swings of temperature from hot days to freezing nights.

Now You Try It, 3

Underline the compound subjects in the following sentences. If there is no compound subject, write *none* above the sentence. Correct all errors in subject-verb agreement.

none
EXAMPLE: **Either the television or the VCR was broken.**

1. A large order of fries and a double cheeseburger was found in the seat of the abandoned car.

2. The actors or one of the stagehands are always leaving the door open.

3. The brushes and the paint was always kept in the garage.

4. The excessive heat and the high humidity was driving us all crazy.

5. Rhythm and blues is Brett's favorite kind of music.

S/V AGR

Editing Practice, 1 **(Corrected sentences appear on page 316.)**

Correct all errors in the following paragraphs using the first correction as a model. The number in parentheses at the end of each paragraph indicates how many errors you should find.

In Mozart's opera, *Don Giovanni,* comedy and melodrama ~~is~~ are mixed together in an unusual way. For example, the character and personality of Don Giovanni is surprisingly complex. His charm and bravery makes him almost a hero at times. Yet at other times, his aristocratic arrogance and deliberate cruelty to women makes him a complete villain. The seduction of a willing woman and a rape is the same to him. (4)

The role and character of his servant Leporello is also unusual. At first, his constant complaining and caustic asides to the audience makes Leporello seem to be just a conventional comic sidekick. Yet in some ways, his observations and reactions to his master's behavior becomes the center of attention. Leporello's admiration for the Don's charm and his repulsion at the Don's treatment of women reflects the audience's equally mixed feelings. (4)

Editing Practice, 2 **(Corrected sentences appear on page 316.)**

Correct all errors in the following paragraph using the first correction as a model. The number in parentheses at the end of the paragraph indicates how many errors you should find.

Barbara Kingsolver is the author of six books and a number of short stories. Her books and stories ~~has~~ *have* attracted a wide following. One of her most recent novels is *Animal Dreams*. Codi, her sister, and their father is the focus of our attention. The story deals with Codi's reluctant return home to a small town in Arizona to take care of her father, who is dying. The events that take place in the story are seen either from Codi's perspective or from her father's point of view. The past and the present constantly runs together in their minds. One of the main themes in the book is Codi's discovery of how deeply her present life and actions has been affected by dimly remembered events in her childhood. At first, it seems that Codi's father is totally out of touch with reality because he seems hopelessly stuck in the past. However, as Codi begins to reconstruct a clearer picture of her own childhood, it is her father's vivid memories that actually provide the key to her adult understanding of her past. (3)

Editing Practice, 3

Correct all errors in the following paragraph using the first correction as a model. The number in parentheses at the end of the paragraph indicates how many errors you should find.

The town and its inhabitants gradually ~~takes~~ *take* on greater and greater importance. Codi gradually begins to see how important the little town and its inhabitants is to her past and present life. The town, because of its unbroken connection from the past to the present, gradually becomes more and more

important to Codi. In fact, the town and its people evolves to become one of the central characters in the book. Finally, it is the town and its people, living and dead, that brings Codi back to life as a complete person who can connect her past to her present. In addition to its serious themes, the book is very funny. Kingsolver's sharp eye and wit makes every scene and conversation vivid and convincing. (4)

Writing Practice

Using the Editing Practice essays in this lesson as a model, write a paragraph or two about some complex fictional character from a movie, play, or book. What are the conflicting personality features that make this person interesting? Try to use as many examples of compound subjects as you can. Then, use the Proofreading Checklist to show that the verbs you have used with compound subjects are correct.

PROOFREADING CHECKLIST

Eliminating Compound-Subject Errors in Your Writing

- ▶ Two or more singular nouns joined by *and* form a compound subject that requires a plural verb.
- ▶ Anytime there is an *and* in the subject part of the sentence, replace the entire subject portion of the sentence with the pronoun *they* to see whether there is a compound subject.
- ▶ If *they* makes sense as a paraphrase of the subject, then the subject is a compound and probably requires a plural verb.

THE BOTTOM LINE

A *noun or pronoun* and another *noun or pronoun* joined by *and* make a compound subject.

UNIT FOUR
PUTTING IT ALL TOGETHER

Errors in subject-verb agreement result when the writer makes the verb agree with a word that is not the actual subject. Failure to identify the correct subject is most likely to happen in the following situations.

S/V AGR

Lost-Subject Errors

When many words separate the subject from the verb, writers tend to make the verb agree with a word near the verb rather than with the more distant, actual subject.

Anytime the subject is long or complicated, check for this kind of error by jumping to the *first* word in the sentence that makes sense as the subject of the verb. In all likelihood, this word is the actual subject. If it is not the subject, continue reading from the beginning of the sentence until you find the subject.

There Is/There Was Errors

When a sentence points out the existence of something using a *there is/there was* construction, writers tend to make the verb singular even when the actual subject is plural.

Check for this kind of error every time you use *there is/there was* to mean "there exists"; make the verb agree with the first word *after* the verb that makes sense as the subject.

Compound-Subject Errors

When there is a compound subject, writers sometimes think of the compound as a single unit and mistakenly use a singular verb. Except for a few fixed phrases that are always used in the singular, subjects that include *and* are compound subjects and as such are grammatically plural when it comes to subject-verb agreement.

Check for a compound subject and for an error in subject-verb agreement anytime there is an *and* in the subject part of the sentence. To be sure that you have used the correct verb form with a compound subject, substitute *they* for the entire subject portion of the sentence.

Review

Underline the subjects in every sentence. Then, correct all errors using the first correction as a model. The number in parentheses at the end of each paragraph indicates how many errors you should find.

Although European explorers came to the New World in search of gold, the new fruits and vegetables of the New World ~~was~~ were much more important to the Old World than all the gold they ever found. Before contact with the New World, there was no tomatoes, corn, or potatoes in the Old World. However, for many of us, the greatest gift of all the New World's many agricultural products were the food and beverage that we call *chocolate*. All products containing chocolate in any form comes from the seeds of the cacao tree. The Mayas in Central America was the first to discover how to produce chocolate from cacao seeds. (4)

A number of large, melon-shaped pods grow directly on the trunk and larger branches of the cacao tree. Each of these pods contain up to forty almond-shaped seeds. The seeds, after being removed from the pod, fermented, and dried, is transformed into the commercial cocoa bean. (2)

The first step in producing chocolate from the cacao beans are to remove the outer shells. What remains after the shells have been removed are called *nibs*. Nibs contain a high percentage of a natural fat called *cocoa butter*. When nibs are heated and ground, the cocoa butter is released. The mixture of cocoa butter and finely ground nibs form a liquid called *chocolate liquor*. The chocolate liquor, after being cooled and molded into little cakes, are what we know as baking chocolate. Baking chocolate and sugar is at the heart of all those wonderful chocolate goodies that we would all die for. (5)

UNIT FIVE
Pronouns

OVERVIEW

Terms That Can Help You Understand Pronouns

If you are not familiar with any of the following terms that appear in this unit, look them up in the Guide to Grammar Terminology beginning on page 1. The numbers in parentheses indicate the lessons in which each term appears.

agreement (21)
noun (20, 22, 23, 24)
object (22)
personal pronoun (21, 22, 24)
preposition (22)
pronoun (20, 22, 23, 24)
pronoun antecedent (20, 21)
relative pronoun (23)
sexist language (24)
subject (22, 23)
verb (22, 23)

PRON

The Nuts and Bolts of Pronouns

Pronouns are an important part of many languages. For one thing, they help us avoid having to use the same words over and over (as in *Ms. Ramone stopped by yesterday, and Ms. Ramone took us for a ride in Ms. Ramone's new car*). Pronouns are useful because they can easily fit into almost any sentence.

But the adaptability of pronouns also creates problems. Because they can refer to so many things, writers must take care to make the reference of each pronoun clear. Here are some common difficulties involving pronouns:

- Making clear what a pronoun refers to (see Lesson 20).

  EXAMPLE: **✗ Our dog gets so mad at the cat that it chases its tail.**

  Our cat gets the dog so mad it chases its own tail.

- Making a pronoun and the word it refers to both single *or* both plural (see Lesson 21).

  EXAMPLE: **✗ The person who called didn't leave their phone number.**

  The person who called didn't leave a phone number.

- Choosing between similar pronouns: *I* or *me*? *she* or *her*? *he* or *him*? (see Lesson 22); *who*, *whom*, or *that*? (see Lesson 23).

  EXAMPLE: ✗ **Dolly and me went skiing.**

  Dolly and I went skiing.

  EXAMPLE: ✗ **Our group decided whom would type our paper.**

  Our group decided who would type our paper.

- Using nonsexist language to ensure that nouns and pronouns appropriately refer to both males and females (see Lesson 24).

  EXAMPLE: ✗ **Everyone should have complected his assignment.**

  Everyone should have completed the assignment.

Can You Detect Pronoun Problems?

(Corrected sentences appear on page 317.)

Correct all errors in the following paragraph using the first correction as a model. The number in parentheses at the end of the paragraph indicates how many errors you should find.

My friend Richard told me that Clyde, the guy ~~whom~~ *who* sits next to him in his English class, decided to quit school because he'd rather be a rock singer. Richard and me both laughed at this at first, but maybe it is a smart decision. Clyde has changed his major at least four times this year; that is what Richard told me. Although a person might change their major a few times, changing it too often indicates a good deal of uncertainty and can put him back several years. (5)

Clyde usually managed to bring up rock music in discussions with Richard, our classmates, and I. Often, Clyde's comments would seem completely irrelevant, but everybody bit their tongue and let him go on and on about Madonna, Bon Jovi, or another rock star that somehow Clyde managed to fit into the discussion. Of course, a student has a right to speak up. However, they shouldn't bring up their pop idols at every opportunity. (4)

LESSON 20

Vague Pronouns

Sample Errors

SAMPLE 1: **Contrary to her campaign promises, the governor announced cutbacks in welfare and an increase in education spending. ✗ That is sure to anger voters.**

SAMPLE 2: **Two of our favorite hobbies are fishing and skiing. ✗ It requires a lot of money for good equipment.**

What's the Problem?

Many pronouns refer back to a previous **noun** or **pronoun**, which is called the **pronoun antecedent**. A problem occurs when this antecedent is missing or unclear. This lesson focuses on three pronouns that are often used vaguely: *this*, *that*, and *it*. Keep in mind, though, that *this*, *that*, and *it* can serve other functions in English in addition to taking the place of an antecedent.

PRON

What Causes the Problem?

A speaker can use *this*, *that*, and *it* without creating much confusion because physical gestures (such as pointing) can clarify what *this* or *that* is. Readers also have ways to figure out what a vague pronoun refers to. However, a writer who uses pronouns precisely has a much greater chance of being understood than one who forces readers to work to figure out the meaning of the pronouns.

Diagnostic Exercise **(Corrected sentences appear on page 317.)**

Using the first correction as a model, correct all vague uses of *this*, *that*, and *it* in the following paragraph. The number in parentheses at the end of the paragraph indicates how many changes you should make.

The program

"Star Wars" was the name of a military program as well as a movie. ~~It~~ ^ was a large research-and-development program calling for military defense in outer space. This was initiated by President Reagan in the 1980's, and it had the official title of "Strategic Defense Initiative." The public never embraced that as much as the catchier title "Star Wars." (2)

Fixing This Problem in Your Writing

Here is one way to avoid vague use of *this*, *that*, and *it*.

ANTECEDENT TIP: Locate what you think the pronoun refers to (the antecedent). Make sure this antecedent is a person, place, or thing—not another part of speech or an entire sentence. Make sure there is not a "pseudo-antecedent"—another person, place, or thing that the pronoun could possibly be referring to.

In Sample 1, *That* seems to be referring to the entire idea of the first sentence. One way to correct the problem is to add a noun after *That*, changing *That* into an adjective, which doesn't require an antecedent.

SAMPLE 1: **Contrary to her campaign promises, the governor announced cutbacks in welfare and an increase in education spending. ✗ That is sure to anger voters.**

CORRECTION: **Contrary to her campaign promises, the governor announced cutbacks in welfare and an increase in education spending. That *inconsistency* is sure to anger voters.**

In the following revision, the writer has revised the sentence before the pronoun to provide an antecedent, *reversal.*

CORRECTION: **The governor announced cutbacks in welfare and an increase in education spending, a *reversal* of her campaign promises. *That* is sure to anger voters.**

For Example . . .

In Sample 2, *It* could refer to *fishing, skiing*, or *fishing and skiing*, but if the last of these possibilities is intended, the correct pronoun is the plural form *They*. Another likely possibility is that the writer really wants *It* to refer to *good equipment* even though the sentence is not constructed to make such a reference. Here are two corrections that eliminate the pronoun:

SAMPLE 2: **Two of our favorite hobbies are fishing and skiing. ✗ It requires a lot of money for good equipment.**

CORRECTION: **Two of our favorite hobbies, fishing and skiing, require a lot of money for good equipment.**

CORRECTION: **Two of our favorite hobbies are fishing and skiing. <u>Good equipment</u> requires a lot of money.**

PRON

Now You Try It, 1 **(Corrected sentences appear on page 317.)**

If the underlined pronoun is vague, correct the sentence using any method described earlier. If the pronoun is not vague, write *OK* above it and underline the antecedent.

EXAMPLE: **I hurried to answer the phone, and this ^mad rush^ caused me to fall and sprain my ankle.**

1. In 1920, the largest known meteorite was found. It weighed some 65 tons.

2. The printer for the computer is not working, and I have a paper that is due in an hour. I knew this was going to happen!

3. The Nobel Prize is the most valuable award for literature, but two writers have declined it. [*Hint:* Can *it* logically refer to *literature*?]

4. So far, the polls indicate that the mayor will be reelected. That is a surprise.

5. A deer poked its head up from the grass where a fawn was resting, and then I saw it run away.

PRON

Now You Try It, 2 **(Corrected sentences appear on page 317.)**

If the underlined pronoun is vague, correct the sentence using any method described earlier. If the pronoun is not vague, write *OK* above it and underline the antecedent.

EXAMPLE: **My roommate told me her teacher gave a lecture on the Industrial Revolution. ~~It~~ ^The lecture^ lasted almost two hours.**

1. Alena called today to talk about the antismoking law passed by the city government. This took almost an hour of my time.

2. We need a new mayor, but that won't happen anytime soon.

3. Cincinnati was a boom town because of its strategic location. In the early 1800's, it was built on the increasingly busy Ohio River.

4. A car pulled in front of the truck that was behind me. It was speeding.

5. World War I was ended by the Versailles Treaty; this also led to the formation of the League of Nations.

Now You Try It, 3

Write a sentence using *this*, *that*, or *it* to refer clearly to the underlined word.

EXAMPLE: **My roommate had a serious <u>illness</u> last summer.**

It caused her to drop her summer courses.

1. A hubcap seems to have fallen off my <u>car</u>.

2. Over there is the main <u>cafeteria</u>.

3. When he discovered that today is his girlfriend's birthday, Bill rushed to the <u>mall</u>.

4. My English teacher read aloud a <u>poem</u>.

5. Even though I looked everywhere, I still can't find my <u>wallet</u>.

Editing Practice, 1 **(Corrected sentences appear on page 318.)**

Correct all errors in the following paragraphs using the first correction as a model. The number in parentheses at the end of each paragraph indicates how many changes you should make.

PRON

Some great books do not become great until long after they were written.
situation
This ^ is particularly evident with a book written by William Bradford. He wrote *Of Plymouth Plantation,* one of the oldest books written by Europeans exploring and colonizing the Western Hemisphere. This was not widely known until 1856, when it was published, but it was written some two hundred years earlier. (1)

This book, written by the governor of Plymouth Colony, chronicles the story of the Pilgrims until 1646. Bradford's book offers considerable detail on the day-to-day lives of the colonists. It contains the oldest-known copy of the Mayflower Compact, which was an agreement among the Pilgrims for a democratic-style government. It disappeared about the time of the American Revolution but was discovered many years later and finally published. (1)

Editing Practice, 2 **(Corrected sentences appear on page 318.)**

Correct all errors in the following paragraphs using the first correction as a model. The number in parentheses at the end of each paragraph indicates how many changes you should make.

Slavery has been a sore spot in the history of the United States. ~~It~~ ^Slavery^ is especially troubling considering the role of African Americans in the founding of the country. In 1774, a group of slaves in the American colonies made a famous appeal to Thomas Gage, who was the royal governor of Massachusetts Colony. It proclaimed that they as slaves had a right to the freedoms that the colonists sought from Britain. This was shared by Benjamin Franklin, Alexander Hamilton, and other colonists opposing slavery. (2)

When the Revolution began, African Americans were excluded from the American army. That changed, however, when the British encouraged the slaves to join their army. Approximately five thousand African Americans would eventually join the American army. This allowed many to win freedom as a result of their service, but America as a whole would still condone slavery until the Civil War. (2)

PRON

Editing Practice, 3

Correct all errors in the following paragraph using the first correction as a model. The number in parentheses at the end of the paragraph indicates how many changes you should make.

I'm trying to make the transition from playing "jungle ball" volleyball to regulation volleyball. This ^transition^ isn't easy. One major difference is it requires more teamwork, and that means paying more attention to how I set the ball to my teammates. In jungle ball, each player tends to play almost any ball within reach (or at least this is what my team does). That sort of play is fun and gives

us a good workout, but too often we have collisions when each person tries to spike every ball over the net. Still, jungle ball has given me some practice in serving, hitting, and occasionally even setting the ball. (3)

Writing Practice

Write a paragraph or two explaining your first efforts to learn a new sport or hobby. Try to include *this*, *that*, and *it* (any combination) at least five times. Use the Proofreading Checklist to correct any pronoun errors in your sentences.

PROOFREADING CHECKLIST

Using Clear Pronouns in Your Writing

- When using *this*, *that*, and *it* to refer to something you just wrote, look for the antecedent—the person, place, or thing that the pronoun is renaming. The antecedent should be a noun or a pronoun, not a verb or an entire sentence.
- Make sure there is no "pseudo-antecedent"—another person, place, or thing that the pronoun could possibly refer to—that could cause confusion.
- You can correct a vague pronoun by adding cues around it to let readers know what the pronoun refers to (such as adding a noun after *this* or *that* to make the pronoun an adjective).
- You can also correct a vague pronoun by rewording what comes before the pronoun so there is only *one* possible antecedent.

THE BOTTOM LINE

When using a pronoun, be sure that *it* has a clear antecedent.

LESSON 21

Pronoun Agreement

PRON AGR

Sample Errors

SAMPLE 1: ✗ **A teacher should explain their assignments carefully.**

SAMPLE 2: ✗ **Did everybody cast their vote in the last election?**

What's the Problem?

Personal pronouns include *I, he, she, it, they, we,* and all their varied forms, such as *me, him, his, her, its, their,* and *them*. A personal pronoun often refers back to a person, place, or thing (called a **pronoun antecedent**). This pronoun and antecedent should be in **agreement**; that is, they should deal with the same number, person, and gender (see Lesson 24 for information about agreement involving gender).

This lesson focuses on one of the more widespread problems: making sure the personal pronoun agrees in number with an antecedent. In Sample 1, the antecedent of *their* is *teacher*. An error occurs because *their* is plural (more than one person) while *teacher* is singular (one person). In Sample 2, *everybody* is singular, while *their* is again (and always) plural. Thus, the pronouns are not agreeing with their antecedents about how many people are involved.

What Causes the Problem?

One reason errors occur in pronoun-verb agreement is that sometimes an antecedent seems to refer to many people, even though technically it includes only one person (even if that one person can be anybody). In Samples 1 and 2, *teacher* and *everybody* are generalizations about each teacher or person, thus giving the feeling that they are plural. Nonetheless, they are grammatically singular.

Another reason this error occurs is that writers do not want to be sexist. If Samples 1 and 2 used *his* instead of *their*, the writer would avoid an agreement error but would be considered sexist for excluding females (see Lesson 24). Writers should avoid both problems—agreement errors as well as sexist use of pronouns.

Diagnostic Exercise **(Corrected sentences appear on page 318.)**

Correct all errors in the following paragraph using the first correction as a model. The number in parentheses at the end of the paragraph indicates how many errors you should find.

Soldiers commit

~~A soldier commits~~ ^ a war crime when they violate norms for acceptable behavior in times of war. Few people want war, but most want their rights and those of others to be respected as much as possible when war occurs. For instance, almost everybody agrees that a prisoner should have their physical needs attended to and should not be physically or mentally tortured. An officer who orders their troops to massacre civilians is also considered to be committing a war crime; the My Lai massacre during the Vietnam War is an example. (2)

Fixing This Problem in Your Writing

As seen in the sample sentences, many agreement errors involve one particular pronoun (*they*) and its various forms (*their*, *them*).

"ARE" TIP: When using *they, their,* or *them,* make sure the antecedent is also *plural.* One way to do so is to see whether this antecedent would take the plural verb *are* after it. If this plural verb does *not* seem to fit, the antecedent is probably *singular* and thus not in agreement with *they, their,* or *them.*

In Sample 1, *their* must be referring to *teacher*, which is clearly singular. Sample 2 is trickier, though, because *everybody* has a plural "feel" about it. But would you say *Everybody are*?

SAMPLE 2: **✗ Did everybody cast their vote in the last election?**

TIP APPLIED: **✗ Everybody are?**

Everybody cannot take *are* as a verb and therefore cannot be plural. The tip shows that Sample 2 incorrectly uses the plural *their* to refer to the singular *everybody*.

Following are two ways to correct this type of pronoun error.

CORRECTION STRATEGY A: **Use an antecedent that you are certain is plural.**

SAMPLE 1, CORRECTED: **Teachers should explain their assignments carefully.**

CORRECTION STRATEGY B: **Revise so you don't need a personal pronoun.**

In Sample 2, you could easily use *a* instead of *their*.

SAMPLE 2, CORRECTED: **Did everybody cast a vote in the last election?**

For Example . . .

The following sample is correct. The pronoun *they* is plural, and so is its antecedent (*voters*).

SAMPLE: **All voters should make sure they are registered.**

TIP APPLIED: **Voters are**

PRON AGR

This next sentence is also correct. The writer offers us a choice by using *his or her*. Each is singular, as is *somebody*.

SAMPLE: **I saw that somebody left his or her book under the desk.**

This final sentence has an error because *person* is singular while *their* is plural. Following the sentence are two ways to correct the error by using Correction Strategy B.

SAMPLE: **✗ A person should have some fun in their lives every now and then.**

CORRECTION: **A person should have some fun every now and then.**

CORRECTION: **A person should have some fun in life every now and then.**

Now You Try It, 1 **(Corrected sentences appear on page 318.)**

In each sentence underline the pronoun once and the antecedent twice, connecting them with a line to show their relationship. Write *plural* or *singular* above the pronoun and antecedent. Correct any agreement problems. If a sentence has no agreement problem, write *OK* above it.

singular plural his or her

EXAMPLE: **Everybody in my composition class had ~~their~~ first essay returned.**

1. A doctor has to have insurance covering them against malpractice.

2. Some of the founders of communism, if they were alive today, might be surprised about what has happened to the Soviet Union.

3. A college student has to pick a field that interests them, but they also have to keep an eye on the job market. [*Hint:* A sentence can easily have more than one agreement error.]

4. I invited my roommates to go out to eat, but they had already eaten.

5. Anybody who hasn't turned in their test should do so now.

PRON AGR

Now You Try It, 2 **(Corrected sentences appear on page 318.)**

In each sentence underline the pronoun once and the antecedent twice, connecting them with a line to show their relationship. Write *plural* or *singular* above the pronoun and antecedent. Correct any agreement problems. If a sentence has no agreement problem, write *OK* above it.

singular All the teachers are plural

EXAMPLE: **~~Every teacher I have~~ this quarter ~~is~~ giving their final exam on the same day!**

1. Not only does a spider spin a web, but they can do so all their lives.

2. Almost everyone has to take this course to obtain their degree.

3. Most people who can recall the assassination of John F. Kennedy seem to remember exactly what they were doing when they heard the news.

4. Did somebody take my book instead of theirs?

5. Out of thirty people in my dorm, nobody wants to room with me.

Now You Try It, 3

Complete each sentence. In addition, refer to the underlined word by selecting one or more of the following pronouns: *he*, *him*, *his*, *she*, *her*, *they*, *them*, or *their*.

EXAMPLE: **Does <u>anybody</u> want** to sell his or her car?

1. <u>Everybody</u> in this room
2. Although <u>politicians</u> should be given due respect,
3. Did <u>everyone</u> have an opportunity to
4. <u>Each</u> of you should
5. I asked each <u>person</u> in my math class to

Editing Practice, 1 **(Corrected sentences appear on page 319.)**

Correct all errors in the following paragraphs using the first correction as a model. The number in parentheses at the end of each paragraph indicates how many errors you should find.

PRON AGR

No other European country has ever spread ~~their~~ ^its people and culture around the globe more than the United Kingdom. Each country, of course, has had their effects on the world. However, by the end of the nineteenth century, the United Kingdom had its culture firmly planted around the world, in such diverse places as Canada, the Caribbean, India, Australia, and South Africa. (1)

Not everyone in the United Kingdom approved of their country's attempt to colonize the world, but most Britons supported colonization because of the economic benefits of commerce with the colonies. A British citizen had much to gain from their country's colonization, but the people within the colonies suffered a loss of freedom and dignity by being controlled by a far-away government. (2)

Editing Practice, 2 **(Corrected sentences appear on page 319.)**

Correct all errors in the following paragraphs using the first correction as a model. The number in parentheses at the end of each paragraph indicates how many errors you should find.

Almost everybody who has taken an English class has written a book report about something ~~they have~~ ^he or she has^ read for the class. For one assignment, my English instructor, Ms. Kaplan, asked everyone to read two books that they wanted to read. In high school, almost every English teacher I had made a similar assignment, but they usually asked us to write a summary to prove we had read the book. (2)

Ms. Kaplan, though, said that she didn't want to "test" us about the books we read or make us feel that we had to scrutinize each page for their "hidden" meaning. She simply asked us to announce the books we read and then be ready to recommend or not recommend them to the rest of the class. Almost everybody seems to have read their first selection and truly enjoyed it. One classmate was so enthusiastic about *The Catcher in the Rye*, the novel they read for the assignment, that I decided to read it next. (3)

PRON AGR

Editing Practice, 3

Correct all errors in the following paragraphs using the first correction as a model. The number in parentheses at the end of each paragraph indicates how many errors you should find.

My literature class read Mary Shelley's *Frankenstein,* published in 1818. ~~Almost everyone has~~ ^Most people have^ seen a Frankenstein movie, but they probably haven't read the novel and noticed how much liberty a Hollywood director takes when they translate a classic novel to the big screen. (1)

A typical moviegoer might be surprised when they discover that in the original novel the monster learned to speak in complete sentences. Movie directors like to put metal bolts in the necks of their Frankenstein monsters, but Shelley's monster had none. Also, a person might be amused or frightened by a Frankenstein movie, but on reading the novel they would probably think more about the relationships among science, society, and nature. (2)

Writing Practice

Write a paragraph or two describing the positive and negative effects that a horror film might have on a moviegoer. Try to use *they*, *their*, or *them* at least five times. Use the Proofreading Checklist to correct any errors in pronoun-antecedent agreement in your sentences.

PROOFREADING CHECKLIST

Using Pronouns in Your Writing

- Locate each use of *they*, *their*, or *them* along with their antecedents (the person, place, or thing that these pronouns refer to).
- If the antecedent is *singular*, there is an agreement error. If you're not sure whether the antecedent is singular, see whether you can use *are* after it. If you can use *are*, the antecedent is plural, meaning there is *no* error.
- You can usually correct the error by rewording the antecedent so that it is plural.
- Another correction strategy is to reword the sentence so that you do not need a pronoun at all.

THE BOTTOM LINE

Pronouns should agree with *their* antecedents.

LESSON 22

I *or* Me? She *or* Her? He *or* Him?

Sample Errors

SAMPLE 1: **✗ Kathy Wong and <u>me</u> took the same math class.**

SAMPLE 2: **✗ Frank sang a song for <u>I</u> alone.**

What's the Problem?

Personal pronouns do something that most other **pronouns** and **nouns** do not do; their appearance can vary dramatically, depending on how they are used. Only *you* and *it* have the same **subject** and **object** forms. The other personal pronouns have different subject and object forms:

SUBJECT FORM:	**I**	**he**	**she**	**we**	**they**
OBJECT FORM:	**me**	**him**	**her**	**us**	**them**

The subject form should be used (1) when the pronoun is the subject of a verb or (2) when the pronoun comes after a linking verb (such as *is*, *am*, *was*, *were*, *are*). Sample 1 is an error because the subject form *I* should be used.

The object form is most often used (1) when the pronoun receives the action or (2) when the pronoun comes after a preposition. Sample 2 is a problem because the personal pronoun follows a preposition (*for*) and should be in the object form (*me*).

What Causes the Problem?

Often an error of pronoun form is created when people "listen" to the words to decide which form "sounds" appropriate. For instance, many people use *I* in formal situations because it sounds more formal (see Sample 2); yet *me* is often technically the correct choice. The problem of pronoun form is especially common in sentences that have compound objects (**✗** *Pedro invited <u>Diane and I</u> to dinner*).

In formal writing, however, writers can't always trust the sound of the sentence. Listening to how a sentence sounds can be helpful in determining whether it is clear and flows well, but don't rely on this approach to help you decide whether you have used the correct form of personal pronouns.

Diagnostic Exercise **(Corrected sentences appear on page 319.)**

Correct all errors in the following paragraph using the first correction as a model. The number in parentheses at the end of the paragraph indicates how many errors you should find.

My roommate and ~~me~~ I visited her friend Jeff, who lives in a cabin he built from scratch. That's a formidable project for I. My roommate asked Jeff whether he would mind if her and I stayed at his place for a few days in the summer. He said that was fine if we would help him build a new storeroom, and we quickly agreed to help him out. I'm not much of a carpenter, but Jeff said he'd be patient and help me learn. For an inexperienced builder such as I, building even a small storeroom is a major challenge, but I am looking forward to learning some carpentry skills. (3)

Fixing This Problem in Your Writing

Following are two tips for avoiding most errors involving the form of personal pronouns.

> NEXT-WORD TIP: Use the *subject form* if a **verb** comes right afterward (or very soon afterward). Use the *object form* in all other instances.

> PRECEDING-WORD TIP: Use the *object form* if a **preposition** or **verb** immediately precedes the pronoun, and use the *subject form* in all other instances.

Applying the Next-Word Tip to each of the following sentences, notice how the subject form (underlined once) is quickly followed by a verb (underlined twice).

Felipe and she wrote a poem together.

Because he almost fell, Bill started to climb more carefully.

But in the next three samples, the personal pronouns are not quickly followed by a verb. Therefore, the object forms are correct.

By helping me, Victoria proved to be a good friend.

The cook gave Jill and me a free sample.

While visiting his aunt, Bart made a cake just for her.

Caution: The Preceding-Word Tip does not apply when the personal pronoun comes after a form of the verb *be,* as in *I am he.* In this construction, the subject form is, indeed, supposed to be used. Such a sentence is more common in speech than in academic writing, but the exception is worth remembering.

For Example . . .

In Sample 1, *me* is followed by the verb *took.* Also, there is not a verb or preposition right before *me.* Thus, both tips show that an error exists, because the subject form should be used.

SAMPLE 1: ✗ **Kathy Wong and me took the same math class.**

verb ↓

TIP APPLIED: ✗ **Kathy Wong and me took the same math class.**

CORRECTION: **Kathy Wong and I took the same math class.**

Consider the term itself: *subject form.* A subject is a noun or pronoun that performs an action. Thus, use the subject form when the pronoun has a verb, as in *I took.*

Is Sample 2 really an error? The word *alone* is not a verb, meaning the subject form should *not* be used.

SAMPLE 2: ✗ **Frank sang a song for I alone.**

not a verb ↓

TIP APPLIED: **Frank sang a song for I alone.**

CORRECTION: **Frank sang a song for me alone.**

Now You Try It, 1 **(Corrected sentences appear on page 319.)**

For each sentence, first underline all personal pronouns. If the pronoun has a verb after it, underline this verb *twice*. When a verb comes after the pronoun, you should use the subject form (*I, he, she, we, they*). Write *OK* above all pronouns that are correctly used, and correct all pronoun errors.

EXAMPLE: **I thought my cat was missing, but Marsha said it was with ~~she~~ her.**

1. The pharaoh visited the burial tomb intended for just he.
2. Alex saw the rest of the class in the hall, and they motioned for him to join them. [*Hint:* The words *to join* are not a verb form in this sentence.]
3. This cake is for me, not you.
4. Huey and me went out for pizza late last night.
5. Mom promised to write to us as soon as she arrived in Florida, and today I received a card from she.

PRON CASE

Now You Try It, 2 **(Corrected sentences appear on page 319.)**

For each sentence, first underline all personal pronouns. If the pronoun has a verb after it, underline this verb *twice*. When a verb comes after the pronoun, you should use the subject form (*I, he, she, we, they*). Write *OK* above all pronouns that are correctly used, and correct all pronoun errors.

EXAMPLE: **That table was reserved for Velda and ~~I~~ me.**

1. Just between you and I, we are having a pop quiz on Friday.
2. On the way to class, Randall saw Carla, who said she would have to call him later because she didn't have time to stop and chat.
3. Are you ready to meet with them?
4. If not for I, you would not be having a birthday at all today.
5. Jane and me are going to the women's basketball game tonight.

Now You Try It, 3

Finish each sentence so that the underlined pronoun is appropriately used.

EXAMPLE: **I thought that Shirley and <u>he</u>** *were engaged.*

1. Yesterday, Sarah and <u>I</u>

2. My aunt wrote me and said that my mother and <u>she</u>

3. A letter supposedly written by <u>me</u>

4. Gloria walked into the room late; unexpectedly, the teacher and <u>she</u>

5. That chair is for <u>him</u>

Editing Practice, 1 **(Corrected sentences appear on page 320.)**

Correct all errors in the following paragraphs using the first correction as a model. The number in parentheses at the end of each paragraph indicates how many errors you should find.

Writing has never been the easiest task for someone like ~~I~~ *me* who has not written a great deal in the past; however, I am gaining more experience in my technical writing class. Three other students and I are supposed to work on a group paper. One member, Suzanne, and me are supposed to write a definition section of our paper, which is on ethical behavior in accounting. I have two friends who are accountants; I don't necessarily agree with they about morality or ethics but believe their input would be useful. My group agreed to supplement our library research by interviewing these two accountants. (2)

An objective analysis of the issue is supposed to be included in the section that Suzanne and me were assigned. The interviews were useful because the two accountants each presented different perspectives. They also admitted that the issue of ethics was confusing for they as well as I. (3)

PRON CASE

Editing Practice, 2 **(Corrected sentences appear on page 320.)**

Correct all errors in the following paragraphs using the first correction as a model. The number in parentheses at the end of each paragraph indicates how many errors you should find.

My roommate, Rusty, asked me to join a money-making enterprise concocted by ~~he~~ *him* and his father. The plan they devised sounds simple: Rusty's dad would purchase fifty compact refrigerators that we would lease out to college students living in the dorms. Rusty's dad would supply the capital, while Rusty and me would do the labor. When Rusty told me the plan, I was skeptical. I talked it over with he and agreed to help when I figured I had little to lose. (2)

Rusty's dad lives in town and owns a place where we could store any refrigerators Rusty and me could not lease. We placed ads and notices around town and in the school paper. The week before class began, thirty students came by to do business. It wasn't stressful, but we had to stay around all day waiting on people. Rusty and me won't get rich from this business, but it helps pay the bills. (2)

Editing Practice, 3

Correct all errors in the following paragraphs using the first correction as a model. The number in parentheses at the end of each paragraph indicates how many errors you should find.

My parents were a great influence on me, but I was influenced by family members besides ~~they~~ *them*. My sister, Monica, and Uncle Ed taught me a great deal. Monica and me were close in age, and we were inseparable. Her greatest influence is that she taught me not to dwell on the bad things that happen. On a bike ride once, a car ran into her and broke her leg. She eventually laughed it off and said she'd learn to wear brighter clothes when riding. (1)

Uncle Ed was like a second dad. My dad and him were very close, and I would join them on long walks in the summer. When I was small, they would take turns carrying Monica and I when we were tired. Next to my dad, Uncle Ed was the gentlest man I've known. He taught me through example to control my temper and care for the feelings of people other than I. (3)

Writing Practice

On your own paper, write a paragraph or two describing how two or three family members or friends have influenced you. Try to use any combination of the pronouns covered in this lesson (*I, me, she, her, he, him*). Use the Proofreading Checklist to correct any pronoun errors in your sentences.

PROOFREADING CHECKLIST

Using Correct Forms of Pronouns in Your Writing

- When using a personal pronoun, see if it has a verb (usually, any verb will quickly follow the pronoun). If there is a verb, you should usually use the *subject form* of the pronoun: *I, he, she, we,* and *they*.
- Another way to decide which form to use is to look at the word right before the pronoun. If this word is a preposition or a verb, use the *object form* of the pronoun: *me, him, her, us,* and *them*.
- Remember the exception: In formal writing, the subject form is used if the pronoun comes right after a *to be* verb (such as *is, was, were,* and *are*).

THE BOTTOM LINE

The subject forms of personal pronouns have a distinct characteristic: *They are followed* more often than not by verbs.

LESSON

Who, Whom, *and* That

Sample Errors

SAMPLE 1: ✗ **The woman <u>that</u> read my paper liked it.**

SAMPLE 2: ✗ **I met a person <u>who</u> you would like.**

What's the Problem?

Who, whom, and *that* are **relative pronouns**—special **pronouns** that always refer to a preceding **noun**. Writers are often confused about which of these three pronouns to use in a sentence, and the rules are not altogether clear or consistent about such issues as whether or not *that* can refer to people. The safest choice is to use *that* to refer to ideas or things, not to people. For instance, many readers would consider *that* in Sample 1 to be inappropriate because *that* refers to a person (*a woman*).

Many writers use only *who* or *whom* to refer to people. But how do you know which of these two to use? Here is the formal rule for making this decision:

PRON CASE

> **When the relative pronoun is the <u>subject</u> of the <u>verb</u> that immediately follows it, use *who*; otherwise, use *whom*.**

Sample 2, for instance, should use the object form *whom* because this pronoun is not the subject of the verb *would like*.

What Causes the Problem?

In the quick give-and-take of conversation, speakers often avoid the complicated choice between *who* and *whom* by using *that* to refer to people; or speakers use *who*, when they should use *whom*. Listeners usually don't comment on any "error" that speakers might make in choosing the most appropriate pronoun form among *that*, *who*, or *whom*.

Thus, many writers simply haven't become sensitive to the distinctions among these relative pronouns. Nonetheless, many readers (unlike listeners) are more than willing to point out errors of this kind, so we suggest that you use these pronouns carefully.

Diagnostic Exercise **(Corrected sentences appear on page 320.)**

In the following passage, every *that* is underlined. Using the first correction as a model, change each inappropriately used *that* to *who* or *whom*. The number in parentheses at the end of the paragraph indicates how many errors you should find.

An experience that we all have had is working for a bad boss. One boss ~~that~~ *whom* we have all had is the petty tyrant, a person that loves to find fault with every employee that works in the building. It seems that the petty tyrant is more interested in finding employees that he or she can belittle than in getting the job done. Even worse than the petty tyrant is a supervisor that is inconsistent. An inconsistent boss is a person that the employees can never depend on. A game that this kind of boss loves is playing favorites. One day, this boss is your best buddy; the next day, the boss acts as if he or she doesn't know the name of a person that has worked with the company for ten years. (6)

Fixing This Problem in Your Writing

To use the appropriate relative pronoun in formal writing, look at the noun that the pronoun refers to. (The noun will always be the word right in front of *that.*) If the noun refers to a thing or idea, use *that.* However, if the noun refers to a person, use either *who* or *whom.*

Use *who* if the relative pronoun is the subject of the following verb. But if the pronoun is *not* the subject of the following verb, use *whom.*

All this information can be a bit confusing, but it can be boiled down to the following tips.

> **"THAT" TIP:** Look at the word that the pronoun renames. Use *that* only if this word refers to something nonhuman.

> **"WHO/WHOM" TIP:** Look at the word immediately after *who* or *whom.* If this word is a *verb,* use *who.* But if this word is a *noun* or *pronoun,* use *whom.*

The *That* Tip indicates that Sample 1 should be changed because *that* is inappropriately used to refer to a person. Next, the *Who/Whom* Tip indicates that the more appropriate pronoun is *who*, because a verb comes immediately after it.

SAMPLE 1: ✗ **The woman that read my paper liked it.**

human

"THAT" TIP APPLIED: ✗ **The woman that read my paper liked it.**

verb

WHO/WHOM TIP APPLIED: **The woman who read my paper liked it.**

CORRECTION: **The woman who read my paper liked it.**

For Example . . .

In the following sample sentence, the verb *would like* immediately follows *who*. Thus, *who* is the subject of the verb, and the sentence does not need to be reworded.

I met a fellow student who would like to know you.

PRON CASE

In Sample 2, however, the pronoun *you* immediately follows *who*, so we should change *who* to *whom*:

SAMPLE 2: ✗ **I met a person who you would like.**

pronoun

WHO/WHOM TIP APPLIED: ✗ **I met a person who you would like.**

CORRECTION: **I met a person whom you would like.**

In this next example, the verb *was* immediately follows *who*. Therefore, *who* is the subject, and the sentence is OK as it is.

The clerk who was at the desk called the office.

But in this final example, the noun *Alicia* immediately follows *who*. Thus, *Alicia* is the subject of the verb *called*, and we should change *who* to *whom*:

✗ **The clerk who Alicia called found a room for us.**

CORRECTION: **The clerk whom Alicia called found a room for us.**

Now You Try It, 1 **(Corrected sentences appear on page 320.)**

Underline the word which *that* refers to. If *that* is used to refer to a thing or idea, write *OK* above it. However, if *that* refers to a person, cross out *that* and write *who* or *whom* above it.

EXAMPLE: **A teacher ~~that~~ whom I had in high school is my instructor in English.**

1. The young woman that answered the phone took my order.

2. Senator Blather ignored the reporters that had been waiting patiently outside his office.

3. I called the couple that had answered the ad.

4. The information that Robert had received proved to be incorrect.

5. The director repositioned the actors that the camera was blocking.

Now You Try It, 2 **(Corrected sentences appear on page 320.)**

Underline the word which *that* refers to. If *that* is used to refer to a thing or idea, write *OK* above it. However, if *that* refers to a person, cross out *that* and write *who* or *whom* above it.

EXAMPLE: **The person ~~that~~ who wrote these instructions left out a vital step.**

1. Here is the cake that you wanted me to bring.

2. I need to know the name and address of the mechanic that supposedly fixed your car.

3. A guy that I knew back in elementary school happens to sit next to me in my chemistry class.

4. Who was the president that succeeded Richard Nixon?

5. On Thursday of last week, the newspaper that first reported a presidential scandal published a correction.

Now You Try It, 3

Complete each group of words so that *who* or *whom* is used appropriately.

EXAMPLE: **Much to my surprise, someone whom** I had never even met before called me up for a date.

1. Please see whether you can get in touch with the person who

2. Don't even think about asking me who

3. Are you talking to the guy whom

4. I was tripped by someone whom

5. If you really need to talk to someone, find a person who

Editing Practice, 1 **(Corrected sentences appear on page 321.)**

Correct all errors in the following paragraphs using the first correction as a model. The number in parentheses at the end of each paragraph indicates how many errors you should find.

PRON CASE

I have several teachers ~~whom~~ ^who use some form of group work. My freshman composition class involves group activities, but Ms. Roberts, whom teaches the course, uses groups in ways that are new to me. (1)

Ms. Roberts believes that we need to become accustomed to working in groups even though they are not effective when they comprise people that prefer to learn independently. Of course, any group is likely to have at least one person that would prefer to work alone, but usually the group can adjust when it's just one or two individuals that learn little from group activities. Early in the course, Ms. Roberts asked us to write a brief essay describing how we have functioned in groups; she then used these essays to help assign us to groups. My group is composed of people with who I can work well. (4)

Editing Practice, 2 **(Corrected sentences appear on page 321.)**

Correct all errors in the following paragraphs using the first correction as a model. The number in parentheses at the end of each paragraph indicates how many errors you should find.

Most Americans ~~that~~ ^who^ have a religious affiliation are Christians, but other religions are thriving within the United States. Jews are a relatively small minority in this country, but their religion is one who was already established by the time of the American Revolution. Muslims, whom are a growing presence in the United States, actually outnumber Christians worldwide. (2)

Some religious denominations are much smaller in terms of the number of people that subscribe to their beliefs, yet these religions have found a niche in American society. For instance, one small religious group, referred to as Ethical Culture, is composed of some 7,000 members and was founded in 1876 by Felix Adler, a humanist philosopher that stressed the importance of ethics and morality. (2)

Editing Practice, 3

Correct all errors in the following paragraphs using the first correction as a model. The number in parentheses at the end of each paragraph indicates how many errors you should find.

Dorothy L. Sayers was an English writer ~~that~~ ^who^ wrote some of the best detective novels ever. She is best known for a series of novels that features Lord Peter Wimsey. In the British tradition, Lord Peter is not a police officer or private detective but an amateur sleuth that manages to become involved in an amazing number of murders that involve friends or relatives. (1)

Lord Peter deliberately adopts the manners of an over-refined aristocrat that doesn't seem to have any brains. Other characters dismiss him as a person

who they do not need to take seriously, a fact that often leads to the criminal's exposure. The author also uses Lord Peter's foolishness to satirize the artificiality of the members of the aristocracy that Lord Peter comes into contact with. (3)

Writing Practice

On your own paper, write a paragraph or two about your favorite detective or law officer from a book, movie, or TV series. Include as many uses of *who*, *whom*, and *that* as you can. Use the Proofreading Checklist to show that each use of *that* refers to ideas or things and that *who* and *whom* are used appropriately to refer to people.

PROOFREADING CHECKLIST

Distinguishing among That, Who, and Whom in Your Writing

- When you use the relative pronoun *that* to refer to an immediately preceding noun, check whether this noun refers to a person. If it does, the safest approach is to change *that* to *who* or *whom* according to the next guidelines:
- If the word *immediately* following the relative pronoun *that* is a verb, use *who*.
- If the word *immediately* following the relative pronoun *that* is a noun or a pronoun, then use *whom*.

PRON CASE

THE BOTTOM LINE

A writer *who* wishes to follow conventions for formal writing should use *who* or *whom*—not *that*—to refer to people.

LESSON

Sexist Use of Pronouns

Sample Errors

SAMPLE 1: ✗ **Each person should try to do <u>his</u> best.**

SAMPLE 2: ✗ **A kindergarten teacher helps <u>her</u> students gain social as well as academic skills.**

What's the Problem?

Sexist language, even when unintentional, is a form of bigotry, and there are two major problems with using such language. First, because it excludes one gender or another, it is demeaning and perpetuates discrimination and stereotyping. Second, a writer who uses even a few instances of sexist language is likely to offend readers, who, in turn, will be less likely to respect the writer's overall point or less likely to react in the way the writer wishes. Sexist language, then, is not a grammar issue as much as a style or usage issue.

SEXIST PRON

Sexist language takes many forms, but we focus on one of the most common types: *gender-exclusive pronouns*. These are certain **personal pronouns** used in ways that inappropriately exclude one gender. That is, they are used in ways that suggest *only* males or *only* females are being discussed. The personal pronouns that can be misused in this way are *he, his, him, she,* and *her*.

Sample 1, for example, suggests that only males should do their best, while Sample 2 implies that only females can be kindergarten teachers. Of course, a writer can use pronouns such as *he* or *her* when they logically refer only to males (a father) or only to females (a bride).

What Causes the Problem?

At one time, it seemed perfectly acceptable to use the generic *he* to refer to *all* people. The *generic he* is simply the use of the masculine pronoun to refer to words (such as *anyone* or *a parent*) that can be female as well as male. It also once seemed appropriate to associate one gender with particular professions (such as nurses = women and doctors = men).

Today, however, people are aware of the subtle discrimination of using the generic *he,* and more people are entering professions that once seemed exclusively the domain of just one gender. In short, writers' language should reflect the changed attitudes of society toward the roles of males and females.

Diagnostic Exercise **(Corrected sentences appear on page 321.)**

Correct all instances of sexist language in the following paragraph using the first correction as a model. The number in parentheses at the end of the paragraph indicates how many problems you should find.

My psychology teacher, Ms. Crystal, had each member of the class complete a questionnaire that would help him ^*or her* consider an appropriate career. I had already decided on a career, but she said the questionnaire would offer options. I've always wanted to be an electrical engineer because I like to design things; an engineer spends much of his time drawing designs and writing specifications. Ms. Crystal said my survey results indicated I should consider being an accountant. She also told me, however, that the survey was just one resource for choosing a career. I agree. Each person has to consider what he knows better than anyone else: his own interests. (3)

SEXIST PRON

Fixing This Problem in Your Writing

Keep in mind that writers often do not intentionally use sexist language. Following is a way to check your writing for this problem.

> GENERAL-REFERENCE TIP: *First,* look for abstract references to people (**nouns** and **pronouns** that refer not to actual individuals but to people in general). *Second,* see whether you later refer to this abstraction by using a personal pronoun that includes only one gender. If so, the language is probably sexist.

In Sample 1, the abstract reference is underlined and the gender-exclusive pronoun is underlined twice.

SAMPLE 1: ✗ **Each person should try to do his best.**

Following are two of many ways to avoid sexist language.

CORRECTION STRATEGY A: **Use plural forms and "genderless" pronouns. Reword the sentence so that any abstract reference to people is in the *plural* form. Do the same with any pronoun that refers to this antecedent.**

Sample 1 has been changed to allow the use of the genderless *their*.

CORRECTION: **People should try to do their best.**

If you use *they*, *them*, or *their*, make sure that the word it refers to is also plural (see Lesson 21).

CORRECTION STRATEGY B: **Avoid using any personal pronoun in this situation. Reword the sentence so you do not need a personal pronoun at all—no *he, his, him, she,* or *her*.**

CORRECTION: **A person should put forth 100 percent effort.**

SEXIST PRON

For Example . . .

Using the General-Reference Tip, you can see that Sample 2 has an abstract reference to a type of person (underlined) followed by a gender-exclusive personal pronoun (underlined twice).

SAMPLE 2: **✘ A kindergarten teacher helps her students gain social as well as academic skills.**

The error can be corrected simply by using the plural form of *teacher*, allowing you to use the genderless *their*. Notice how making these changes also requires changing the verb *helps* to *help*.

CORRECTION STRATEGY A: **Kindergarten teachers help their students gain social as well as academic skills.**

The problem can also be fixed by using Strategy B. All you need to do is delete the personal pronoun *her*.

CORRECTION STRATEGY B: **A kindergarten teacher helps students gain social as well as academic skills.**

Now You Try It, 1 **(Corrected sentences appear on page 321.)**

If a sentence contains sexist language, show where it is by underlining the abstract reference to people and double-underlining the gender-exclusive pronoun. Correct any instance of sexist language. If a sentence avoids sexist language, write *OK* above it.

EXAMPLE: **Somebody left ~~his~~ ^a set of car keys on the television.**

1. A senator has to be responsible to his constituents.

2. Boxer Vic Towell once knocked down his opponent fourteen times within ten rounds of their championship fight.

3. We must hire a secretary, and she has to have computer skills.

4. I prefer a teacher who knows his subject material but who allows students to figure out some things for themselves.

5. Everybody should cast his vote in the next election! [*Hint: Everybody* is singular, so avoid correcting the error by just changing *his* to *their*.]

SEXIST PRON

Now You Try It, 2 **(Corrected sentences appear on page 321.)**

If a sentence contains sexist language, show where it is by underlining the abstract reference to people and double-underlining the gender-exclusive pronoun. Correct any instance of sexist language. If a sentence avoids sexist language, write *OK* above it.

EXAMPLE: **~~A parent~~ ^Parents should let ~~her~~ ^their children have some independence.**

1. The mechanic says he can repair my car by Monday.

2. If you ever put your children into day care, meet with the person who will actually watch your children and see whether she is patient and congenial.

3. Has everyone done his homework?

4. A chef rarely talks to his customers, but yesterday the chef at my favorite restaurant greeted us.

5. I've never met anyone who brushes his teeth as often as you!

Now You Try It, 3

In a nonsexist sentence of your own, use each abstract reference plus any of these pronouns: *he, his, she, her, they,* or *their.* The pronoun should refer to the abstract reference.

EXAMPLE: **Nobody** in my algebra class did his or her homework.

1. A pilot
2. Everyone
3. A student
4. Someone
5. Any politician

Editing Practice, 1 **(Corrected sentences appear on page 322.)**

Correct all instances of sexist language in the following paragraphs using the first correction as a model. The number in parentheses at the end of each paragraph indicates how many problems you should find.

~~A college student has~~ College students have many options about what ~~he~~ they might study. I am torn between geology and teaching. On the one hand, I have long been interested in being a geologist in the private sector, perhaps for an oil company. A geologist spends much of his time outdoors collecting samples, and I like working outdoors. A geologist also works in his office or lab, but I like this sort of work as well. (2)

On the other hand, my mother is a teacher and has encouraged me to follow in her footsteps. Almost every teacher has a good deal of stress put on her by students, parents, and administrators; however, a teacher also has many rewards, such as knowing that she has helped somebody succeed in his life and intellectual development. I am seriously considering teaching earth science so that I can combine my interest in teaching with geology. (3)

SEXIST PRON

Editing Practice, 2 **(Corrected sentences appear on page 322.)**

Correct all instances of sexist language in the following paragraphs using the first correction as a model. The number in parentheses at the end of each paragraph indicates how many problems you should find.

At one time or another, almost everybody has wondered what it would be like if he ^*or she* were born at another time or place. I don't think a person is necessarily unhappy or out of place simply because he's had such thoughts. Perhaps it's a way to explore possibilities in his own present circumstances. (2)

When I was much younger, I wondered what it would be like to be an early colonist in the Americas. The life of a colonist was not easy; he had to cope with starvation, the wilderness, and financial ruin. When I was a teenager, I dreamed (like many other kids) of being an astronaut—again, a person who often puts his life in danger to explore a new world. Even today I think about such adventures, and perhaps it's all a clue that I would not be happy confined in an office. I'm not saying that being a businessperson is dull, but everyone needs to find the sorts of challenges and environments that reflect his own dreams and goals. I imagine that sounds like a cliché, but I often think many people consider jobs only in terms of how they'll affect their bank accounts. (3)

Editing Practice, 3

Correct all instances of sexist language in the following paragraphs using the first correction as a model. The number in parentheses at the end of each paragraph indicates how many problems you should find.

A stamp collector has to be patient; there are hundreds of thousands of stamps, and it may take ~~him~~ ^*a collector* a long time to collect even a fraction of these or find a truly rare stamp. It seems that everybody keeps his eyes out for old or colorful stamps, making stamp collecting somewhat competitive. (1)

Anybody can hang onto a stamp he likes or thinks to be valuable. A true collector not only collects stamps but also systematically stores them (perhaps in labeled envelopes or stamp books) and tries to learn the history of stamps (such as when they appeared and for what occasion). Consequently, a person needs to be systematic in the way he approaches finding, storing, and researching stamps. Somebody who just throws stamps into his desk drawer isn't—to my way of thinking—a serious collector. (3)

Writing Practice

On your own paper, write a paragraph or two explaining a particular job or hobby and the skills it requires. Try to use at least four abstract references to people followed by *he, his, him, she, her, they, them,* or *their.* Use the Proofreading Checklist to correct any sexist language in the sentences you write.

SEXIST PRON

PROOFREADING CHECKLIST

Using Nonsexist Pronouns in Your Writing

- First, look for words that refer to people in an abstract or general way, rather than to specific or real people.
- Next, see whether you later refer to this abstraction by using a gender-exclusive pronoun (*he, his, him, she,* or *her*). If so, there is likely to be sexist language.
- To correct the problem, see whether you can change each gender-exclusive pronoun to the plural forms *they*, *them*, or *their.*
- Another way to correct the problem is to reword the sentence so that it avoids personal pronouns altogether.

THE BOTTOM LINE

A writer can use language more effectively if *he or she* avoids using the generic *he*.

UNIT FIVE
PUTTING IT ALL TOGETHER

Here is an overview of the tips for dealing with pronouns.

Vague Pronouns

ANTECEDENT TIP: Locate what you think the pronoun refers to. Make sure this antecedent is a noun, not any other part of speech or an entire sentence. Make sure there is no other person, place, or thing that the pronoun could possibly refer to (see Lesson 20).

EXAMPLE: **I got a bonus for helping during the Christmas rush.**

a bonus

✗ It was ^ bigger ^ than I expected.

Pronoun Agreement

PRON

"ARE" TIP: When using *they, their,* or *them,* be sure the antecedent is plural. One way to do so is to see whether this antecedent would take the plural verb *are* right after it. If not, the antecedent is probably singular (see Lesson 21).

singular plural

EXAMPLE: **✗ Somebody left their gloves on the floor.**

I or *Me, She* or *Her, He* or *Him*

NEXT-WORD TIP: Use the *subject form* (*I, she, he*) if a verb comes right after (or very soon after) the pronoun. Use the *object form* in all other instances (see Lesson 22).

PRECEDING-WORD TIP: Use the *object form* (*me, her, him*) if a preposition or verb immediately precedes the pronoun, and use the *subject form* in all other instances.

I

EXAMPLE: **Stephanie and ~~me~~ ^ met for lunch.**

Who, Whom, and *That*

"THAT" TIP: Look at the word that the pronoun renames. Use *that* only if this word refers to something nonhuman (see Lesson 23).

"WHO/WHOM" TIP: Use *who* or *whom* to refer to people. *Who* should have a verb right after it. *Whom* should have a noun or pronoun right after it.

EXAMPLE: **There is a teacher <u>who</u> taught in the high school <u>that</u> I went to. She's the one <u>whom</u> I had for math.**

Sexist Use of Pronouns

GENERAL-REFERENCE TIP: Look for abstract references to people. If you refer back to this abstraction by using a pronoun that applies only to females or only to males, the language is probably sexist (see Lesson 24).

EXAMPLE: **~~A police officer~~** *Police officers* **should never consider ~~himself~~** *themselves* **above the law.**

Review

Correct all errors in the following paragraph using the first correction as a model. The number in parentheses at the end of the paragraph indicates how many errors you should find.

Yesterday, I received a call from my neighbor Ellen, ~~whom~~ *who* wanted me to meet her friend Janie. She just arrived in town and is staying with Ellen for a short time. Ellen and me have been friends a long time, so I was glad to meet a friend of hers. Janie, who is an electrician, is looking for a job, and I know a number of contractors that work in the area. An electrician can get a job if he is really experienced and willing to work his way up the pay scale. Typically, an electrician is experienced because their skills are so technical that they do a lot of hands-on learning. (6)

UNIT SIX
Verb Tense

OVERVIEW

Terms That Can Help You Understand Verb Tense

If you are not familiar with any of the following terms that appear in this unit, look them up in the Guide to Grammar Terminology beginning on page 1. The numbers in parentheses indicate the lessons in which each term appears.

adjective (28)
participle (26, 27, 28)
past participle (27, 28)
past tense (25, 27)
perfect tense (27)
present participle (26, 28)
present tense (25, 26)
progressive tenses (26)
tense (25, 26, 27)

The Nuts and Bolts of Verb Tense

This unit deals with the most common problems writers are likely to encounter when they are deciding which verb tense to use.

VT

Lesson 25: Present, Past, and Tense Shifting
The term *tense shifting* refers to jumping from one tense to another, usually between the present and past tenses. Tense shifting is often inappropriate, but sometimes it is required. Knowing whether to shift requires an understanding of the fundamentally different roles of the present and past tense. The **present tense** is used to make statements of fact or generalizations. The **past tense** is used to describe events that are completed in the past.

Lesson 26: The Progressive Tenses
The **progressive tenses** are used for describing an action in "progress" now (the *present progressive*) or at some past moment in time (the *past progressive*). Certain verbs that refer to unchanging, steady-state conditions are incompatible with the progressive tenses.

Lesson 27: The Past and the Perfect Tenses
The **perfect tenses** are formed with the helping verb *have* in some form. If you use a present tense form of *have*, you create the *present*

perfect (*Pat has lived in London for two years now*). If you use a present tense form of *have*, you create the *present perfect.* The present perfect describes an action that began in the past and has continued in an unbroken manner up to the present moment. For example, the sentence *Pat has lived in London for two years now* indicates that Pat moved to London two years ago and still lives there. The present perfect can also indicate an action begun and completed at an unspecified time in the past, for example, *Pat has lived in London, Paris, and several other cities.*

If you use a past tense form of *have*, you create the *past perfect.* The past perfect is used to connect two past events when the earlier event is completed before the more recent event. The sentence *Pat had lived in London before she got married* tells you that Pat was already living in London at the time of her wedding. You can't tell from this sentence whether she lived in London after the wedding or where she lives now.

▶ Lesson 28: Using Participles as Adjectives

Participles are derived from verbs. Participles are used to modify nouns. The *present participle* ends in *-ing*; the *past participle* usually ends in *-ed.* The two types of participles mean very different things. For example, there is a world of difference between *a boring teacher* and *a bored teacher.* This lesson deals with techniques that help writers decide which participle to use for the meaning they intend.

Can You Detect Problems Involving Verb Tense?

(Corrected sentences appear on page 322.)

VT

Correct all errors in the following paragraph using the first correction as a model. The number in parentheses at the end of the paragraph indicates how many errors you should find.

My wife and I really disagree about old movies. ~~I am loving~~ ^love to watch them, unlike my wife. She would just as soon watch paint dry as sit through an old black-and-white film. The other night, as we watched Hitchcock's 1938 classic mystery *The Lady Vanishes*, she fell asleep. After the movie finished, I woke her up and started telling her about what an amused movie it was. She was not impressed. To her, the poor quality of the print, with its flickering light and uneven focus, makes watching that movie a chore rather than a pleasure. (4)

LESSON 25

Present, Past, and Tense Shifting

Sample Errors

SAMPLE 1: ✗ **Whenever we went to a restaurant, my father always makes a fuss about ordering exactly the right wine.**

SAMPLE 2: ✗ **She went to Tulane University, which was in New Orleans.**

What's the Problem?

Readers usually expect a piece of writing to maintain a consistent use of **tense** from beginning to end. For example, in Sample 1, the writer starts in the **past tense** (*we went*) and then, for no apparent reason, shifts to the **present tense** (*my father always makes a fuss*).

However, sometimes the opposite is true: the sentence is wrong if we don't shift. For example, in Sample 2, the writer needs to shift the past tense *was* to the present tense *is* because, as the sentence is written, it implies something that the writer does not mean: that Tulane University is no longer in New Orleans.

VT

What Causes the Problem?

Once writers commit themselves to a tense (either present or past), they must stick with it *unless* there is a reason to shift tenses. In Sample 1, however, there is no reason for the shift from past tense to present tense. Readers find such inappropriate *tense shifting* distracting at best and often misleading. Sometimes, though, as we saw in Sample 2, there are reasons to shift from one tense to another. The trick, of course, is knowing what the reasons for shifting are.

The differences between the past tense and the present tense go beyond just their difference in time. The two tenses have different functions, and we shift between them as we have need of those functions. The past tense is used to describe an event that happened in the past *(The phone rang during dinner last night),* while the present tense is used to make a statement or generalization that is not tied to a past event *(The phone always rings during dinner).*

Diagnostic Exercise **(Corrected sentences appear on page 322.)**

Correct all errors in the following paragraph using the first correction as a model. The number in parentheses at the end of the paragraph indicates how many errors you should find.

Last summer we took a trip to Provence, a region in the southeast corner of France, which ~~bordered~~ borders on Italy. The name *Provence* referred to the fact that it was the first province created by the ancient Romans outside the Italian peninsula. Today, Provence still contained an amazing number of well-preserved Roman ruins. While there were a few big towns on the coast, Provence was famous for its wild country and beautiful scenery. Provence was especially known for its abundance of wildflowers in the spring. These flowers were used to make some of the world's most expensive perfumes. (6)

Fixing This Problem in Your Writing

Your writing needs to show whether you are telling about events that happened and were completed in the past (in which case you would use the *past tense*) or whether you are making a statement of fact or a generalization whose validity is not limited to the past (in which case you would use the *present tense*).

People use the past tense to tell stories. For example, most novels are written in the past tense. The present tense is used for "timeless" statements and generalizations. For example, most nonfiction writing that deals with description or analysis is written in the present tense. (Notice that this paragraph uses the present tense to make a "timeless" generalization.) Writing contains a great deal of tense shifting because the past and present tenses have complementary functions. For example, generalizations (in the present tense) often need the support of concrete examples, which are often descriptions of events (past tense). Stories (past tense) often include generalizations about what happened that are true not only for the time of the story but also will continue to be true indefinitely (present tense). Following are some suggestions that will help you in deciding which tense to use.

VT

PAST TENSE TIP: Use the past tense when describing or discussing events that were completed in the past.

EXAMPLE: **The Great Depression in the 1930's <u>was</u> worsened by incorrect government policies.**

PRESENT TENSE TIP: Use the present tense to make statements of fact or generalizations that are true now and will continue to be true indefinitely unless something happens to change the situation.

EXAMPLE: **My wife's favorite movie <u>is</u> *Casablanca.***

This sentence is written in the present tense because it states a fact that will continue to be true indefinitely. The statement does not mean that, at some future time, the writer's wife could not change her mind. It means that the current state is likely to continue until and unless something happens to change that state.

HABITUAL-ACTIONS TIP: Use the present tense to describe habitual or repeated actions.

EXAMPLE: **Sam <u>is</u> always late for meetings.**

This sentence is a generalization about Sam's habitual behavior. It would still be a valid statement even if Sam showed up early for his next meeting.

VT

For Example . . .

Here is an example of how to shift from tense to tense according to the meaning you need to express:

Shakespeare <u>wrote</u> *Hamlet* around 1600. The action of the play <u>is</u> set in Elsinore Castle in Denmark. Critics <u>have</u> always considered this one of Shakespeare's most complex plays.

The first sentence is in the past tense because it describes an event (Shakespeare's writing of *Hamlet*) that was completed in the past (Past Tense Tip). The second sentence is in the present tense because it is a "timeless" statement of fact about the setting of the play (Present Tense Tip). The third sentence is in the present tense because it describes the habitual behavior of critics (Habitual-Actions Tip).

Now You Try It, 1 **(Corrected sentences appear on page 323.)**

Correct the present and past tense errors in the following sentences by drawing a line through each error and writing the correct tense above it. If the sentence is correct, write *OK* above it.

EXAMPLE: **We all knew that Sacramento ~~was~~ *is* the capital of California.**

1. Juan always got a headache whenever he works at the computer without taking a break.

2. In general, the main cause of depressions and unemployment was the reluctance of governments to go into debt to stimulate the economy.

3. Last year, we visited George Washington's plantation. It was located just down the river from Washington.

4. Last year, I was nearly hit by a taxi in London because I forget to look to the right when I step off the curb.

5. Last weekend, we went for a hike on the trail that went through the woods.

Now You Try It, 2 **(Corrected sentences appear on page 323.)**

Correct the present and past tense errors in the following sentences by drawing a line through each error and writing the correct tense above it. If the sentence is correct, write *OK* above it.

EXAMPLE: **When we went on vacation last year, it never ~~gets~~ *got* above 50°F.**

1. The drainage in the area was awful back then; I always get my feet wet when I go there.

2. It always seemed to rain when we go on vacation.

3. Painters today are still influenced by the art styles that come from prewar Germany.

4. I always use the phone that we installed in the den.

5. One of the things we remember about Teddy Roosevelt is how he always seems to be grinning with those big white teeth.

Now You Try It, 3

Correct the present and past tense errors in the following sentences by drawing a line through each error and writing the correct tense above it. If the sentence is correct, write *OK* above it.

EXAMPLE: **After the game, we ~~stop~~ *stopped* by to see Harry and Sally.**

1. I remember the time when the Dodgers play in Brooklyn.
2. Whenever Stanford beat California, the San Francisco newspapers always made a big deal out of it.
3. It is not easy keeping the money that we work so hard to get.
4. The police routinely stop every car that had a missing brake light.
5. Walt Disney drew Mickey Mouse showing only three fingers. This simplification saved thousands of dollars every year in production costs.

Editing Practice, 1 **(Corrected sentences appear on page 323.)**

Correct all errors in the following paragraphs using the first correction as a model. The number in parentheses at the end of each paragraph indicates how many errors you should find.

A few years ago, we spent a week in Italy on the Amalfi Coast, which ~~was~~ *is* south of Naples. This mountainous stretch of coast ran east to west from Sorrento to Salerno. The name comes from the name of the town of Amalfi, which was in the middle of the coastline. Amalfi, which dated from the fourth century A.D., was a major city during the Middle Ages. However, much of the ancient city no longer existed. It was destroyed by the sea in 1343. (4)

We stayed in Ravello, a little town on the top of a ridge line that overlooked Amalfi. Ravello was best known for an international music festival that was held every summer near the Palazzo Rufolo. The beautiful palace garden is the inspiration for the magic garden in Wagner's opera *Parsifal*. (4)

VT

Editing Practice, 2 **(Corrected sentences appear on page 323.)**

Correct all errors in the following paragraphs using the first correction as a model. The number in parentheses at the end of each paragraph indicates how many errors you should find.

Although William Shakespeare died in 1616, performances of his plays ~~were~~ *are* alive and well today. A number of theaters and summer festivals were devoted to performing his plays. In England, the Royal Shakespeare Company performed in London and Stratford-upon-Avon (the small town where Shakespeare was born). In Canada, there was a highly successful Shakespeare festival every summer in Stratford, Ontario. In the United States, there were theatrical organizations devoted to performing Shakespeare's plays in Washington, D.C., New York, San Diego, and the small college town of Ashland, Oregon. (4)

Ashland's Shakespeare Festival begins almost by accident as an outgrowth of the old Chautauqua circuit that provides entertainment to rural America before the days of radio and movies. After the collapse of Chautauqua, Ashland finds itself with a good-sized summer theater facility, and faculty from the college decide to stage a few Shakespearean plays. (4)

Editing Practice, 3

Correct all errors in the following paragraphs using the first correction as a model. The number in parentheses at the end of each paragraph indicates how many errors you should find.

A few years ago, I was a juror in a murder trial. The defendant was a member of the local mob who ~~is~~ *was* accused of conspiring to kill the head of another gang. The prosecution's entire case rested on the testimony of a police informant who had been a friend of the accused. According to the judge, the rules of evidence in a conspiracy case were quite different from the rules governing evidence when the defendant was accused of actually committing a criminal act. (2)

The process of jury deliberation was very interesting. As we discussed the evidence, we had amazingly different recollections about what we had heard. We even have different memories of basic factual information. What was remarkable was that we eventually reached a consensus and delivered a verdict that we all feel was fair. (2)

Writing Practice

On a separate sheet of paper, write about some event you experienced in the past, using one of the Editing Practice essays as a model. Then, step back from that experience, and make some generalizations about it. Use the Proofreading Checklist to show that every use of the present tense and the past tense in your essay is correct.

PROOFREADING CHECKLIST

Using the Present and the Past Tense Correctly in Your Writing

- Do not shift tenses unless there is a reason for doing so. However, there are many occasions that require writers to shift tenses. To understand which tense to use, you must understand the different uses of the present tense and the past tense.
- Use the past tense to describe events that were completed in the past.
- Use the present tense to make statements of fact or generalizations that will continue to be true indefinitely.
- Use the present tense to describe habitual or repeated actions.

VT

THE BOTTOM LINE

Keep the verbs in a sentence in the same tense unless you *have* a reason for tense shifting.

LESSON

The Progressive Tenses

Sample Errors

SAMPLE 1: **I can't talk to you right now. ✗ I finish my homework.**

SAMPLE 2: **✗ I am knowing the answer.**

SAMPLE 3: **✗ Ms. Higa was owning a house in the country last year.**

What's the Problem?

The **progressive tenses** are formed by using the helping verb *be* in some form followed by a **present participle** (a verb form ending in *-ing*).

- The tense is *present progressive* when the helping verb *be* is in one of its three present tense forms (*am, are, is*); for example: *I am smiling; They are smiling; She is smiling.*
- The tense is *past progressive* when the helping verb *be* is in one of its two past tense forms (*was, were*); for example: *He was smiling; They were smiling.*
- The tense is *future progressive* when the helping verb *be* is used with *will*; for example: *They will be smiling.*

There are two sources of mistakes with the progressive. The first is using the present tense where the present progressive is called for. The second is using the progressive with certain verbs that do not permit a progressive.

What Causes the Problem?

Most verbs cannot be used in the present tense without sounding stilted or even ungrammatical *unless* they are used to make "timeless" statements (see Lesson 25). To describe an action that is ongoing at some moment in time, people usually use the present, the past, or the future progressive as appropriate. For example, Sample 1 becomes grammatical when we change the present tense to a present progressive: *I am finishing my homework.*

However, there is a group of exceptional verbs that usually cannot be used in any progressive tense. We will call these *steady-state verbs*. The verbs (*know* and *own*) in Samples 2 and 3 are such verbs.

Diagnostic Exercise **(Corrected sentences appear on page 324.)**

Correct all errors in the following paragraph using the first correction as a model. The number in parentheses at the end of the paragraph indicates how many errors you should find.

Every weekday morning at 6 A.M., my alarm ~~is going~~ goes off. By 6:15, the breakfast dishes are on the table, and the coffee brews. I always am getting the children up next. It is very hard for them to get going. On Mondays, they are resembling bears coming out of hibernation. While they take their showers with their eyes still closed, I get everyone's clothes ready. Since the youngest child still is needing a lot of help getting dressed, I usually am spending some extra time with her talking about the day's events. By 7 A.M., we all sit at the table for breakfast. The children are loving pancakes and waffles, but there just isn't time to make them except on weekends. Breakfast goes by quickly, unless somebody is spilling the milk or juice. I am wishing we had more time in the morning, but every morning I am being amazed when I am looking back and realizing that we got it all done again. (14)

VT

Fixing This Problem in Your Writing

PROGRESSIVE TIP: Use the progressive tense when you are describing an event that is taking place at a particular moment of time, either now (present progressive), during some past moment of time (past progressive), or during some future moment of time (future progressive).

EXAMPLE: **Can you call back later? We <u>are eating</u> dinner now.**

In this sentence, the present progressive indicates that the action (*eating*) is ongoing at the present moment.

EXAMPLE: **We <u>were eating</u> dinner when we heard the news.**

In this sentence, the past progressive indicates that the action was ongoing at a particular moment of past time (*when we heard the news*, in this case).

EXAMPLE: **The tide <u>will be coming</u> in when they start back.**

In this sentence, the future progressive indicates that the action will be ongoing at a particular moment of future time (*when they start back,* in this case).

ONGOING-ACTION TIP: Do not use the progressive to refer to ongoing actions or conditions that continue indefinitely—ones that are not tied to some point in time or to some set period of time.

The basic function of the progressive tenses is to signal an action or condition that is in *progress* (as the name of the tense indicates) at some point in time or over some period of time. The fact that the progressive sentences are linked to some point or period of time means that they have a strong sense of being temporary. This temporariness is particularly important in the distinction between the "timeless" nature of the present tense as opposed to the "temporary" nature of the present progressive.

For example, compare the following two sentences:

I <u>live</u> in Santa Cruz.

I <u>am living</u> in Santa Cruz.

Both sentences are grammatical, but they mean slightly different things. The present tense in the first sentence implies that the writer is a permanent resident of Santa Cruz, while the present progressive in the second sentence implies that the writer is only there "for now"—in other words, that the writer is there only temporarily.

STEADY-STATE VERB TIP: Verbs that refer to unchanging, steady-state conditions are incompatible with the progressive tenses. These verbs tend to fall into certain broad categories: mental activity, emotional condition, and possession.

The progressive tenses indicate action that is temporary in nature. The use of the progressive tenses is incompatible with certain steady-state verbs whose meaning implies a continuous condition or state. These verbs tend to fall into three broad categories:

- Mental activity: *believe, doubt, forget, imagine, know, mean*
- Emotional condition: *appreciate, care, dislike, envy, fear, hate, like, love, need, prefer, want*
- Possession: *own, belong, contain, consist of, possess*

This list is far from complete. Moreover, many verbs are incompatible with the progressive tenses in certain meanings but not in other meanings. For example, verbs of perception cannot be used in the progressive when they describe something (✘ *The soup* <u>*is tasting*</u> *salty*), but they can be used in the progressive when a subject performs the action of the verb (*The cook* <u>*is tasting*</u> *the soup to see whether it is ready to serve*).

For Example . . .

Sample 2 and Sample 3 are steady-state verbs incorrectly used in the progressive tenses.

SAMPLE 2: **✘ I <u>am knowing</u> the answer.**

When a person knows the answer to a question, that knowledge is not tied to just a specific moment in time; a person does not know something one minute and then not know it the next. Taking the verb out of its progressive form makes the sentence grammatical as a simple statement of fact:

VT

SAMPLE 2, CORRECTED: **I <u>know</u> the answer.**

SAMPLE 3: **✘ Ms. Higa <u>was owning</u> a house in the country last year.**

The verb *own* is incompatible with the progressive tenses. The verb *own* implies that ownership is not limited to a set period of time. Even though we can assume that Ms. Higa no longer owns the house now, her right of ownership *when she owned the house* was not temporary. Taking the verb out of its progressive form makes the sentence grammatical as a statement about the past:

SAMPLE 3, CORRECTED: **Ms. Higa <u>owned</u> a house in the country last year.**

Now You Try It, 1 **(Corrected sentences appear on page 324.)**

The following sentences contain verbs in their dictionary form (underlined). Above each underlined verb, write the correct form of the verb using either the present tense, the past tense, or one of the three progressive tenses as appropriate.

believed
EXAMPLE: **Many people in Columbus's time believe that the world was round.**

1. We had to hurry because a big line form in front of the box office for tickets to the opening-night performance.
2. When we got to the restaurant, the host tell us that there would be a twenty-minute wait.
3. The plane arrive right now.
4. The boss believe that you may be right after all.
5. The noise sound very far away.

Now You Try It, 2 **(Corrected sentences appear on page 324.)**

The following sentences contain verbs in their dictionary form (underlined). Above each underlined verb, write the correct form of the verb using either the present tense, the past tense, or one of the three progressive tenses as appropriate.

will be snowing
EXAMPLE: **By the time we get to Lake Wobegon, it snow.**

1. When I was growing up, I always hate the uniforms we were required to wear in school.
2. I think that it is going to rain all weekend.
3. Right now, that seem to be our best choice.
4. They won't hear the phone ring, because they work outside.
5. I am sorry that I can't stop to talk to you now; I go to an important meeting.

Now You Try It, 3

The following sentences contain verbs in their dictionary form (underlined). Above each underlined verb, write the correct form of the verb using either present tense, past tense, or one of the three progressive tenses as appropriate.

EXAMPLE: **All during the movie, the person behind us ~~talk~~ ^was talking.**

1. We certainly appreciate your kindness to us during our stay with you.
2. Dr. Smith can't see you now; she meet with another student.
3. I am no longer missing class, because I have a more reliable car now.
4. Tomorrow at this time, we fly to Madrid.
5. We need to get some fresh air while the paint was drying.

Editing Practice, 1 **(Corrected sentences appear on page 324.)**

Correct all errors in the following paragraph using the first correction as a model. The number in parentheses at the end of the paragraph indicates how many errors you should find.

You all ~~are knowing~~ ^know the old joke that research is showing that the amount of sleep that we are needing is always five minutes more. I am never using the snooze button on my alarm clock because I am hitting it without actually waking up. In fact, I am finding that I must put my clock clear across the room so that I am being forced to actually get out of bed to turn it off. (6)

I am not a morning person, to put it mildly. I am hating getting up, and I am being nauseated by the thought of breakfast. Since I am so dopey in the mornings, I have learned to be methodical. While the water warms up in the shower, I set my clothes out. I fix two pieces of toast while I make the coffee. As I leave for the office, I grab the morning paper to read on the bus while I ride to work. When I finally do get to work, I am almost resembling a normal person. (7)

Editing Practice, 2 **(Corrected sentences appear on page 324.)**

Correct all errors in the following paragraphs using the first correction as a model. The number in parentheses at the end of each paragraph indicates how many errors you should find.

This year, both my husband and I ~~go~~ *are going* to school in programs that are requiring a lot of writing. We are both pretty good writers and are tending to get good grades on our papers. However, we are going about the process of writing in completely different ways. He is compulsive about how he writes his papers. First, he is brainstorming the topic and grouping all his thoughts into clusters. From the clusters, he makes a list of topics that he is wanting to include in his paper. Then, he writes draft after draft until he gets it right. (6)

I am completely the opposite. I am thinking that I would go crazy if I wrote the way my husband does. I am spending just as much time on my papers as he does, but I write in a completely different way. I am spending my time thinking about my papers before I ever write a word. I write my papers in my head. When I am feeling that I know what I want to say, I sit down and write a complete draft. I am needing to go over this draft for mechanical errors and punctuation, but I rarely make any big changes (5)

Editing Practice, 3

Correct all errors in the following paragraphs using the first correction as a model. The number in parentheses at the end of each paragraph indicates how many errors you should find.

I really enjoy cooking. Even though it is something that we ~~are needing~~ *need* to do every day, I find it very relaxing. I am liking to cook Italian food. When I was living in Italy, I was loving eating in restaurants. In Italy, people are going out to restaurants to try foods from different regions in Italy. Soon I was knowing something about the different regional dishes. I was appreciating most the importance of fresh ingredients. (5)

In my own cooking, I am liking to keep things relatively simple. Also, since I am trying to eat a low-fat diet, I am not liking the creamy dishes of northern Italy. Instead, I am preferring to cook the country dishes from the South, especially the ones that are having a lot of vegetables. The only problem that I have with these recipes is that they are using a lot of cheese. And, much as I am loving cheese, its fat content makes it a killer. (5)

Writing Practice

On your own paper, write about some process you engage in, such as your morning routine, your writing process, or how you cook. Use the proofreading checklist below to make sure that you have used the present and progressive tenses correctly.

PROOFREADING CHECKLIST

Using Present and Progressive Tenses in Your Writing

- Use the progressive tenses when you are describing an event that is taking place at a particular moment or period of time.
- Do not use the present or past progressive to refer to ongoing states or to conditions that continue indefinitely.
- Verbs that refer to unchanging, steady-state conditions are incompatible with the progressive tenses.

THE BOTTOM LINE

Use the progressive tenses only for events that *are taking place* at a particular moment or period of time.

LESSON

The Past and the Perfect Tenses

Sample Errors

SAMPLE 1: **✗ We regretted our choice ever since we bought that car.**

SAMPLE 2: **✗ When we bought the house last year, it was empty for ten years.**

What's the Problem?

The **perfect tenses** are formed with the helping verb *have* in some form followed by the **past participle** form of a second verb. When the present tense forms of *have* (*have, has*) are used, the resulting construction is called the *present perfect* tense; for example: *We have seen that movie*; *Raoul has answered that question before.*

The past tense of *have* (*had*) is used to form the *past perfect* tense; for example: *Juan had reported the accident before the police arrived.*

The most common mistake is that writers use the past tense when they should have used either the present perfect or the past perfect tense.

You should use the present perfect tense to indicate an action that began in the past and continues to the present (*Senator Longterm has served for 18 years*) or an action that began and ended at an unspecified time in the past (*Senator Longterm has won three elections*).

The past perfect tense indicates an action that took place in the past before another past action (*I had admired Senator Longterm before the newspaper revealed the scandal*) or a past action that ended at a specific time (*I had met the senator in 1989*).

What Causes the Problem?

The present perfect and the past perfect tenses allow us to show rather subtle differences in past time relationships. Very often in conversation, speakers fail to use the perfect tenses, especially the past perfect, because they do not always plan out their sentences. Consequently, writers also tend to use the past tense incorrectly for all time relationships in the past.

Diagnostic Exercise **(Corrected sentences appear on page 325.)**

Correct all errors in the following paragraph using the first correction as a model. The number in parentheses at the end of the paragraph indicates how many errors you should find.

Unfortunately, most people ~~were~~ ^have been^ involved in an automobile accident at some time. I was involved in several but my luckiest accident was one that never happened. Just after I got my driver's license, I borrowed the family car to go to a party. Although it was a very tame party, I left feeling a little hyper and silly. It was night, and there were no street lights nearby. I parked a little distance from the house, so my car was by itself. I got into the car and decided to show off a little bit by throwing the car into reverse and flooring it. I went about 20 yards backward before I thought to myself that I was doing something pretty dangerous. I slammed on the brakes in a panic. I got out of the car and found that my back bumper was about 4 inches from a parked car that I never saw. Whenever I feel an urge to push my luck driving, I remind myself of the accident that almost happened. (6)

VT

Fixing This Problem in Your Writing

> **PRESENT PERFECT TIP:** Use the present perfect when a past action continues in an unbroken manner up to the present moment.

The difference between the past and the present perfect is that the past tense refers to a *completed* past event, but the present perfect refers to something that started in the past and that has continued in an unbroken manner up to the present time. Compare the following sentences:

PAST: **Louise lived in Chicago for ten years.**

PRESENT PERFECT: **Louise has lived in Chicago for ten years.**

In the first sentence, we know that Louise does not live in Chicago anymore; the period of her residence ended some time in the past. In the second sentence, the present perfect means that the ten-year period continues and that Louise *still* lives in Chicago.

For Example . . .

Let's look at the first sample sentence:

SAMPLE 1: **✗ We regretted our choice ever since we bought that car.**

The problem is the incompatibility between the over-and-done-with meaning of the past tense and the fact that the writer still regrets the choice of car today.

PRESENT PERFECT TIP APPLIED: **We have regretted our choice ever since we bought that car.**

The present perfect and the **progressive** both emphasize action that takes place over a span of time. Writers often use the two tenses together; for example: *We have been regretting our choice ever since we bought that car.*

PAST PERFECT TIP: Use the past perfect to show that one event in the past was completed *before* a more recent event took place.

The past perfect tense enables us to describe the time sequence between two different past events, one of which happened before the other.

SAMPLE 2: **✗ When we bought the house last year, it was empty for ten years.**

There are two past events here: (1) a ten-year period before last year during which time the house had stood empty and (2) the moment last year when the writer bought the house.

PAST PERFECT TIP APPLIED: **When we bought the house last year, it had been empty for ten years.**

Often, writers use the past perfect to imply that one past event *caused* a later past event. For example, the sentence *They had gotten into a big fight just before they broke up* implies that they broke up *because* of their big fight.

Now You Try It, 1 **(Corrected sentences appear on page 325.)**

The following sentences contain mistakes involving the use of the past, the present perfect, and the past perfect tenses. Make the necessary changes as shown in the following example.

had lost

EXAMPLE: **Germany ~~lost~~ ^ the war long before Hitler committed suicide in his bunker in Berlin.**

1. Senator Blather campaigned in every district for the last six months.

2. It rained every weekend since Easter.

3. Holmes suspected Lord Bumfort because Holmes noticed the unexplained mud on His Lordship's shoes.

4. Holmes explained the clues to Watson three times before Watson finally understood.

5. I saw that movie a dozen times this year.

Now You Try It, 2 **(Corrected sentences appear on page 325.)**

The following sentences contain mistakes involving the use of the past, the present perfect, and the past perfect tenses. Make the necessary changes as shown in the following example.

had left

EXAMPLE: **When we got to the airport, we realized that we ~~left~~ ^ our passports at home.**

VT

1. Before I got sick, I was working about 60 hours a week.

2. The committee met every week this term.

3. The plane returned to the airport after the pilot noticed that fuel was leaking from an engine.

4. In the last ten years, the company expanded into nearly every major market in the country.

5. The defendant's lawyers filed a motion before their time expired.

Now You Try It, 3

The following sentences may contain mistakes involving the use of the past, the present perfect, and the past perfect tenses. Make the necessary changes. If the sentence is correct, write *OK* above it.

EXAMPLE: **Alice** *had* ^ **called her parents three times before they finally answered the phone.**

1. Apparently the driver suffered a heart attack before the accident occurred.

2. We struggled with that problem all afternoon.

3. Poor Watson searched the manor for days before Holmes finally found the missing jewels in the carriage house.

4. The members of the orchestra played together for years.

5. The overture began before the audience had time to take their seats.

Editing Practice, 1 **(Corrected sentences appear on page 325.)**

Correct all errors in the following paragraph using the first correction as a model. The number in parentheses at the end of the paragraph indicates how many errors you should find.

America *has* ^ **had a love affair with the automobile ever since its invention. However, our attitudes about automobile safety were always ambiguous, even contradictory. Over the years, we were willing to pay a lot of money for automobiles that go faster and faster, but we always seemed to be unwilling to deal with the safety consequences of this increased speed. An interesting case in point is the recent decision by the federal government to eliminate the 55-mile-per-hour speed limit on interstate highways. We had this speed limit since the 1970's. Interestingly, the speed limit was put into effect not as a safety measure but as a way to save gasoline during the oil embargo at the time. (4)**

Editing Practice, 2 **(Corrected sentences appear on page 326.)**

Correct all errors in the following paragraph using the first correction as a model. The number in parentheses at the end of the paragraph indicates how many errors you should find.

My friend Dale ~~was~~ ^had been^ living on his parents' farm his whole life when he made himself unwelcome at home. Just before Dale got his license, his father bought a new car that was his pride and joy. One day, after Dale and his best friend were out someplace fooling around, Dale got home late for one of his chores: rounding up the cows for milking. Dale drove his dad's new car into the pasture to get the cows, something his father expressly prohibited. When he was out in the pasture, the horn got stuck, so Dale pulled out various wires until the horn stopped. That night, after his father went to bed, Dale sneaked into the barn and rewired the horn in the dark. The next morning, when his father started the car, it burst into flames. (4)

Editing Practice, 3

Correct all errors in the following paragraphs using the first correction as a model. The number in parentheses at the end of each paragraph indicates how many errors you should find.

Among all the bad news we ~~had~~ ^have had *or* have been having^ recently, there is one piece of encouraging information. The number of deaths resulting from traffic accidents steadily declined over the past few years. Researchers cited a number of reasons: improved safety of vehicles, increased use of seat belts and air bags, and fewer drunk drivers. Automobile manufacturers were always very reluctant to mention safety, because their entire marketing strategy was based on selling the glamour of cars and driving. Fortunately, this situation changed since the federal government mandated national safety standards. Now, companies compete over who achieved the highest levels of safety. (5)

VT

Perhaps the biggest single factor in declining death rates in this decade was the increased use of seat belts. Now, most of us would never start the car until we fastened our seat belt first. Another big change affecting the accident rate was the general decline in the use of alcohol throughout society in recent years. Americans just do not drink as much as we used to. (3)

Writing Practice

On your own paper, write a short essay about an automobile accident or some aspect of automobile safety. Try to use a mixture of past and the two perfect tenses. Use the Proofreading Checklist to show that the tenses in your essay are correct.

PROOFREADING CHECKLIST

Using the Past and the Perfect Tenses in Your Writing

- Use the *past tense* to describe an event that occurred at some point or fixed period in the past. The event belongs entirely in the past. There is no implication that the event continued over time up to the present.
- Use the *present perfect tense* to describe an action that began in the past and that has continued in an unbroken manner up to the present moment.
- Use the *past perfect tense* to connect two past events; the earlier event is completed before the more recent past event, sometimes with an implication that the first event caused the second.

VT

THE BOTTOM LINE

Use the past tense for single events that *ended* in the past. Use the present perfect for actions that *have begun* in the past and continue up to the present. Use the past perfect for showing that an earlier event *had ended* before a later event started.

LESSON

Using Participles as Adjectives

Sample Errors

SAMPLE 1: ✗ **The movie was about a <u>frightened</u> old house.**

SAMPLE 2: ✗ **After the three-hour exam, there was a break for the <u>exhausting</u> students.**

What's the Problem?

A **participle** is a word used as an **adjective**, a word that modifies a noun. Participles are unusual noun modifiers because they come from verbs that have been turned into adjectives. There are two different routes by which most verbs can be turned into adjectives:

- Adjectives that end in *-ing* are called **present participles.**
- Adjectives that end in *-ed* are called **past participles.** (A relatively small number of verbs have irregular past participle forms.)

The problem is that the two different types of participles mean completely different things.

VT

What Causes the Problem?

Every participle comes from an underlying verb. In using a participle to modify a noun, a writer is making a statement about the relationship of the noun to that underlying verb. That noun is either the subject of the underlying verb or the object of the underlying verb. For example, the present participle phrase *a <u>boring</u> teacher* means that the teacher (subject) is boring the students; however, the past participle phrase *a <u>bored</u> teacher* means just the opposite—that the students bore the teacher (object).

If you are not careful to work out the correct relationship of the noun to the verb underlying the participle, you may use the wrong participle to express the intended meaning.

As this example shows, you may be able to write a grammatical sentence using either the past participle form or the present participle form of the verb, but the meaning of the sentence will depend on your choice.

Diagnostic Exercise **(Corrected sentences appear on page 326.)**

Correct all errors in the following paragraph using the first correction as a model. The number in parentheses at the end of the paragraph indicates how many errors you should find.

The Smithsonian Institution is an ~~amazed~~ amazing system of museums and art galleries in Washington, D.C. The Smithsonian is a requiring stop for every concerning visitor to Washington. Recently, I spent a fascinated day at the National Museum of Natural History. The only problem is that there is so much to see that the overwhelming visitors find themselves frantically rushing from one interested exhibit to another without taking the time to understand all the information in the exhibits. One solution to this frustrated problem is to take a tour. The guide points out important highlights of the show. (6)

Fixing This Problem in Your Writing

To find out whether you have used the right participle, you must look at the relationship between the participle and the noun it modifies. The easiest way to do this is to change the participle back into its underlying verb form and see what role the noun plays—subject or object—and then choose the participle form accordingly.

VT

> SUBJECT TIP: Use the present participle form (*-ing*) if the noun being modified plays the role of the subject of the verb underlying the participle.

Now apply this tip to Sample 1:

SAMPLE 1: ✗ **The movie was about a <u>frightened</u> old house.**

Ask yourself this question: Is *house* the subject of *frighten*? Can old houses frighten people? Clearly, the answer is yes, they can. Now ask yourself the opposite question with *house* as the object of *frighten*: Can people frighten an old house? Clearly, *house* can't be the object of *frighten*.

SUBJECT TIP APPLIED: **The movie was about a <u>frightening</u> old house.**

OBJECT TIP: Use the past participle form (*-ed*) if the noun being modified plays the role of the object of the verb underlying the participle.

Now apply this tip to Sample 2:

SAMPLE 2: **✗ After the three-hour exam, there was a break for the <u>exhausting</u> students.**

Ask yourself this question: Did something exhaust the students, or were the students exhausting something? Clearly, a *yes* answer to the first question, in which *students* is the object, makes more sense. When the noun being modified is the object, then you must use the *-ed* past participle.

OBJECT TIP APPLIED: **After the three-hour exam, there was a break for the <u>exhausted</u> students.**

For Example . . .

Let's apply these two tips to the following sentence:

✗ After their <u>thrilled</u> ride through the rapids, the <u>exhausting</u> rafters rested for a while in calmer water.

VT

Clearly, *thrilled ride* is incorrect, because *ride* is the subject of the verb *thrill*: (*The ride thrilled the rafters*); it is not the object ✗ (*The rafters thrilled the ride*). You must use the present participle *-ing*: *thrilling ride.*

Likewise, *exhausting rafters* is incorrect, because *rafters* is the object of the underlying verb *exhaust* (*The ride exhausted the rafters*); it is not the subject ✗ (*The rafters exhausted the ride*).

You must use the past participle *-ed*: *exhausted rafters.*

CORRECTION: **After their <u>thrilling</u> ride through the rapids, the <u>exhausted</u> rafters rested for a while in calmer water.**

Now You Try It, 1 (Corrected sentences appear on page 326.)

The following sentences contain underlined participles. If the participle is wrong, replace it with the correct one. Confirm correct answers by turning the participle into a verb and using the noun as a subject or an object, as appropriate.

The quiz surprised the students.

EXAMPLE: **The professor gave a quiz to the ~~surprising~~ ^surprised^ students.**

1. A <u>watching</u> pot never boils.

2. We realized that we had a <u>troubled</u> problem on our hands.

3. Most good department stores will replace <u>damaging</u> furniture if the customer has a receipt.

4. It was a terribly <u>embarrassed</u> situation for all of us.

5. Do you know Sherlock Holmes's famous question about the <u>barking</u> dog?

Now You Try It, 2 (Corrected sentences appear on page 326.)

The following sentences contain underlined participles. If the participle is wrong, replace it with the correct one. Confirm correct answers by turning the participle into a verb and using the noun as a subject or object, as appropriate.

The meal nourished the children.

EXAMPLE: **I prepared a ~~nourished~~ ^nourishing^ meal for my children.**

1. We all enjoyed such a <u>gripped</u> movie.

2. The <u>extracting</u> ore is sent to a mill for further processing.

3. The <u>sprawled</u> suburbs went on for miles and miles.

4. The movie was a <u>smashed</u> success at the box office.

5. Unable to endure the dentist's silly jokes any longer, the <u>provoking</u> patient took matters into his own hands.

Now You Try It, 3

The following sentences contain participles. If the participle is wrong, replace it with the correct one. Confirm correct answers by turning the participle into a verb and using the noun as a subject or an object, as appropriate.

EXAMPLE: **The ~~threatened~~ threatening clouds foretold an afternoon shower.**

The clouds threatened.

1. The press was very cautious in how it handled the reporting incident.

2. The accident was caused by a loading gun kept in a drawer.

3. The press followed the unfolded scandal with glee.

4. The audience was startled by the disembodying voice of the three witches.

5. The invaded floodwaters had covered all the town's access roads.

Editing Practice, 1 **(Corrected sentences appear on page 326.)**

Correct all errors in the following paragraphs using the first correction as a model. The number in parentheses at the end of each paragraph indicates how many errors you should find.

I have quite ~~conflicted~~ conflicting feelings about the National Museum of Natural History. On the one hand, it is in a depressed building. Even a casual visitor can't help noticing the water-staining walls and crumbled plaster in the remote hallways. Clearly, a penny-pinched Congress has not adequately provided the museum with the needing funds. One recent report said that repairing storm-damaging roofs alone would absorb the whole maintenance budget for the year. (6)

On the other hand, the new exhibits are lively and colorful. We can only hope that in these difficult times, Congress can develop a balancing plan that maintains the old building and provides for excited new exhibits. (2)

Editing Practice, 2 **(Corrected sentences appear on page 327.)**

Correct all errors in the following paragraph using the first correction as a model. The number in parentheses at the end of the paragraph indicates how many errors you should find.

One of the things that strikes visitors to Hawaii is the ~~amazed~~ *amazing* variation in climate. Waikiki Beach, for example, only has about 20 inches of rain a year. Without irrigation, Waikiki would be a dusty plain, as it was shown in photographs from missionary times. However, Manoa Valley, the valley behind the beach, has gradually increased amounts of rainfall until, at the back of the valley, less then 10 miles from Waikiki Beach, there is an astonished 130 inches a year. Another interested fact about the valleys in Hawaii is that, despite the astonished rainfall at the backs of the valleys, there are only a few rivers. The reason for this surprised fact is that the volcanic soil is remarkably porous. The rain is absorbed into the ground before it can run off. In most places in the world, such overwhelmed rain could not be held by the saturating soil and would create streams and rivers to carry off the excess water. (7)

Editing Practice, 3

Correct all errors in the following paragraphs using the first correction as a model. The number in parentheses at the end of each paragraph indicates how many errors you should find.

Milan has become Italy's ~~undisputing~~ *undisputed* financial capital. Despite its central role in modern Italy, Milan is not a recognizing tourist destination comparable to Venice, Rome, or Florence. Milan is not a well-preserving Renaissance city; it is a modern industrializing city that seems more German than Mediterranean. (3)

Milan does have one undisputing claim to fame: Leonardo da Vinci's *Last Supper*. The painting is in an otherwise undistinguishing building attached to

the church of Santa Maria delle Grazie. There are several astonished features about the painting. First is its surprised size: it covers the entire end of the building. Second, it incorporates existed features of the building. For example, the beams that support the building appear to continue right into the creating room in the painting. (6)

Writing Practice

On your own paper, write about a visit to a museum or other famous place and your reactions to it. Use as many present and past participles as you can. Then, use the Proofreading Checklist to show that your use of present and past participles is correct.

PROOFREADING CHECKLIST

Using Present and Past Participles in Your Writing

- Participles are verbs that have been turned into adjectives. There are two types of participles. *Present participles* are formed by adding *-ing* to verbs. Most past participles are formed by adding *-ed* to verbs.
- You can tell which participle to use by looking at the relationship between the verb underlying the participle and the noun it modifies.
- Use the *-ing* present participle when the noun being modified is the *subject* that is doing the action of the verb underlying the participle.
- Use the *-ed* past participle when the noun being modified is the *object* of the verb underlying the participle.

THE BOTTOM LINE

Use *-ing* if the noun *being* modified serves as the subject.
Use *-ed* if the noun being *modified* serves as the object.

UNIT SIX
PUTTING IT ALL TOGETHER

The first three lessons in Unit Six discuss how to use different tenses, and the last lesson covers participles.

- Lesson 25: Present, Past, and Tense Shifting
  This lesson explores the fundamentally different meanings of the present tense and the past tense. The *past tense* refers to a completed, past event (*John found his keys*). Use the *present tense* for "timeless" statements of facts (*The world is round*); for generalizations (*Children love parades*); and for descriptions of habitual, repeated actions (*I get up at seven every morning*)—none of which really refers to the present moment.

- Lesson 26: The Progressive Tenses
  The progressive tenses describe ongoing actions that are "in progress" at a moment in time. Use the *present progressive* for the present moment (*I am working as fast as I can*); the *past progressive* for a moment in past time (*They were waxing the car when I came in*); and the *future perfect* for a moment in future time (*They will be eating dinner when we get there*).

- Lesson 27: The Past and the Perfect Tenses
  The perfect tenses describe action that is completed with respect to a second moment in time. Use the *present perfect* to describe an action that began in the past and that has continued up to the present (*We have had rain all this week*). Use the *past perfect* to show that one past-time event took place before a second, more recent event (*I had returned my library books before I got the overdue notice*).

- Lesson 28: Using Participles as Adjectives
  Participles modify nouns and are of two types: *present* participles (*an amusing child*) and *past* participles (*an amused child*). The difference between the types of participles comes from the relation of the noun being modified to the verb that underlies the participle. With present participles, the noun is the *subject* of the verb (*Children amuse*). With past participles, the noun is the *object* of the verb (*Somebody amused the children*).

VT

Review

Correct all errors in the following paragraphs using the first correction as a model. The number in parentheses at the end of each paragraph indicates how many errors you should find.

Thanks to federal regulations, industrial pollution ~~was~~ *has been* significantly reduced over the past several decades. However, we begin to realize that there is another form of water pollution that was completely outside state and federal regulation: "nonpoint-source" pollution. Regulations dealt with pollution that has a distinct point of origin—a factory or a plant, for example, whose discharge into the air or water can be directly measured. "Point-of-origin" pollution is consisting of relatively high levels of pollution in a small area. The effects that a particular point-of-origin pollution had on the immediate area over time is relatively easy to identify. It is nearly as easy to see what effects a reduction in pollution had over time in the same area. (6)

Nonpoint-source pollution is a different matter altogether. Every time we are starting our car, we release a relatively small amount of pollutants of various types into the atmosphere. These pollutants are dispersed over such a wide geographic area that nobody can tell where they came from or even when they are put into the air. The problem that defeated environmentalists for years is how to deal with such overwhelmed numbers of little polluters. A similar problem existed for years with runoff. Every time it rains, water is washing off the grease, oil, and litter from all our roads, driveways, and parking lots. The amount of pollution per square foot of paved surface is not very great, but when the runoff from millions of square feet of pavement flows into open drains and then directly into nearby streams, the cumulative effect can sometimes be devastating. (6)

UNIT SEVEN
Articles

OVERVIEW

Terms That Can Help You Understand Articles

If you are not familiar with any of the following terms that appear in this unit, look them up in the Guide to Grammar Terminology beginning on page 1. The numbers in parentheses indicate the lessons in which each term appears.

article (29, 30, 31)
common noun (29)
count noun (29)
definite article (30, 31)
indefinite article (30, 31)
noncount noun (29, 30, 31)
proper noun (29)

The Nuts and Bolts of Articles

One of the most complicated and confusing aspects of English for non-native speakers is the use of **articles**. There are two types of articles, **definite** (*the*) and **indefinite** (*a* and *an*, together with *some*, which behaves like an indefinite article). The choice among these articles—and the additional option of using no article at all—is determined by the nature of the noun that the article modifies. This unit will examine how both the form of nouns and the meaning of nouns affect the choice of articles.

There are two main groups of nouns: proper nouns and common nouns. **Proper nouns** name particular people, places, and institutions and are usually capitalized. Most categories of proper nouns do not involve the use of articles. For example:

PEOPLE: **Ms. Chin, Martin Luther King, Barbara Walters**

PLACES: **Chicago, State Street, Niagara Falls, China, Mexico City**

INSTITUTIONS: **General Motors, Apple Computer, Columbia University**

However, as you doubtless already know, some proper nouns are used with the definite article *the*. While many such uses are completely idiomatic, some uses of *the* actually follow rules of their own. Just for fun, see whether you can figure out the rules for using *the* with certain classes of proper nouns, based on the following examples. (*Hint:* Think about the difference in meaning between the nouns that don't use articles and the ones that use *the*.)

No article	**Used with *the***
Mt. Everest, Mt. McKinley, Pikes Peak, Mt. Hood, Mt. Washington	The Alps, The Rockies, The Sierra Nevadas, The Andes, The Himalayas
Lake Como, Golden Pond, Lake Ontario, Walden Pond	The Atlantic, The Mediterranean Sea, The Pacific, The Indian Ocean

(Answers appear on page 327.)

This unit focuses on the other type of nouns—common nouns. **Common nouns** are not capitalized and are not the names of particular people, places, or institutions. For example, *Ms. Chin* is the name of a particular person, but the common noun *woman* is not. The choice of which article to use with a common noun (or whether to use any article at all) depends on three questions, each of which is discussed in its own lesson:

- *What is the form of the noun?* Is it singular or plural? Is it a count noun or a noncount noun? (Lesson 29: Incorrect Plurals and Articles with Noncount Nouns)
- *Does the reader know which specific noun you are referring to?* (Lesson 30: Definite and Indefinite Articles: Known or New?)
- *Is the noun being used to make a generalization?* Does the noun refer to things in general, or does it refer to a particular thing? (Lesson 31: Making Generalizations without Articles)

This unit is somewhat different from other units in the book. In the other units, the lessons are only loosely connected. Usually, you can do one lesson in a unit without doing any other lessons first. In this unit, however, that is not the case; the three lessons are tightly connected. You need to do all three lessons in order. The three lessons work together to give you a specific technique called a *decision tree* for deciding which article (if any) you should use with a given common noun. This technique is found in the final section of Unit Seven: "Putting It All Together."

Can You Detect Problems Involving Articles?

(Corrected sentences appear on page 327.)

Correct all errors in the following paragraphs using the first correction as a model. The number in parentheses at the end of each paragraph indicates how many errors you should find.

We live in ~~the~~ *a* time of the great technological change. The engine that is driving this change is the computer. It is hard to believe how quickly the computers have become the absolutely essential part of our personal and professional lives. Many of us first used computers as the greatly improved typewriters. With computers, we were able to edit and revise the essays with a few keyboard commands without going to trouble of having to retype entire document over again. In business world, computers were first used as the greatly improved desk calculators. With computers, we could create spreadsheets that would do tiresome calculations for us. (9)

As the computers have become more common and more powerful, they have begun to redefine what it means to write and to calculate. For example, it used to be that distinction between writing term paper and publishing book was as different as day and night. That is no longer the case. What I write at my computer in my office can be sent out over network and be more widely distributed than any published book ever was. It used to be that jobs of bookkeeper and the financial planner were completely different. That is no longer the case. With the financial planning software, I can do analysis of dozens of alternative business choices and decide which one works best, and even throw in strategy for minimizing taxes at the same time. (10)

LESSON 29

Incorrect Plurals and Articles with Noncount Nouns

Sample Errors

SAMPLE 1: ✘ **There have been many studies about the effects of violences on children watching TV.**

SAMPLE 2: ✘ **The customs agent might ask to see a luggage.**

What's the Problem?

A large group of nouns in English cannot be used in the plural. For example, the word *violences* in Sample 1 has incorrectly been made plural. Another peculiarity of this group of nouns is that they cannot be used with the article *a* or *an*. For example, in Sample 2, we cannot say "a luggage."

What Causes the Problem?

A noun that cannot be used in the plural and that cannot be used with the article *a* or *an* is called a **noncount noun** (or a *mass noun*). Since non-native speakers of English have great difficulty in recognizing noncount nouns, they are likely to treat a noncount noun as though it were a regular **count noun** and incorrectly to pluralize it or to use the article *a* or *an* with it.

Diagnostic Exercise **(Corrected sentences appear on page 327.)**

Correct all errors in the following paragraph using the first correction as a model. The number in parentheses at the end of the paragraph indicates how many errors you should find.

ART

The ~~modernizations~~ [modernization] of agriculture has meant a huge increase in just a few crops—wheats and rices for a human consumption, corns for an animal consumption, and cottons for industrial productions. This specialization in a few crops is called a *monoculture*. A monoculture has some disadvantages: it reduces a biodiversity and requires huge amounts of energies and fertilizer. (11)

Fixing This Problem in Your Writing

The reason why nouns in this group are called "noncount" is that they cannot be counted with number words like *one, two, three.* For example, we cannot say "one luggage, two luggages." This fact also explains why we cannot use the article *a* or *an* with noncount nouns. Historically, the article *a* or *an* came from the number word *one.*

PLURAL TIP: The easiest way to test whether a word is a noncount noun is to make the noun plural. If the plural of the word is not grammatical or does not make sense in the context of the sentence, then the word is a noncount noun. (Note that when the tested noun is a subject, the verb will change to agree.)

For Example . . .

In the expression *Talk is cheap, talk* is a noncount noun because the plural *Talks are cheap* is not grammatical without completely changing the meaning of the expression. However, in the sentence *I went to the talk,* the noun *talk* is a count noun because we can make it plural: *I went to the talks.* In the first sentence, the noncount noun *talk* means "the process of talking." In the second sentence, the count noun *talk* means a "lecture."

Although it is difficult to predict which nouns are noncount nouns, many noncount nouns do occur in relatively well-defined classes based on their meaning. Here are examples:

Abstractions (the largest single group of noncount nouns): faith, hope, charity, beauty, luck, peace, flexibility, knowledge, reliability, intelligence . . .
Liquids and gases: water, coffee, tea, wine, blood, gasoline, air, oxygen . . .
Materials: gold, silver, paper, wool, silk, wood, glass, chalk, sand, plastic . . .
Food: bread, butter, rice, cheese, meat, jam, chicken, beef, salt, sugar . . .
Languages: English, Chinese, Spanish, Russian . . .
Academic fields: anthropology, chemistry, physics, literature . . .
Sports and games: tennis, bridge, soccer, football, baseball, chess . . .
Gerunds (words ending in *-ing* used as nouns): smiling, wishing, walking . . .
Weather words: weather, fog, snow, rain, pollution, thunder, wind, hail . . .
Natural phenomena: gravity, electricity, space, energy, matter . . .

People tend to use abstract noncount nouns to make generalizations about categories of things or events, especially when the things or events refer to abstractions. Conversely, when talking about some particular, specific thing or event, people tend to use count nouns.

GENERALIZATION TIP: When a noun is used to make a generalization—especially if the noun refers to an abstraction—check to see whether that noun is a noncount noun.

For Example . . .

In the following sentence, compare the words *experimentation* and *experiment.*

Experimentation without an appropriate way to evaluate the results of the experiment is a misuse of the scientific process.

In this sentence, the noun *experimentation* is an abstract noun that refers to the general process of conducting tests. *Experimentation* is, thus, a word that might be a noncount noun. To confirm this suspicion, try to make it plural.

GENERALIZATION TIP APPLIED: **✗ Experimentations without an appropriate way to evaluate the results of the experiment is a misuse of the scientific process.**

The related word *experiment* in the same sentence refers to an actual test; thus, it is probably a count noun. To confirm this expectation, make it plural:

PLURAL TIP APPLIED: **Experimentation without an appropriate way to evaluate the results of the experiments is a misuse of the scientific process.**

There is one other odd feature about noncount nouns. While noncount nouns cannot have a plural meaning, sometimes they can be used with the plural marker *-s* to mean something like "different kinds of." For example, *tea* is a noncount noun; when it is used with an *-s*, it means "different kinds of teas," as in the sentence *That store carries teas from all over the world.* In this sentence, *teas* is still a noncount noun because it does not have a plural meaning.

Now You Try It, 1 **(Corrected sentences appear on page 328.)**

In the following sentences, many noncount nouns have been incorrectly used in the plural or with the article *a* or *an*. Underline the incorrectly used noncount nouns, and make any necessary corrections.

EXAMPLE: **Supervisors are people charged with the responsibility of carrying out the supervisions of other employees.** [supervision]

1. Having a flicker in my computer screen caused me an anxiety about saving my works.
2. My roommate and I finally unplugged the TV set during the week because we couldn't stand the silly nonsenses in all the commercials.
3. Most people need to pay a high price for popularities.
4. Everyone in the legal profession has an obligation to uphold the enforcements of the laws.
5. A record of traffic tickets is an evidence of a tendency to drive dangerously.

Now You Try It, 2 **(Corrected sentences appear on page 328.)**

In the following sentences, many noncount nouns have been incorrectly used in the plural or with the article *a* or *an*. Underline the incorrectly used noncount nouns, and make any necessary corrections.

EXAMPLE: **The company has been successful because of a good management.**

1. After being pursued by a mysterious villain, the hero seeks the protections of his friends.
2. The company is trying to prolong the storage of food by treating it with radiations.
3. The teacher offered the young people some good advices.
4. We assured them of our complete cooperations in these matters.
5. To be a writer, you must have lots of good ideas and lots of informations.

Now You Try It, 3

Each line below contains two nouns. The first is a noncount noun, and the second is a count noun. Write a sentence that uses both nouns (in either order).

EXAMPLE: **guilt, example**

The joke "Guilt is a gift that keeps on giving" is an example of black humor.

1. pollution, automobile
2. homework, assignment
3. equipment, coach
4. congestion, road
5. violence, term paper

Editing Practice, 1 **(Corrected sentences appear on page 328.)**

Correct all errors in the following paragraphs using the first correction as a model. Make whatever other changes are necessary. The number in parentheses at the end of each paragraph indicates how many errors you should find.

Jewelry

Gold has long been one of the most valued of metals. ~~A jewelry~~ ^ made of gold has been discovered at an excavation in Iraq that dates from 3500 B.C. The high level of artistries in the workmanships suggests that the craft of working golds had been evolving for centuries before then. (3)

From ancient times to today, gold has been highly prized for a number of reasons. Its soft yellow color makes it intrinsically beautiful; unlike irons, coppers, and most other metal, a gold does not rust; and gold can be easily shaped into any desired form. (3)

ART

Editing Practice, 2 **(Corrected sentences appear on page 328.)**

Correct all errors in the following paragraphs using the first correction as a model. Make whatever other changes are necessary. The number in parentheses at the end of each paragraph indicates how many errors you should find.

One of the most remarkable Americans who ever lived was Benjamin Franklin. He was born in 1706 in Boston. His ~~educations were~~ *education was* quite limited because his father, who made candles and soap, was unable to send him to school beyond the age of ten. It is amazing that one of the most educated men in the Age of Reasons was entirely self-taught. Franklin learned to be printer, and by the time he was twenty-four, Franklin was the owner of his own print shop in Philadelphia. He began publishing a highly successful newspaper, writing much of the materials himself as his own editor. Through the newspaper and other publishings, Franklin became one of the most important public figures in the thirteen colonies. (4)

Adding to his already-substantial fames was his work as an inventor and scientist. Two of his most famous inventions were bifocal eyeglasses and a much more efficient stove, called the Franklin Stove. His research on electricities made him world famous. (2)

Franklin's great personal reputations and knowledge of civic affairs made him a natural political leader. He had enormous influences on the Revolutionary War. For example, he helped draft the Declaration of Independence and was one of its signers. However, his most important impacts on the war were his role in obtaining the diplomatic supports and eventual military intervention of France on the side of the colonies. After the war, Franklin's wisdoms and common senses played a key role in resolving fundamental conflicts in the creations of the Constitution. (7)

Editing Practice, 3

Correct all errors in the following paragraphs using the first correction as a model. Make whatever other changes are necessary. The number in parentheses at the end of each paragraph indicates how many errors you should find.

Probably the most important aspect of gold is its rareness. The fact that there ~~are~~ *is* always more ~~demands~~ *demand* for gold than there is availability of gold means that gold has great economic values. Several times in histories, our quest for gold has led to several great discoveries (albeit accidentally). For example, in the Middle Ages in Europe, alchemists, half-scientists and half-magicians, believed that inexpensive metals like leads could be turned into gold. The works of the alchemists never succeeded, but their researches were the foundation for the science of chemistries. The search for gold was also the main motivation for the early exploration of the New World and Australia. (6)

Today, we do not use gold for a money. Instead, gold is used to stand behind paper currency. Some economists have urged the United States to return to the gold standard, a system in which the government agrees to redeem its paper money for a fixed amount of gold. The advantage of the gold standard is that it prevents an inflation. (2)

Writing Practice

Many nouns can be used either as a noncount noun or as a count noun, but with different meanings. Following are some such nouns. Use each in two sentences that use the noun both ways. Explain the differences in meaning.

EXAMPLE: **chicken**

NONCOUNT: **We seem to have <u>chicken</u> for dinner every night. <u>(meat)</u>**

COUNT: **The <u>chickens</u> were running around everywhere. <u>(living animals)</u>**

1. lamb
   Noncount:
   Count:

2. glass
   Noncount:
   Count:

3. iron
   Noncount:
   Count:

4. football
   Noncount:
   Count:

5. coffee
   Noncount:
   Count:

PROOFREADING CHECKLIST

Using Noncount Nouns in Your Writing

- Noncount nouns are nouns that cannot be used in the plural. They cannot be counted with numbers or used with the article *a* or *an*.
- The easiest way to see whether a word is a noncount noun is to see if it can be used in the plural. If the plural is ungrammatical in the intended meaning, then the word is a noncount noun.
- Noncount nouns are often used to make generalizations, especially generalizations about abstractions. Thus, words used as generalizations about abstractions should always be tested to see whether they are noncount nouns.

THE BOTTOM LINE

Count *nouns* can be made plural, but noncount nouns cannot be made plural.

LESSON 30

Definite and Indefinite Articles: Known or New?

Sample Errors

SAMPLE 1: ✘ **Masanori really had the good idea.**

SAMPLE 2: ✘ **Effie went into a phone booth and picked up a receiver.**

What's the Problem?

English has two fundamentally different types of articles: **definite** and **indefinite**. Every time you use an article, you must correctly decide which type is appropriate. Since the factors that govern the choice between definite and indefinite articles are complex and subtle, it is easy to make a choice that sends a message you do not really intend. However, before discussing the problems of article selection, let's clarify some terminology.

The **definite article** is always *the*, which is used with all types of **common nouns:** singular and plural, **count** and **noncount.** The situation with indefinite articles is more complicated. The **indefinite articles** *a* and *an* are used *only* with singular count nouns. With plural count nouns and all noncount nouns, the word *some* is used instead of *a* or *an*. Since the rules that govern *some* are exactly parallel to the rules that govern *a* and *an*, this lesson will group them all together as indefinite articles.

What Causes the Problem?

ART

Let's illustrate the basic distinction between definite and indefinite articles with the singular count noun *truck*.

- Using the definite article *the* (*the truck*) means two things, *both* of which must be true: (1) the writer has a particular truck in mind, *and* (2) the writer can reasonably assume that the reader can identify *which* truck the writer has in mind.
- Using the indefinite article *a* or *an* (*a truck*) means *either* (1) that the writer does *not* have a particular truck in mind *or* (2) that, even if the writer has a particular truck in mind, he or she does not assume that the reader can identify *which* truck the writer has in mind.

For example, in Sample 1, the reader has no idea what Masanori's good idea is, so the definite article *the* should be changed to the indefinite article *a*: *Masanori really had* a *good idea*.

Diagnostic Exercise **(Corrected sentences appear on page 329.)**

Correct all errors in the following paragraph using the first correction as a model. The number in parentheses at the end of the paragraph indicates how many errors you should find.

Doctors have long known that we need to have iron in our diet. Recently, however, ~~the~~ *a* new study has revealed that we may be getting too much iron. The human body keeps all an iron it digests. An only way we lose stored iron in a body is through bleeding. John Murray, the researcher at the University of Minnesota, discovered that people who live on the very low iron diet may have the greatly reduced risk of the heart attack. Another study found that diets high in meat have the strong correlation with a high risk of heart disease. Apparently, when people have the high level of iron, excess iron may worsen the effect of cholesterol. (9)

Fixing This Problem in Your Writing

Here is a useful strategy for testing your use of definite and indefinite articles: if you have a specific person, place, or thing in mind when you use a noun, test the second assumption: can you reasonably assume that the reader will be able to identify which meaning you have in mind? If this assumption can be met, use "the"; if this assumption cannot be met, then you must use an indefinite article, either "some" or "a" or "an" depending on the initial sound of the noun being modified. Here are some tips that will help you decide whether you can reasonably assume the reader will be able to identify which meaning you have in mind:

PREVIOUS-MENTION TIP: Use the definite article if you have already mentioned the noun.

TIP APPLIED: **My cat nearly caught a bird. The bird barely escaped with its life.**

The first mention of *bird* requires an indefinite article. From that point on, the definite article *the* is always used to refer to that bird because the reader knows which bird the writer means: the one that the writer's cat nearly caught.

For Example . . .

DEFINED-BY-MODIFIERS TIP: Use the definite article if the noun is followed by modifiers that uniquely identify the noun.

TIP APPLIED: **There was an accident at the corner of Fifth Street and Riverside Drive.**

The reader can tell which corner the writer has in mind because the modifier *of Fifth Street and Riverside Drive* automatically defines the corner.

NORMAL-EXPECTATIONS TIP: Use the definite article if the noun meets our normal expectations about the way things work.

SAMPLE 2: **✗ Effie went into a phone booth and picked up a receiver.**

Even though the receiver has not been mentioned or defined by modifiers, you would use the definite article *the* because the reader expects phone booths to contain telephones with receivers.

CORRECTION: **Effie went into a phone booth and picked up the receiver.**

UNIQUENESS TIP: Use the definite article if the noun has a uniqueness that everybody would be expected to know about.

TIP APPLIED: **The sun was beginning to rise above the horizon.**

Unless you are writing a science-fiction novel, there are only one sun and only one horizon, and everybody already knows about them.

Now You Try It, 1 **(Corrected sentences appear on page 329.)**

The following sentences contain one or more correct uses of the word the (underlined). Assume that there is no previous context that these sentences refer to. In each case, indicate which of the four tips in this lesson provides your reason for using the definite article.

EXAMPLE: **I am having trouble with my computer; there is a strange flicker on the screen.**

REASON: **Normal expectations.**

1. We heard a car stop outside the house. A girl got out of the car and came toward us.
   Reason:
2. Joel Cairo came into the office and put a package on the desk.
   Reason:
3. I wish I had the time to read the books on the *New York Times* list.
   Reason:
4. Yesterday we watched a little-league baseball game. The players were not very good, but they were fun to watch.
   Reason:
5. Professor Chou wrote a well-known paper on the fall of the Roman Empire.
   Reason:

Now You Try It, 2 **(Corrected sentences appear on page 329.)**

Fill in the blanks with the correct article: *the, a, an,* or *some.*

EXAMPLE: **When I got home, I went into __the__ kitchen and fixed myself __a__ sandwich.**

1. _______ new airport in Denver had problems with its baggage system.
2. Some people came in and bought _______ postcard and _______ stamps.
3. Just before we landed, an attendant came down _______ aisle and collected _______ headphones from _______ passengers.
4. Most folk tales seem to involve _______ young hero who is required to perform _______ dangerous deeds.
5. During the performance, there was _______ loud cry from the back of _______ auditorium.

Now You Try It, 3

On a separate sheet of paper, write two sentences that use each of the following nouns. In the first sentence, use the noun with the appropriate indirect article *a*, *an*, or *some*. In the second sentence, refer to the noun using the definite article *the*.

EXAMPLE: **ball gowns**

ANSWER: **We saw some beautiful ball gowns in a catalog. The girls picked out the ball gowns they liked the best.**

1. pickup truck
2. jokes
3. misunderstanding
4. confusion
5. ammunition

Editing Practice, 1 **(Corrected sentences appear on page 329.)**

Correct all errors in the following paragraph using the first correction as a model. The number in parentheses at the end of the paragraph indicates how many errors you should find.

All of us have seen movies that were completely forgettable except for ~~the~~ a single scene. For some reason, this scene has always stuck in our minds. Often, a scene is not even a major part of a plot. It is usually some little piece of character development that struck us, or it is the funny or whimsical episode. For example, a few years ago I saw the French film whose title I can no longer even recall. In this otherwise forgettable movie, there was the long scene that showed someone fixing dinner and chopping the big pile of garlic while carrying on the long and animated conversation with the dinner guests. Everything in a scene was perfectly normal except that the cook was wearing the mask and snorkel while he prepared a garlic. (10)

Editing Practice, 2 **(Corrected sentences appear on page 329.)**

Correct all errors in the following paragraph using the first correction as a model. The number in parentheses at the end of the paragraph indicates how many errors you should find.

My nomination for the Unforgettable Scenes from Forgettable Movies Award is ~~the~~ *a* scene in one of Humphrey Bogart's last movies, *Beat the Devil*. A movie is set in rural Italy on the Amalfi Coast. Bogart and Sydney Greenstreet are taking the taxi up the narrow mountain road. Just below a top, a taxi stalls, and they have to get out to push it. A driver walks alongside a driver's seat and steers as Bogart and Sydney Greenstreet push from behind. Bogart and Greenstreet get into the terrible argument as they are pushing, and a taxi driver is dying to hear what they are talking about. All three men get so involved in an argument that they forget what they are doing. (10)

Editing Practice, 3

Correct all errors in the following paragraphs using the first correction as a model. The number in parentheses at the end of each paragraph indicates how many errors you should find.

Probably ~~a~~ *the* classic example of an unforgettable episode from a less-than-memorable movie is the cartoon characters created for the opening credits in the Peter Sellers movie *The Pink Panther*. As you may or may not recall, there are no panthers in a movie, pink or otherwise. A term *Pink Panther* refers to the fabulous diamond. It is called the Pink Panther because a diamond has the pink shadow in its center. In the movie, Peter Sellers plays Inspector Clouseau, the comically inept Parisian policeman. Clouseau is after the international jewel thief, who, of course, is intent on stealing a Pink Panther. (8)

The Pink Panther cartoon was so popular that a whole series of Inspector Clouseau comedies starring Peter Sellers are now known as the Pink Panther movies. A Pink Panther character has taken on the life of its own, independent of an original movie. (3)

Writing Practice

On your own paper, write a paragraph or two that describes your favorite unforgettable scene from a forgettable movie. Use the Proofreading Checklist to examine all the definite and indefinite articles in your essay and to make certain that they are correct.

PROOFREADING CHECKLIST

Using Definite and Indefinite Articles in Your Writing

- Use the definite article *the* when you are referring to a specific person, place, or thing *and* you can reasonably assume that the reader knows which specific person, place, or thing you are referring to.
- If you do not have a particular example of the noun in mind *or* you cannot assume that the reader will know what it is, then use the indefinite article *a* or *an* with singular count nouns, and use *some* with plural count nouns and all noncount nouns.
- Here are some situations in which the definite article *the* is likely to be correct:
  - The noun has been *previously mentioned.*
  - The noun is *defined by modifiers.*
  - Readers would *normally expect your meaning.*
  - Readers would know your meaning because *the noun is unique.*

THE BOTTOM LINE

Use *the* only when *the* reader knows what *the* noun refers to.

LESSON 31

Making Generalizations without Articles

Sample Errors

SAMPLE 1: **✗ The barn is always full of <u>some</u> cats.**

SAMPLE 2: **✗ Our family usually has <u>the</u> fish for dinner on Fridays.**

What's the Problem?

Non-native speakers of English (and sometimes native speakers) incorrectly use an **article** with a **noncount noun** or with a plural **count noun** to make a generalization.

What Causes the Problem?

Generally speaking, nouns in English must be preceded by an article or some similar modifier. However, there is one major exception to this rule that non-native speakers often overlook: to signal a generalization about a noun, use *a noncount noun or a plural count noun with no article or other noun modifier.*

For example, in Sample 1, the writer uses the plural count noun *cats.* In this sentence, the word *cats* does not refer to any particular actual cats; instead, the writer is making a generalization about the category of animals that inhabit the barn. Therefore, Sample 1 should not include the indefinite article *some.* (See Lesson 30 for an explanation of why *some* is treated as a kind of indefinite article.)

SAMPLE 1, CORRECTED: **The barn is always full of cats.**

NO ART

In Sample 2, the writer uses the definite article *the* with the noun *fish.* In this sentence, the word *fish* does not refer to any actual fish that the family had on any particular day. Sample 2 is a generalization about the family's typical meal on Fridays. Therefore, Sample 2 should not include the article *the.*

SAMPLE 2, CORRECTED: **Our family usually has fish for dinner on Fridays.**

Diagnostic Exercise **(Corrected sentences appear on page 330.)**

Correct all errors in the following paragraph using the first correction as a model. The number in parentheses at the end of the paragraph indicates how many errors you should find.

~~The~~ scientists have long known that the honeybees are somehow able to tell some other bees where to look for some food. In the 1940's, Karl von Frisch of the University of Munich discovered that the type of the dance that the bees make when they return to their beehive is significant. It seems that the honeybees are able to signal both the direction of the food that they found and its approximate distance from their hive to the bees who had remained at the hive. (6)

Fixing This Problem in Your Writing

Anytime writers use a noncount noun or a plural count noun, they must monitor the meaning of the noun to see whether they are using that noun to make a generalization. If that is the case, then they would expect to use no article. Following are some tips that may help you recognize when a noun is being used in a general sense.

ADVERB-OF-FREQUENCY TIP: Look for such adverbs of frequency as *always, often, generally, frequently,* or *usually.*

Adverbs of frequency are often used in sentences that describe habitual or repeated actions—typically a sign of a generalization. Notice that both of the sample sentences use adverbs of frequency.

NO ART

SAMPLE 1, CORRECTED: **The barn is <u>always</u> full of cats.**

SAMPLE 2, CORRECTED: **Our family <u>usually</u> has fish for dinner on Fridays.**

PRESENT TENSE TIP: Sentences used for making generalizations are often written in the present tense.

Writers usually use the present tense to make generalizations (see Lesson 25: Present, Past, and Tense Shifting), so be especially sure to check noncount nouns and plural count nouns in sentences that use the present tense to see whether these nouns are being used to make generalizations. Notice, for instance, that both of the sample sentences are in the present tense.

"MOST" TIP: A noun that can be modified by the word *most* is probably being used to make a generalization.

For Example . . .

You can modify the noun in the following sentence

Textbooks have really gotten to be expensive

by adding the word *most* to confirm that you are using *textbooks* as a generalization; thus, it will be used without any article.

TIP APPLIED: **Most textbooks have really gotten to be expensive.**

NO-MODIFIERS TIP: A noun used for making a generalization is not usually restricted by any modifiers that follow the noun.

Modifiers after a noun usually restrict the meaning of the noun so that it is not a generalization about all nouns.

For Example . . .

Compare the following two sentences.

NO MODIFIER AFTER THE NOUN: **Cheese is very salty.**

MODIFIER AFTER THE NOUN: **The cheese in the refrigerator is very salty.**

The first sentence is an unrestricted generalization about all cheese; therefore, we do not use an article. The second sentence is talking only about the cheese that is in the refrigerator. Since we are referring to a particular piece of cheese, we must use the definite article *the* in this sentence.

Now You Try It, 1 **(Corrected sentences appear on page 330.)**

In the following sentences, underline any noncount nouns and plural count nouns that are used for making generalizations. Cross out any articles incorrectly used with these nouns. Assume that there is no previous context that these sentences refer to.

EXAMPLE: **In the late afternoon, there is usually a buildup of ~~some~~ clouds.**

1. Advances in the technology make it very difficult for the school systems to prepare the students for the workplace.
2. The development is always limited by the resources that are available.
3. The sticks and stones will break my bones, but the words will never hurt me. [children's rhyme]
4. We have to be careful driving on the wet roads just after the summer showers because the oil on the pavement has not been washed away yet.
5. The natural gas is formed by the decay of the plants and animals.

Now You Try It, 2 **(Corrected sentences appear on page 330.)**

In the following sentences, underline any noncount nouns and plural count nouns that are used for making generalizations. Cross out any articles incorrectly used with these nouns. Assume that there is no previous context that these sentences refer to.

EXAMPLE: **~~The~~ mammals feed their newborn offspring by nursing.**

1. As a general rule, the cost of modernizing the kitchens will be recovered when the house is sold.
2. The key issue in any scientific controversy is agreeing on what constitutes some relevant evidence.
3. The tropical diseases are poorly understood because so little research has been devoted to them.
4. The appointment of ambassadors requires the congressional approval.
5. In many towns, the shopping malls have taken the business from older stores.

Now You Try It, 3

For each of the following nouns, write a sentence that uses the noun to make a generalization. Use the noun either as a singular noncount noun or as a plural count noun without an article.

EXAMPLE: **confrontation** *The school started training sessions to help the students cope with confrontations that could lead to violence.*

1. conflict

2. transportation

3. stereotype

4. beef

5. drug

Editing Practice, 1 **(Corrected sentences appear on page 330.)**

Correct all errors in the following paragraph using the first correction as a model. The number in parentheses at the end of the paragraph indicates how many errors you should find.

The history of ~~the~~ furniture reflects the history of the culture. Relatively little is known about the furniture of the ancient societies, simply because furniture is usually made of the perishable materials—wood and sometimes fabric—that have not survived. Our limited knowledge of Egyptian, Greek, and Roman furniture is based mostly on the paintings and the sculptures. The only actual surviving pieces of furniture are from the burials. For example, King Tut's tomb in Egypt contained piles of elegantly decorated royal furniture. About the only surviving examples of everyday Roman furniture are from the two cities near Naples that were buried under the tons of volcanic ash from the eruption of Mt. Vesuvius on August 24, 79 A.D. (8)

Editing Practice, 2 **(Corrected sentences appear on page 330.)**

Correct all errors in the following paragraphs using the first correction as a model. The number in parentheses at the end of each paragraph indicates how many errors you should find.

The American linguist Deborah Tannen is best known for her books about the differences in the language of ~~the~~ men and women. Her books show that the men tend to use language in a very competitive way. For example, the conversations among a group of men are marked by some competition to be the center of the attention. (3)

Women tend to be careful about taking the turns in the conversations. Even in the animated conversations, the interruptions tend to be supportive rather than confrontational. (3)

Editing Practice, 3

Correct all errors in the following paragraph using the first correction as a model. The number in parentheses at the end of the paragraph indicates how many errors you should find.

Dr. Tannen maintains that ~~the~~ conversational styles are generally the result of the way that children grow up. The little boys and little girls have the very different forms of the social interaction. The different conversational styles that they learn to use are a natural result of their different social needs. For example, until the puberty, the sexes are largely self-segregated—boys play with boys, and girls play with girls. The nature of their play is quite different. The boys' play is based on the competition. The girls' play is much more cooperative and democratic. (6)

Dr. Tannen believes that neither form of the conversation is superior to the other. However, there are often some big problems when the men and

women talk to each other, because each group assumes that the other group plays by the same rules that it does—but the other group doesn't! (2)

Writing Practice

On a separate sheet of paper, write a paragraph or two of generalizations about the differences in male and female language that you have observed. If you come from another country, do you think that Dr. Tannen's observations about Americans' conversational styles can be applied to your country? Use the Proofreading Checklist to identify every noncount noun and plural count noun in your essay, and see whether they are used for making generalizations. Correct any errors you might have made.

PROOFREADING CHECKLIST

Using Nouns for Making Generalizations in Your Writing

- Whenever you use a noncount noun or a plural count noun, be sure to check to see whether you are using that noun to make a generalization. If you are making a generalization, you probably won't want to use the indefinite articles *a*, *an*, or *some*.
- Here are four tips that will help you recognize when a noun is being used to make a generalization.
  - Look for adverbs of frequency such as *generally, usually, often,* and *always*.
  - Writers often use the present tense when they want to make generalizations.
  - To test whether a noun is being used to make a generalization, see if you can put *most* in front of the noun.
  - Nouns used for generalizations tend *not* to be followed by modifiers.

THE BOTTOM LINE

Check noncount and plural count *nouns* to see whether they make a generalization. If so, they do not need *articles.*

UNIT SEVEN
PUTTING IT ALL TOGETHER

Every time you use a common noun, you must choose whether to use an article or not; if you do need to use an article, you must choose which one it should be. These choices are governed by four sets of decisions:

- Decision 1: *Generalization?* Is the noun (whether a noncount noun or a plural count noun) being used for making a generalization (see Lesson 31)? If the answer is yes, use *no* article at all. If the answer is no, then you must make the following decision.
- Decision 2: *Known or New?* Is your intended meaning of the noun "known" to the reader or is it "new" (see Lesson 30)? If the intended meaning is known to the reader, use the definite article *the*. If the meaning will be new, use an indefinite article: *a*, *an*, or *some*. The choice of indefinite article is determined by the next two decisions.
- Decision 3: *Plural or Singular?* If the new noun is plural, then you must use *some*. If the new noun is singular, then you must decide whether it is a count or a noncount noun. That brings you to the final decision.
- Decision 4: *Count or Noncount?* If the singular noun is a count noun, then you must use the indefinite article *a*. If the singular noun is a noncount noun, use *some* (see Lesson 29).

Review

The *decision tree* on page 261 shows you how these four sets of decisions flow step by step from Decision 1 to Decision 4. Track the choice of articles for the underlined nouns down through the decision tree.

- *Mugs hold more than cups*. (Using no article with the plural nouns *cups* and *mugs* shows that we are making a *generalization* about the nature of all cups and mugs.)
- *Chicken is good for you*. (*Chicken* is a noncount noun. The writer is making a *generalization* about chicken as a category of food.)

- *I want* ***the*** *cup on the bottom shelf.* (Which cup the writer wants is identified by the restrictive modifier *on the bottom shelf.* Therefore, *cup* is a *known* noun, and the writer must use the definite article *the.*)
- *I want* ***some*** *cups.* (Since there is no way that the reader could know which cups the writer has in mind, *cups* is a *new* noun. We use *some* with new plural count nouns.)
- *I want* ***a*** *cup.* (Since there is no way that the reader could know which cup the writer has in mind, *cup* is a *new* noun. We use *a* or *an* with new singular count nouns.)
- *I want* ***some*** *chicken.* (Since there are no modifiers to define which chicken the writer wants, *chicken* is a *new* noun. We use *some* with new noncount nouns.)

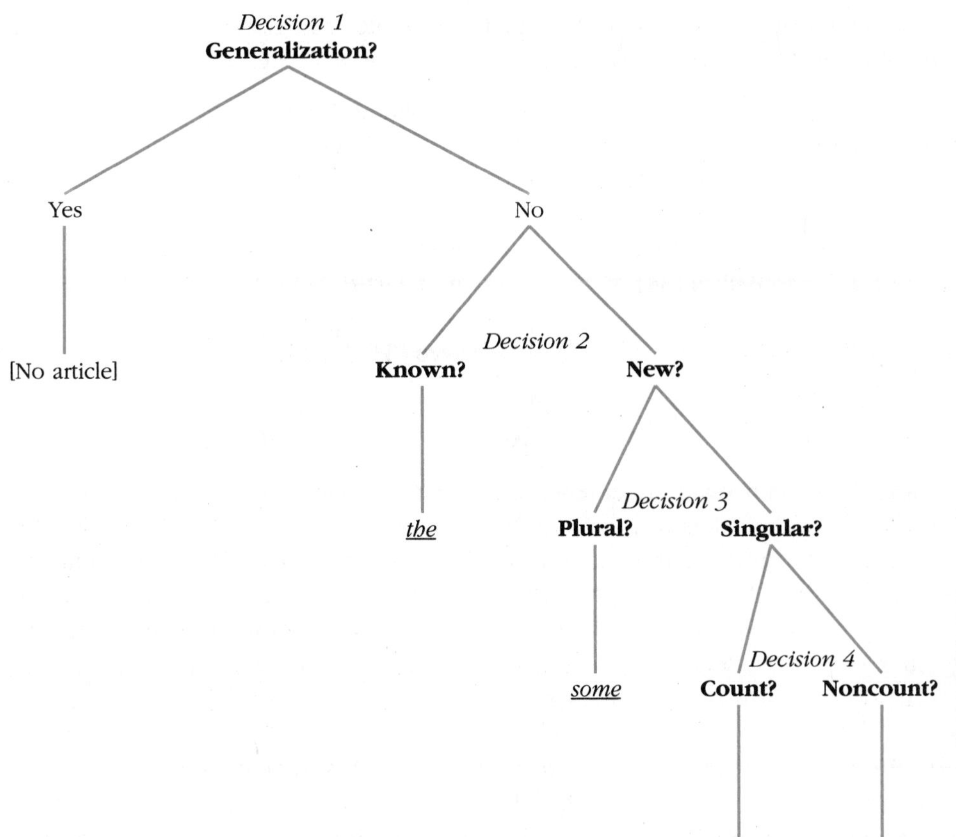

ART

UNIT EIGHT
Sentence Clarity and Style

OVERVIEW

Terms That Can Help You Understand Sentence Clarity

If you are not familiar with any of the following terms that appear in this unit, look them up in the Guide to Grammar Terminology beginning on page 1. The numbers in parentheses indicate the lessons in which each term appears.

active (35)
adjective (33)
complete sentence (33)
coordinating conjunction (34)
dangling modifier (33)
faulty parallelism (34)
gerund (34)
infinitive (34)
misplaced modifier (32)
noun (33, 34)
parallelism (34)
participle (33)
passive (35)
past participle (35)
subject (33)
verb (33, 34, 35)

The Nuts and Bolts of Sentence Clarity

Many things can make a sentence clear or not clear. Indeed, an error of any sort can cause readers to be confused. In this unit, however, we focus on four problems that involve the structure of the entire sentence: dangling modifiers, misplaced modifiers, faulty parallelism, and ineffective use of the passive voice.

The first two problems involve a similar concept: how modifiers relate to other parts of a sentence. The last two problems concern the shape of the verbs or verb forms used in a sentence.

1. *Sentences containing single-word modifiers.* Most modifiers are single words, but these, too, must be placed as near as possible to the word they modify. Notice the different meanings in the following sentences caused merely by moving around a single modifier.

Only Monica wrote to say that she would visit me.

Monica only wrote to say that she would visit me.

Monica wrote to say only that she would visit me.

Monica wrote to say that only she would visit me.

Some misplaced modifiers are more subtle, but they, too, should be avoided in formal writing (see Lesson 32).

2. *Sentences that begin with participial phrases.* A participial phrase is a phrase based on a participle—a word that once was a verb but whose ending has been changed. Each of the following sentences uses a participial phrase correctly, and the participle is underlined.

   Reading over her paper, Alena discovered two misspellings.

   Looking over its shoulder, the creature saw it was being followed.

   It is important that the participial phrase be followed very quickly by the word it is modifying, as in the preceding examples (see Lesson 33).

3. *Sentences that use* and *to connect verb forms which end in* -ing *or appear after* to. If you combine these verb forms, they should all be one or the other—either *-ing* verbs *or* verbs preceded by *to.* The next two examples do not contain errors because the underlined verb forms are parallel.

   Sylvia likes to read poetry and to write her own poems.

   My mother wrote a book about birdwatching, hiking, and collecting leaves.

   If we changed *to read poetry* to *writing poetry,* then the first example sentence would have faulty parallelism. The same problem would occur if we changed *hiking* to *to hike* in the second example (see Lesson 34).

4. *Sentences that needlessly use the passive voice.* In the passive voice, the subject of the sentence is not performing the action; it is *receiving* the action. In the active voice, the subject actually performs an action. Although the passive voice is not necessarily an error, many readers prefer that you use the active voice instead (see Lesson 35).

   PASSIVE VOICE: **The door was slammed by Val.**

   ACTIVE VOICE: **Val slammed the door.**

Can You Detect Problems Involving Sentence Clarity and Style?

(Corrected sentences appear on page 331.)

Using the first correction as a model, make whatever changes are needed to eliminate misplaced modifiers, dangling participles, faulty parallelism, and passive voice. The number in parentheses at the end of each paragraph indicates how many changes you should make.

I first went to college some fifteen years ago but decided to stay at home and raise my two children. Back then, I and most of my fellow students wrote papers the old-fashioned way: by typing them. Realizing the need to be more up to date, ^ *I decided that* my goal this year was to improve my word-processing skills, do most assigned papers on a computer, and to learn how to use a graphics program. My major motivations were keeping up with modern technology and to make it less of a chore to revise my papers. (2)

However, I noticed all the younger students for whom using a computer was second nature. I was intimidated by these students. Feeling insecure, my pride wouldn't allow me to ask them for help, go to the computer lab for tutoring, or to ask my teachers for advice. Then, I began noticing that even many of the younger students were not experts at all. Many, in fact, did not know how to type, turn on a computer, or to insert a disk into the computer. I signed up for a computer class covering the basics, and by the end of the quarter, I could comfortably do all my papers on computer. Next quarter, the graphics programs will be tackled by me. (5)

LESSON 32

Misplaced Modifiers

Sample Errors

SAMPLE 1: **✗ Carole barely took ten minutes to finish the American history test.**

SAMPLE 2: **✗ The landlord told me yesterday the rent was due.**

What's the Problem?

A **modifier** is a word or group of words that describes something, somebody, or an action. A modifier should be placed in a sentence in a position where readers can easily determine what the modifier is describing. For instance, *angry* and *quickly* are modifiers in *The angry teacher quickly left the room.* The word *angry* is clearly modifying *teacher*, while *quickly* is modifying *left.*

A misplaced modifier occurs when readers cannot easily determine what a modifier is supposed to be describing. In Samples 1 and 2, the underlined modifiers should be placed elsewhere to avoid misreading. In Sample 1, *barely* isn't describing how Carole *took*; instead, *barely* is placing a limit on the amount of time—not quite ten minutes. In Sample 2, is *yesterday* describing *when the landlord said something* or is it indicating *when the rent was due?*

In this lesson, we focus on single-word modifiers that are frequently misplaced. A related problem is the dangling modifier, which typically involves groups of words at the beginning of a sentence (see Lesson 33).

What Causes the Problem?

Misplaced modifiers sometimes are difficult to detect because they often do not create an ungrammatical sentence; that is, the sentence structure can look perfectly OK. The problem is that the sentence may not accurately reflect the writer's intended meaning. The meaning of a sentence can change dramatically depending on where a modifier is placed. Compare, for instance, the meaning of *Only I love you* with *I love only you.*

Writers are rarely around to correct any misunderstanding or to answer questions from readers, so extra care with language—such as with modifiers—is especially important in writing.

Diagnostic Exercise **(Corrected sentences appear on page 331.)**

Correct all errors in the following paragraph using the first correction as a model. The number in parentheses at the end of the paragraph indicates how many errors you should find.

My brother called ^today and said he would travel to Europe ~~today~~. He plans to go as soon as his school is out this summer. A travel agent told him it would only cost $400 for a round-trip ticket to London. The agent he spoke with enthusiastically said that he should take advantage of this price. My brother asked whether I wanted to go with him, but I have already committed myself to a summer job. He almost talked for an hour before I convinced him I couldn't go with him. (3)

Fixing This Problem in Your Writing

A good way to start is to locate any modifiers that have the potential to be misplaced. This is not an easy task, but the following tip will help you pick out most such modifiers.

> "OFTEN" TIP: Look for each use of *often* or for any word that could be replaced by *often* (such as *just, simply, hardly, barely, only,* and *nearly*). You might change the meaning of the overall sentence by doing the *often* substitution, but the sentence should still be grammatical.

Once you locate these modifiers, closely examine each to see whether it is placed so that it is clearly modifying the word it most logically describes. For instance, Sample 1 could easily be reworded as follows.

SAMPLE 1: **✗ Carole barely took ten minutes to finish the American history test.**

TIP APPLIED: **Carole often took ten minutes to finish the American history test.**

MM

Now that you have located a *possible* problem, you must decide whether *barely* is truly misplaced. Look at all possible words that the modifier could be describing, and reword the sentence so that readers will not be confused about what is being modified. Often, all you need to do is move the modifier. Since *barely* is placing a limit on *time* (not on *taking*), you should reword Sample 1 as follows.

SAMPLE 1, CORRECTED: **Carole took barely ten minutes to finish the test.**

For Example . . .

By applying the *often* tip to Sample 2, we see that *yesterday* is, indeed, a modifier.

SAMPLE 2: ✘ **The landlord told me yesterday the rent was due.**

TIP APPLIED: **The landlord told me often the rent was due.**

But is *yesterday* misplaced? It is because it could be describing *told* or could be indicating when the rent was due. No one can know how to correct Sample 2 without knowing what the writer intended, but either of these next two revisions would correct the problem.

OPTION 1: **Yesterday, the landlord told me the rent was due.**

OPTION 2: **The landlord told me the rent was due yesterday.**

The *Often* Tip helps us locate a *potential* misplaced modifier in the next sentence.

We seldom watch television.

TIP APPLIED: **We often watch television.**

Can *often* possibly describe anything other than *watch*? No. Thus, the original sentence is fine.

Now You Try It, 1 **(Corrected sentences appear on page 331.)**

First, locate *potential* misplaced modifiers by determining whether any words could be replaced by *often*. Next, write *OK* above each correct sentence, or correct the sentence by moving any misplaced modifier to a position that clarifies what the modifier describes. Your correction might depend on how you interpret the sentence.

often
slowly
EXAMPLE: **The man who had been ^ dancing ~~slowly~~ ^ began laughing.**

1. The teacher almost gave us a pop quiz on the reading material.
2. Hamsters are only pregnant for 16 days.
3. We almost read thirty poems for this class.
4. My biology teacher said that there are 138,000 varieties of butterflies and moths yesterday.
5. We saw a man gesturing angrily talking to an officer.

Now You Try It, 2 **(Corrected sentences appear on page 331.)**

First, locate *potential* misplaced modifiers by determining whether any words could be replaced by *often*. Next, write *OK* above each correct sentence, or correct the sentence by moving any misplaced modifier to a position that clarifies what the modifier describes. Your correction might depend on how you interpret the sentence.

often
nearly
EXAMPLE: **Jean ~~nearly~~ ^ talked for ^ two hours on the phone.**

1. The woman skating slowly asked me to turn off my radio.
2. Ira said yesterday he found my missing car keys.
3. He only bought it for a hundred dollars!
4. We only located three sources for our group paper.
5. Fishing often gives me a good deal of pleasure and time alone.

Now You Try It, 3

Use each word in a sentence so that it clearly modifies an appropriate concept.

EXAMPLE: **barely** *I barely knew you until we dated.*

1. only

2. today

3. quickly

4. just

5. merely

Editing Practice, 1 **(Corrected sentences appear on page 331.)**

Correct all errors in the following paragraphs using the first correction as a model. The number in parentheses at the end of each paragraph indicates how many errors you should find.

My friend Janet ^*regularly* tells me what her literature teacher discusses ~~regularly.~~ Janet said yesterday her literature teacher discussed comic books. That topic does not seem appropriate for a college-level course, but the teacher brought comics up while covering popular literature because comics reveal the values of a culture as well as helping promote these values. (1)

Take, for instance, the popular character Batman. The character today is violent and even scary to law-abiding citizens. The fact that he lurks in the shadows and is a creature of the night frequently is interesting. Perhaps readers envy Batman for being outside the law. Indeed, heroes who border on being lawbreakers commonly are best-selling characters in the comics—a trend suggesting that readers barely seem satisfied with governmental law enforcement and yearn to take matters into their own hands. (3)

Editing Practice, 2 **(Corrected sentences appear on page 332.)**

Correct all errors in the following paragraph using the first correction as a model. The number in parentheses at the end of the paragraph indicates how many errors you should find.

Generally, a

~~A~~ ^ person whose brain is damaged ~~generally~~ runs the risk of aphasia. Sometimes, this disorder, called *dysphasia*, happens when damage occurs to the part of the brain devoted to language production or comprehension. All people with aphasia have some language ability remaining, but it has been impaired in some way. Strokes almost account for 85 percent of aphasia cases. Eating an unhealthy diet, avoiding exercise, or smoking frequently can cause arteries to become clogged, a situation that can lead to strokes. Another cause of aphasia is head injuries from accidents. About a quarter of all penetrating head injuries result in aphasia, with males accounting for most cases. However, nearly a quarter of all cases involve short-term aphasia, with recovery occurring within three months. After six months, though, full recovery is unlikely. (2)

Editing Practice, 3

Correct all errors in the following paragraphs using the first correction as a model. The number in parentheses at the end of each paragraph indicates how many errors you should find.

later

While going to class, I saw a friend who was talking to two men. I ^ discovered ~~later~~ Hank was upset because the two men had been handing out leaflets and warning people abruptly the world would end. I found out that they claimed yesterday the world would be destroyed around 2001. (2)

Hank had politely disagreed with them and asked them for evidence. He said that he had never seen such belligerence on campus; the two men had angered several students by yelling at them and even blocking their paths.

Hank told the two men he would call campus administrators to prevent such harassment, and that is when they decided loudly to speak to him. Eventually, they began shouting at Hank. Hank was concerned that these two people would cause students to be annoyed with anyone who wishes graciously to share his or her beliefs on campus. (2)

Writing Practice

On your own paper, write a paragraph or two about something that took place at school and bothered you. Use the Proofreading Checklist to find and correct any misplaced modifiers in your writing.

PROOFREADING CHECKLIST

Avoiding Misplaced Modifiers in Your Writing

- Look for any use of *often* or any word that could be replaced by *often* (the meaning will change, but the sentence will make sense). These words have the potential to be misplaced modifiers.
- Once you locate these words, closely examine each to see whether it is placed so that it is clearly modifying the word you want it to describe.
- A good rule of thumb is that a modifier should be placed as close as possible to the word it modifies.
- To correct a misplaced modifier, you might simply need to move it to a position closer to the word it modifies—and away from any other word that it could possibly modify.

THE BOTTOM LINE

Modifiers are *usually* placed close to the words they *best* describe.

LESSON 33
Dangling Modifiers

Sample Errors

SAMPLE 1: ✗ **Writing long into the night, my hopes of finishing the paper on time grew.**

SAMPLE 2: ✗ **Damaged beyond all repair, I threw my watch away.**

What's the Problem?

Often, a sentence starts off with a modifier that describes the person, place, or thing that comes right after the modifier. A **dangling modifier** is a problem that occurs when the modifier is not clearly or sensibly describing the word immediately following it. This lesson focuses on one of the most common types of dangling modifiers: the *dangling participle.*

A **participle** is simply a special type of *adjective* (an *adjective* is a word used to describe a person, place, or thing). What makes a participle special is that at first it looks like a verb. Participles modify nouns, as in *the laughing clown* or *a broken glass.*

Usually, a dangling participle involves more than just a participle acting by itself. Instead, the participle is the first word in a group of words that function together to describe something. This entire group is called a **participial phrase**. The following participial phrase (underlined) is used *correctly*; the noun it modifies is underlined twice.

Laughing out loud, Jerry looked really happy.

An error occurs when the phrase is in the wrong place or has nothing in the sentence that it can logically describe.

What Causes the Problem?

To create an interesting style, writers often use a participial phrase at the beginning of a sentence. The error occurs when the phrase cannot logically modify the noun right after it. Participial phrases—like all adjectives—should be placed close to the person, place, or thing they describe. A dangling participle is not placed close to a word it can logically modify. In Sample 1, for example, the noun nearest to the participial phrase is *hopes*, but logically the phrase can't be referring to this word.

Diagnostic Exercise **(Corrected sentences appear on page 332.)**

Correct all errors in the following paragraph using the first correction as a model. The number in parentheses at the end of the paragraph indicates how many errors you should find.

Studying for hours, ^*I felt* my eyes ~~grew~~ ^*grow* tired. I felt I could not read another word. I walked to the store for a drink. When I got there, the store was closed. Deciding against walking another mile to another store, the thought crossed my mind that maybe I would just quit studying and get some sleep. I returned home and tried to decide what to do. Torn between the need to sleep and the need to study, the alarm clock went off and made me realize it was time for class. (2)

Fixing This Problem in Your Writing

Here is a tip to help you see whether a participial phrase is dangling.

> NEW-SENTENCE TIP: Turn the participial phrase into a complete sentence. Be sure the subject of the new sentence is the noun that is closest to the participial phrase in the original sentence. Does the new sentence sound odd? If so, the original sentence has a dangling modifier.

For instance, the introductory phrase in Sample 1 can be turned into a new sentence by (1) using *my hopes* as the subject and (2) using *were* plus the participial phrase as the verb.

SAMPLE 1: ✗ **<u>Writing long into the night</u>, my hopes of finishing the paper on time grew.**

TIP APPLIED: ✗ **My hopes were writing long into the night.**

The test sentence simply doesn't make sense (*hopes* can't write). However, the original sentence was really saying the same thing. Here is one way to correct a dangling modifier.

CORRECTION STRATEGY: Place the correct noun after the phrase. That is, keep the participial phrase where it is, but place the correct person, place, or thing *immediately* after the phrase. For Sample 1, we added *I* since this is the person being described.

SAMPLE 1, CORRECTED: **Writing long into the night, I found my hopes of finishing the paper on time were growing.**

The same tip and correction strategy works for Sample 2.

SAMPLE 2: ✗ **Damaged beyond all repair, I threw my watch away.**

TIP APPLIED: ✗ **I was damaged beyond all repair.**

SAMPLE 2, CORRECTED: **Damaged beyond all repair, my watch was useless, so I threw it away.**

For Example . . .

Try the tip to make sure the following participial phrases are *correctly* used. (The phrases are underlined.) The test sentences make sense, so there are, indeed, no errors in the original sentences.

CORRECT USE: **Walking alone, Mary stopped to pick up a broken watch.**

TIP APPLIED: **Mary walked alone.**

CORRECT USE: **Startled by the noise, I suddenly awoke.**

TIP APPLIED: **I was startled by the noise.**

CORRECT USE: **Running to class, Paulette slipped and fell.**

TIP APPLIED: **Paulette was running to class.**

Now You Try It, 1 **(Corrected sentences appear on page 332.)**

Apply the New-Sentence Tip to each of the following sentences. Write *OK* above the original if the test sentence makes sense, or correct the original if the test sentence sounds odd.

Panic was surprised by the explosion.

the audience panicked.

EXAMPLE: **Surprised by the explosion, ^ ~~panic spread throughout the audience.~~**

1. Excited by the fans, a touchdown was quickly scored by the home team.

2. Hoping there was plenty of air in the tank, the scuba diver decided to explore the sunken wreck a little longer.

3. Waving good-bye to his mother, Paul's eyes grew misty.

4. Using his last check, Deon wrote the clerk a check for gas.

5. Running up the stairs, Colleen's nose broke as she fell.

Now You Try It, 2 **(Corrected sentences appear on page 332.)**

Apply the New-Sentence Tip to each of the following sentences. Write *OK* above the original if the test sentence makes sense, or correct the original if the test sentence sounds odd.

The trip was hit by the speeding car.

the chicken abruptly ended its trip to the other side of the road.

EXAMPLE: **Hit by the speeding car, ^ ~~the chicken's trip to the other side of the road ended abruptly~~.**

1. Reading the contract carefully, it was decided to wait a few days before both parties would sign.

2. Devastated by the bad news, Barney canceled his TV show.

3. Practicing almost every day for a year, Molly's writing improved. [*Hint: Molly's* is an adjective, since it describes *writing*.]

4. Breaking the pencil in anger, Steve's bad temper revealed itself.

5. Feeling hungry because I skipped lunch, supper was appealing.

Now You Try It, 3

Write a sentence correctly using each participle provided below.

EXAMPLE: **Picking up the wallet lying on the sidewalk,** *Shelby looked around for the person who had dropped it.*

1. Looking around at all the people in the audience,
2. Worried about the upcoming test,
3. Talking loudly to herself,
4. Thinking about his plans for the upcoming weekend,
5. Hit by the wildly thrown ball,

Editing Practice, 1 **(Corrected sentences appear on page 332.)**

Correct all errors in the following paragraphs using the first correction as a model. The number in parentheses at the end of each paragraph indicates how many errors you should find.

Oliver turned his leisurely walk

Worried that he would be late for class, ~~Oliver's leisurely walk turned~~ ^ into a trot. He quickly entered the science building. His chemistry teacher seemed to dislike late arrivals. Meeting an old friend who wanted to chat, his chances of arriving on time diminished. Oliver didn't want to be rude, so he left as soon as he could. Thinking about skipping the class altogether, several options went through his mind. He decided he would simply try to walk in without being noticed. (2)

Opening the classroom door as quietly as possible, his arrival seemed to go unnoticed. But then Dr. Wilson said, "Oh, I hope it wasn't too much trouble for you to join us today, Oliver." Attempting to explain why he was detained, his excuse seemed to make things worse. Oliver decided maybe Dr. Wilson was just a bit too touchy. (2)

Editing Practice, 2 **(Corrected sentences appear on page 333.)**

Correct all errors in the following paragraphs using the first correction as a model. The number in parentheses at the end of each paragraph indicates how many errors you should find.

Irritated by the recent turn of events, ~~the~~ ^ *Jacquita realized that her* day just wasn't going well ~~for Jacquita~~. She had no control over the virus that plagued her, but she really couldn't afford to miss the study session for her economics test. She decided to ask a classmate to take notes for her. Calling her friend Jerry, her plan was shot down when he said he too was ill. Jacquita didn't have the phone number of anyone else in the class, so she dragged herself to the study session. (1)

Getting about halfway to the classroom, the need for a quick detour to the rest room interrupted her. Jacquita soon decided that having a stomach virus was not going to be a crowd-pleaser, so she headed back to her dorm room. Overcome by fatigue and illness, sleep came to her almost immediately. Upon awakening, she called her teacher, but he wasn't in. The next day, she found that the study session was canceled because the teacher was sick. (2)

Editing Practice, 3

Correct all errors in the following paragraphs using the first correction as a model. The number in parentheses at the end of each paragraph indicates how many errors you should find.

Having a horrible time finding a birthday present for her boyfriend Shane, ^ *Rose realized that* his few hobbies provided no inspiration ~~for Rose~~. Remembering that he once said he liked electronic "toys," her decision was to go to an electronics store and not leave until she found something there. (1)

Determined to find the right gift, Rose's curiosity was aroused by a foot-long race car with antennae. Since the demo model was fully operational, she took it for a spin down the aisle. Running into a wall, the car's hood flew off,

along with two of its wheels. She decided that particular model wasn't quite sturdy. In fact, all the demos seemed to have been put through quite a bit of wear. She wasn't sure if it was the customers' or the manufacturers' fault, so she played it safe and just bought Shane a new set of speakers for his car. (2)

Writing Practice

On your own paper, write ten sentences so that each correctly uses a participial phrase at the beginning. Place a comma after each participial phrase.

EXAMPLE: *Working all night, Patricia finally finished her paper.*

Use the Proofreading Checklist to be sure that no sentence has a dangling modifier.

PROOFREADING CHECKLIST

Using Introductory Participial Phrases

- Turn the introductory participial phrase into a complete sentence. This new sentence should have the same subject used in the original sentence. The verb of the new sentence should be taken from the original participial phrase.
- If the new sentence sounds strange, there is probably a dangling modifier in the original sentence.
- Fix the error by rewording the original sentence so that the participle is near a word it can logically describe.

THE BOTTOM LINE

Placed correctly, a participial phrase *modifies the nearest noun or pronoun.*

LESSON 34
Parallelism

Sample Errors

SAMPLE 1: **✗ I like <u>to bike</u>, <u>swim</u>, and <u>to go</u> on camping trips.**

SAMPLE 2: **✗ It is hard <u>to make</u> a mistake and <u>starting</u> over again.**

What's the Problem?

The term **parallelism** refers to a series of two of more grammatical elements of the same type joined by the **coordinating conjunction** *and* (or, sometimes, by *or*). When one of the elements breaks the pattern set up by the other elements, the error is called **faulty parallelism**. Both of the following sentences have parallel elements because each underlined element has the same grammatical purpose as the others.

Tim said that he was feeling <u>tired</u>, <u>hungry</u>, and <u>poor</u>. [Each underlined word is an adjective describing Tim.]

Jean <u>ran</u>, <u>jumped</u>, and <u>fell</u>. [Each underlined word is an action.]

Achieving parallelism can be more difficult, though, because there are occasions when the words linked together must have a similar *form* as well as *purpose* in the sentence.

The most common type of faulty parallelism involves different forms of verbs. In Sample 1, there are three verbs in the **infinitive**: *to bike, swim,* and *to go.* However, the forms of their infinitives are not parallel—*to* is used with the first and third verbs but not with the second. We can make them parallel either by repeating the *to* for all three verbs, or by using the *to* only once so that it applies equally for all three (*I like to <u>bike</u>, <u>swim</u>, and <u>go</u> on camping trips*).

In Sample 2, *to make* is an infinitive, but *starting* is a **gerund** (the *-ing* form of a verb that is used as a noun). We can either say *It is hard to <u>make</u> a mistake and <u>to start</u> over again,* or say *It is hard <u>making</u> a mistake and <u>starting</u> over again.* However, what we cannot do is be inconsistent—as in Sample 2, where an infinitive is incorrectly used with a gerund.

What Causes the Problem?

Faulty parallelism usually occurs when writers join elements together with *and*, but fail to check whether the elements all have the same *form*. The error is most likely to occur when there is a choice between forms and it does not make any difference which form is used. For instance, in Sample 1, it makes no difference whether or not we repeat the *to* with a series of infinitive verbs; either choice is fine. In Sample 2, we could choose the infinitives *to make* and *to start* or the gerunds *making* and *starting*. However, we must be consistent in whatever choice we make.

Diagnostic Exercise **(Corrected sentences appear on page 333.)**

Correct all errors in the following paragraph using the first correction as a model. The number in parentheses at the end of the paragraph indicates how many errors you should find.

We all go to college for different reasons—to get an education, meet new people, and ~~to~~ gain the skills for a job. The best programs are ones that reach several of these goals at the same time. I like to take courses that interest me and doing things that will lead to a job. For example, it is great to read about something in a class and then applying it in a practical situation. That is why I am doing an internship program. I have the opportunity to get credits, develop professional skills, and to make important contacts. The internship will be worthwhile even if I have to go to school an extra semester to earn all the credits I need to graduate. (3)

Fixing This Problem in Your Writing

Every time you use an *and* (or an *or*), you are creating parallel elements. You always need to check to see that the parallel elements have exactly the same form. You need to be especially careful to check for parallel elements when you use *and* with infinitives or gerunds.

"AND" TIP: Whenever you use an infinitive or a gerund after an *and* (or an *or*), look to the left side of the *and,* and check every single infinitive or gerund to see that each has the *exact same form* as the infinitive or gerund on the right side of the "and." If the form(s) on the left side of the *and* are not exactly the same as the form on the right side of the *and,* then you have faulty parallelism.

Correcting a case of faulty parallelism once you have found it is not very difficult. Usually, either form will work, since the problem is usually one of being inconsistent in your choice between two equally valid alternatives.

For Example . . .

Here is how we would apply the *And* Tip to the two samples.

SAMPLE 1: **✗ I like to <u>bike</u>, <u>swim</u>, and <u>to go</u> on camping trips.**

The infinitive after *and* is *to go*, which uses the *to.* Starting on the left side of the *and*, we would work backward through the sentence looking at the exact form of each infinitive to see whether or not it also used the *to.* We would find *swim* without the *to* and *to bike* with the *to.* We would correct the faulty parallelism by using *to* with each of the infinitives or by using *to* only once to apply to all three verbs equally.

TIP APPLIED: **I like <u>to bike</u>, <u>to swim</u>, and <u>to go</u> on camping trips.**

I like to <u>bike</u>, <u>swim</u>, and <u>go</u> on camping trips.

SAMPLE 2: **✗ It is hard <u>to make</u> a mistake and <u>starting</u> over again.**

In Sample 2, there is a gerund, *starting*, after the *and.* Starting on the left side of the *and*, we would work backward through the sentence looking for a matching gerund. Instead, we would find the infinitive *to make.* At this point, we would know that we have faulty parallelism. We would need to rewrite the sentence using parallel infinitives or parallel gerunds.

TIP APPLIED: **It is hard <u>to make</u> a mistake and <u>to start</u> over again.**

SAMPLE 2, CORRECTED: **It is hard <u>making</u> a mistake and <u>starting</u> over again.**

Now You Try It, 1 **(Corrected sentences appear on page 333.)**

Underline the verb forms used before and after *and.* If the verb forms are parallel, write *OK.* Rewrite sentences that contain faulty parallelism.

> EXAMPLE: **I want to improve my skills, go on-line, and ~~to~~ surf the Internet.**

1. Today, I have to call my mother, write a report, and to pay my bills.
2. College gives us a chance to be away from home and gaining independence.
3. This book will teach you ways to write better, get good grades, and to amuse your friends.
4. The standard formula for speeches is beginning with a joke and to conclude with a summary.
5. Student representatives on faculty committees are required to attend all meetings, take notes, and to report to the student government.

Now You Try It, 2 **(Corrected sentences appear on page 333.)**

Underline the verb forms used before and after *and* or *or.* If the verb forms are parallel, write *OK.* Rewrite sentences that contain faulty parallelism.

> EXAMPLE: **Japanese cranes need about 30 feet to run, flap their wings, and ~~to~~ fly away.**

1. The porters began sorting the baggage and to clear a space for the groups to assemble.
2. Before I leave, I have to feed the cat, water the plants, and to lock the door.
3. This semester I started working at home in the mornings and to do my schoolwork later in the afternoons.
4. I don't want you to lose the directions or getting lost.
5. I remembered filling out the form, handing it to the clerk, and asking him to check it.

Now You Try It, 3

Complete the following sentences with parallel verb forms. If you use infinitives, try to use at least three verbs. Underline the parallel verb forms.

> EXAMPLE: **The children are eager to** *open their presents, play with their toys, and show them off to their friends.*

1. My boss is anxious for me to

2. It is very important to

3. I hate my friends

4. Texas Slim enjoys

5. You should always try to avoid

Editing Practice, 1 **(Corrected sentences appear on page 333.)**

Correct all errors in the following paragraph using the first correction as a model. The number in parentheses at the end of the paragraph indicates how many errors you should find.

It used to be that schools just taught students to read, write, and ~~to~~ do arithmetic, and that was it. When students left school, there were plenty of blue-collar jobs, for example, on the automobile assembly line. The assembly line required workers who were willing to be punctual, work at a steady pace, and to follow instructions. These jobs often paid pretty well—well enough for a worker to support a family, to buy a new car, and make the down payment on a house. Because the work was broken down into tiny routines, workers never needed to receive any training more sophisticated than basic first aid or even developing technical knowledge relevant to the industry. The work was designed to be simple, make little demand on the workers, and to ensure that nearly anybody could do the job. (4)

Editing Practice, 2 **(Corrected sentences appear on page 334.)**

Correct all errors in the following paragraphs using the first correction as a model. The number in parentheses at the end of each paragraph indicates how many errors you should find.

Nowadays, there are far fewer manufacturing jobs around because companies are able to subcontract to the cheapest bidder, get components manufactured overseas, and ~~to~~ do the same work with fewer workers because of automation. These developments leave Americans jobs that require workers to meet extremely short deadlines, produce customized products, and to do high technology. Routine jobs will be done overseas or by machines. (1)

These changes in the workplace mean that American workers must become much more sophisticated to function in a high-tech world. For example, they need to learn to read technical manuals, communicate with many different technical specialists, and to be able to upgrade themselves constantly. What companies need are students who are able to read, write, and to engage in critical thinking. It is a strange paradox: the more high-tech and specialized our society becomes, the more general our education needs to be. (2)

Editing Practice, 3

Correct all errors in the following paragraph using the first correction as a model. The number in parentheses at the end of the paragraph indicates how many errors you should find.

//

Train robberies in the United States reached their peak in January of 1885, when on average they occurred once every four days. It cost so much money to locate, apprehend, and ~~convicting~~ convict the robbers that it was often more economical to ignore them. Efforts to stop the robberies were hindered by such things as quarreling over word usage, dealing with unscrupulous lawyers, and trying to get Congress to pass effective legislation. In California, a lawyer suc-

cessfully argued that his client did not rob a train; rather, he managed to derail a train, to turn it into a mangled heap of cars, and take money from a "wreck" (technically, not a "train"). Another lawyer argued that it was impossible to "rob" a train—that only people can be robbed. In 1902 Congress finally managed to agree on wording, to define terms clearly, and pass the Train Robbery Act, which spelled out the law on this issue. (2)

Writing Practice

On your own paper, write a paragraph or two about the kinds of education you think you will need for your career. Try to use several parallel verb forms. Use the Proofreading Checklist to check for parallelism.

PROOFREADING CHECKLIST

Keeping Verbs Parallel in Your Writing

- Faulty parallelism results when grammatical elements in a series are not in exactly the same grammatical form. The most common form of faulty parallelism involves verb forms, especially infinitives and gerunds.
- Whenever you use an infinitive or a gerund in a series, look at the exact form of the verb that follows the coordinating conjunction, which is usually *and* or *or*.
- Match the form on the right of the coordinating conjunction with every element in the series on the left of the conjunction. If the forms are not identical, then you have a case of faulty parallelism.

THE BOTTOM LINE

Make verb forms parallel by *using* the gerund (*-ing*) form for verbs in a series or by *making* the verbs infinitives (used with *to*).

//

LESSON 35

Passive Voice

Sample Problems

In the following two sample sentences, the passive-voice verbs are underlined.

SAMPLE 1: **A ball <u>was kicked</u> by me.**

SAMPLE 2: **A report <u>was written</u>.**

What's the Problem?

Passive voice involves the form of the **verb** you use. Passive voice occurs when the grammatical **subject** is the thing that *receives* the action—not the thing that *performs* it. In Sample 1, for instance, the *ball* didn't do the kicking; the ball was the thing that *received* the action. Often, sentences in the passive voice use the word *by* to indicate who performed an action (see Sample 1).

Using the passive voice is not really an error, because there is no universal rule against using it. It can, in fact, be a useful way to call attention to certain words in a sentence that usually would be placed at the end. Suppose, for instance, that the writer of Sample 2 were writing about reports. The use of the passive voice in Sample 2 might, therefore, be appropriate because it puts *a report* up front in the sentence and in the subject position.

However, many readers prefer that writers avoid passive voice. As the name suggests, the *passive* voice can lead to a dull style because it does not stress action. Also, it can "hide" the person or thing doing an action. For example, Sample 2 does not indicate *who* wrote the report. Generally, writers should avoid using passive voice unless they can justify doing so, as noted in the following section.

What Causes the Problem?

Sometimes, people use passive voice because it seems to sound formal and objective. Also, people sometimes use it to be polite. For instance, compare *You must avoid these errors* with the passive-voice version: *These errors must be avoided.* Still, overusing the passive voice can easily lead to boring, stuffy, unclear writing; so this lesson focuses on how to recognize passive voice and how to convert it to active voice.

PASS

Diagnostic Exercise **(Corrected sentences appear on page 334.)**

Are the **boldface** words really in passive voice? Using the first correction as a model, change all passive-voice verbs to the active voice. The number in parentheses at the end of the paragraph indicates how many passive-voice verbs you should find and change.

Matt's apartment manager called him, wanting

~~Matt was called by his apartment manager, who wanted~~ ^ to know why he played his music so loudly. Matt **was surprised** by the phone call; he **didn't think** his music was loud. He **apologized**, but **he said** his radio **was playing** at only a fourth of its potential volume. Apparently, the manager **was satisfied** by this response. Matt **was told** by her that she would speak with the people who complained. I **have heard** that they have a history of complaining. (3)

Fixing This Problem in Your Writing

You can recognize passive voice by applying the following tip.

> FORMULA TIP: The passive voice is produced by a definite formula:
>
> **a *to be* helping verb + a past-participle form of another verb = passive voice**

Let's look at each of these two parts in more detail. Here are the only *to be* verbs in formal English:

is was were are am be being been

A sentence is *not* in the passive voice just because it has a *to be* verb! There also must be a **past-participle** form of another verb. Usually, this immediately follows the *to be* verb. As discussed in the Guide to Grammar Terminology, the term *past participle* refers to the form of a verb you would use after the word *have*, as seen below.

Verb	**Past Participle Form**
eat	eaten
write	written
borrow	borrowed
sing	sung

If you wish to eliminate passive voice, consider the following strategy.

> REVISION STRATEGY: The passive voice can be turned into the active voice by allowing the subject of the passive verb to become what it really is—the thing that *receives* action. In other words, move the subject of the passive verb so it comes *after* the verb.

Informally speaking, you would "flip-flop" what comes before and after the passive verb. That's the first step to turn a passive verb into an active verb. You also need to get rid of the *to be* verb, as follows.

PASSIVE VOICE: **This book was read by Angela.**

REVISION STRATEGY APPLIED: **Angela read this book.**

For Example . . .

The next two examples follow the passive-voice "formula": a *to be* verb + past-participle form of another verb = passive voice.

***to be* verb past participle**
↓ ↓
SAMPLE 1: ✗ **A ball was kicked by me.**

***to be* verb past participle**
↓ ↓
SAMPLE 2: ✗ **A report was written.**

You can turn each example into the active voice by moving the subject to follow the verb. Delete the *to be* verbs and make other *minor* changes for the new sentences to make sense.

REVISION TO ACTIVE VOICE: **I kicked the ball.**

REVISION TO ACTIVE VOICE: **Somebody wrote a report.**

In the second revision, we added *somebody* because the original sentence did not indicate *who* wrote the report. Sometimes, a passive-voice sentence will tell you who or what did an action (look for the tip-off word *by*). At other times, a passive sentence will not specify who did the action.

Now You Try It, 1 **(Corrected sentences appear on page 334.)**

Prove that all sentences in this exercise contain the passive voice. *First*, underline once the *to be* verbs, and underline twice the past-participle verb that comes afterward. *Second*, change the passive sentence into an active one by flip-flopping what comes before and after the verbs you've underlined.

The gardener carelessly left a rake in the yard.
EXAMPLE: **A rake was carelessly left in the yard by the gardener.**

1. The flowers were uprooted by those kids.
2. We are frightened by your yelling.
3. The television was broken by you.
4. I am hurt by your actions.
5. The story was written by Eudora Welty.

Now You Try It, 2 **(Corrected sentences appear on page 334.)**

Prove that all sentences in this exercise contain the passive voice. *First*, underline once the *to be* verbs, and underline twice the past-participle verb that comes afterward. *Second*, change the passive sentence into an active one by flip-flopping what comes before and after the verbs you've underlined.

Julia Child presented a cooking demonstration.
EXAMPLE: **A cooking demonstration was presented by Julia Child.**

1. The food was eaten by the hungry workers.
2. On Saturday, my car was hit by a careless driver who pulled in front of me.
3. All the classrooms were cleaned over the weekend by the custodians.
4. My dancing partner was violently bumped by another dancer.
5. The pesticide was sprayed by the farmer.

Now You Try It, 3

Prove that all sentences in this exercise contain the passive voice. *First*, underline once the *to be* verbs, and underline twice the past-participle verb that comes afterward. *Second*, change the passive sentence into an active one by flip-flopping what comes before and after the verbs you've underlined.

The Senate passed the bill.
EXAMPLE: The bill was passed by the Senate.

1. When a politician is elected by the voters, the politician is obligated to keep in close contact with his or her constituency.

2. During last night's football game, the punt was blocked by our team.

3. The first European flag raised in North America was hoisted by John Cabot in 1497. [*Hint:* The word *raised* is not part of a passive-voice verb because it is not preceded by a *to be* verb.)

4. The first winter Olympic games were hosted by France in 1924.

5. Because the television was broken by somebody, we can't use the VCR.

Editing Practice, 1 **(Corrected sentences appear on page 334.)**

Change all passive-voice sentences to the active voice using the first correction as a model. The number in parentheses at the end of each paragraph indicates how many passive-voice verbs you should find.

My parents greatly influenced me

~~I was greatly influenced by my parents~~ ^ to love reading. Both of them are avid readers, yet I was rarely hassled by them to read. Rather, they let me read at my own pace and pick what I wished to read. (1)

Almost every type of reading material has an appeal for me, but science-fiction stories are most often read by me. They were consumed by me during my teenage years; often, one a week would be read. Now that I'm in college, I have less time to spend on pleasure reading, but some time was carved out of my schedule by me to devote to reading a good book every now and then. (4)

PASS

Editing Practice, 2 **(Corrected sentences appear on page 335.)**

Change all passive-voice sentences to the active voice using the first correction as a model. The number in parentheses at the end of each paragraph indicates how many passive-voice verbs you should find. (Notice, by the way, how unnatural these paragraphs sound because of the "forced" use of the passive voice.)

I consider parking on this campus

~~Parking on this campus is considered by me~~ ^ to be a real problem. The school is in the middle of a large city, and available parking places are searched for by students, teachers, and people working in the city. When more classrooms were needed by the school, the parking lots it once had disappeared. As the city grew, the parking places gave way to more and more stores. All this growth has its advantages, but parking needs were not considered carefully by the school or city. (3)

Parking permits can be bought by students, but the better lots are expensive. Riding the bus is encouraged by the school and city, but it can take forever to get to class from where I live. Most schools seem to have parking problems, but the problem is even worse when the school is in the middle of a busy downtown area. (2)

Editing Practice, 3

Change all passive-voice sentences to the active voice using the first correction as a model. The number in parentheses at the end of each paragraph indicates how many passive-voice verbs you should find.

A pair of travelers were on the side of a dusty road, resting their sore feet.

I saw them,

~~They were seen by me,~~ ^ so I walked up to them and asked them where they were going. My question was not answered. My question was asked again. This time, one man said, "We are traveling north to Maine." I was surprised by this response because I was going to Maine as well. (3)

The travelers said that I could travel with them, so we soon left. The long road was traveled all day by us. Our feet were hurt by the hot gravel. We were not in a hurry, so we stopped frequently to rest. A driver stopped to see whether we wanted a ride. He was friendly and offered directions. Our feelings were hurt by him. He told us that we were crazy to walk a thousand miles to Maine. (3)

Writing Practice

On your own paper write a paragraph or two describing a trip, walk, or bike ride you recently took. Use the Proofreading Checklist to see whether any sentences are in the passive voice. If so, change each passive-voice sentence to the active voice unless there is a strong reason to use the passive voice.

PROOFREADING CHECKLIST

Using the Active Voice in Your Writing

- Look at the verbs of your sentences, and see how many follow the passive-voice formula: a *to be* helping verb + a past-participle form of another verb = the passive voice.
- If you can apply the following steps, the sentences you have identified are probably in the passive voice. Consider changing them into the active voice.
- See whether these sentences can be turned into the active voice by flip-flopping them so that the subjects are moved to follow the verbs.
- Make any other minor changes so that the new sentences are grammatical and haven't changed meaning.

THE BOTTOM LINE

PASS

Writers *use* active voice when the subject of the sentence actually performs the action indicated by the verb of the sentence.

UNIT EIGHT
PUTTING IT ALL TOGETHER

To help keep sentences clear and effective, writers must consider how the different parts of a sentence are working together to create the desired effect and meaning.

In particular, modifiers should clearly describe an appropriate idea. Also, verb forms that are linked by *and* or *or* should be similar, and writers should be cautious in using verbs that are in the passive voice.

Following is a review of the four tips dealing with sentence clarity and style.

Misplaced Modifiers

The *Often* Tip assists in locating the sorts of one-word modifiers that have the *potential* to be misplaced (see Lesson 32).

> "OFTEN" TIP: Look for each use of *often* or any word that could be replaced by *often* (such as *just, simply, hardly, barely, only,* and *nearly*). You might change the meaning of the overall sentence by doing the *often* substitution, but the resulting sentence should still be grammatical.

Once you locate these words, closely examine each to see whether it is placed so that it is clearly modifying the word it most logically describes. For instance, the *Often* Tip helps locate a modifier in the following sentence.

Gary bought a coat for just a hundred dollars.

TIP APPLIED: **Gary bought a coat for <u>often</u> a hundred dollars.**

Of course, the tip only showed where the modifier is. Now, the writer must consider if he or she wants *just* to refer to the amount of money spent or to something else. Depending on what the writer intends, this modifier could also be placed in front of *bought* or a *coat*. In any case, the *Often* Tip alerts the writer to double-check the use of this modifier.

Dangling Modifiers

The New-Sentence Tip can help you determine whether a participial phrase at the beginning of a sentence is clearly modifying the person, place, or thing you want it to modify (see Lesson 33).

> NEW-SENTENCE TIP: Turn the participial phrase into a complete sentence. The grammatical subject of the new sentence should be the same one used in the original sentence. Does the new sentence sound odd? If so, the original sentence has a dangling participle.

In the following sentence, the tip shows that there is *not* a dangling participle, because the test sentence sounds *OK*.

CORRECT: **<u>Hitting the delete key by accident</u>, Paul erased the information he had been putting onto his computer.**

TIP APPLIED: **Paul hit the delete key by accident.**

Avoiding Faulty Parallelism

Words connected by *and* or *or* should have a similar form and function. The *And* Tip helps you detect common types of faulty parallelism involving verb forms that begin with *to* or end with *-ing* (see Lesson 34).

> "AND" TIP: Whenever you use an infinitive or a gerund after an *and* or an *or*, look to the left side of the *and*, and see whether every infinitive or gerund has the *same form* as the infinitive or gerund on the right side of the *and*. If the forms on the left side of *and* are not the same as the form on the right side of *and*, then you have faulty parallelism.

In the following sentence, for example, the *and* connects verb forms that are not the same.

✘ **In his spare time, Rusty likes <u>to drink</u>, <u>to eat donuts</u>, and <u>watch TV</u>.**

CORRECTION: **In his spare time, Rusty likes <u>to drink</u>, <u>eat donuts</u>, and <u>watch TV</u>.**

The Passive Voice

Using the passive voice is not an error, but many readers prefer sentences that use the active voice (see Lesson 35). You can recognize the passive voice by using the following tip.

> FORMULA TIP: The passive voice is produced by a definite formula: a *to be* helping verb + a past-participle form of another verb = passive voice.

In the following passive-voice sentence, the *to be* verb is underlined once, and the past participle is underlined twice. To create the active-voice sentence, we deleted the *to be* verb and flip-flop *the report* and *Theresa*.

PASSIVE VOICE: **The report was written by Theresa.**

ACTIVE VOICE: **Theresa wrote the report.**

Review

Eliminate all misplaced modifiers, dangling participles, faulty parallelism, and passive-voice sentences using the first correction as a model. The number in parentheses at the end of each paragraph indicates how many problems you should find.

This summer, I took a bowling class and learned how to select a comfortable ball, ~~to~~ be consistent in my approach, and aim the ball. I have always liked to bowl or watching my friends bowl. Knowing I had some bad habits, my PE requirements were satisfied by a bowling course. Most of my bad habits were corrected by this course. (4)

Some of my worst habits were to vary my approach almost every time I bowled and throwing the ball with all my strength. It seemed to me that I could only knock the pins over by hurling the ball at them, but my teacher helped me gently release the ball. Amazingly, it just takes a little effort to knock a pin over and starting a chain reaction that knocks several—sometimes all—pins down. By practicing, my average is much higher now. (6)

ANSWER KEY

UNIT ONE OVERVIEW

Can You Detect Problems Involving Sentence Basics?

One of the highest honors that can be given in the movie industry is an Academy Award**, which** is more commonly known as an Oscar. Winning just one Oscar is a notable feat. A few movies, however, are exceptional**;** they have won several Oscars. Four of the most important Oscars are for best actress, best actor, best director, and best picture. Only a few movies have won even three of these four awards. In 1982, *Gandhi* received Oscars for best actor, best director, and best picture. Two years later, *Amadeus* won the same awards**, and** the best actress Oscar went to Sally Field for her role in *Places in the Heart.* In 1988, *Rain Man* captured the same three **Oscars, while** the best actress award . . .

Some movies have done even better with the Academy Awards. Back in 1975, *One Flew over the Cuckoo's Nest* won all four of these **Oscars, a** movie that also helped propel actor Jack Nicholson to fame. The first movie to win all four was *It Happened One Night*, **which** won awards back in 1934.

LESSON 1

Diagnostic Exercise

My roommate has an annoying habit**, leaving** his dirty dishes on the cabinet. I've asked him to at least put them in the sink **or** rinse them off a little. However, he just ignores me. Perhaps I am a little sensitive, but I wish he would clean up after himself **because** it is really embarrassing when friends visit **or** when my parents . . .

Now You Try It, 1

1. We heard a noise**, a** loud, frightful noise.
2. OK
3. A river runs through San Antonio**, a** peaceful, beautiful river.
4. Hearing the hunter approach, Bambi fled.
5. OK

Now You Try It, 2

1. A capital offense is a crime punishable by death**, a** penalty for only the most serious of crimes.
2. Jan told me she plans to become a parapsychologist **because** she really believes a person can communicate with the spirits.
3. I vividly recall January 12, 1995**, the** day my parents made a surprise visit while I was in the middle of holding a wild party.
4. Our astronomy class took a field trip to Mount Palomar, California**, where** one of the world's largest telescopes is located.
5. OK

Editing Practice, 1

Many cities played an important role in the forming of the United States**, especially** Philadelphia**, which** has some of the nation's most important historical treasures. Most of them **are** found around Independence Mall. The most famous is Independence Hall,

where the Declaration of Independence was signed. The Liberty Bell was, at one time, located there as well, but it was moved **because** it . . .

Editing Practice, 2

Several of Babe Ruth's baseball records have been broken**, by** Roger Maris and Hank Aaron, for example. However, Babe may well be the most famous baseball player of all time**, largely** because . . .

Babe's personality frequently made news **even** when his character got him into trouble. In 1922, his behavior resulted in five suspensions, and in 1925 his drinking and quarreling with management resulted in a $5,000 fine**, a** huge amount at the time for even well-paid players. He gained even more fame, though, when he turned himself around**, hitting** a record 60 home runs in 1927. He had a comeback again in the World Series of 1932. After a September attack of what was thought to be appendicitis, he fought back and played all games in the World Series**, in** which he batted .333. . . .

LESSON 2

Diagnostic Exercise

My friend Miranda is a junior majoring in government**, and** she plans to go to law school. Most law schools do not require applicants to major in certain areas, but she's been told that majoring in government helps prepare students for law. Most law schools do require a very high grade-point average and a good score on the law school examination. Her grades are high**;** she has about a 3.8 GPA at present. Still, law schools have high entrance requirements, and she studies more than anyone else I know. She plans to take the law school examination soon**, and** she . . .

Now You Try It, 1

1. OK
2. A pidgin language is not a natural language**;** people invent it when they need to communicate but do not share a common language.
3. OK
4. I write using a computer**, and** I don't know what I'd do without it.
5. It's about time you arrived**.** I was getting very worried!

Now You Try It, 2

1. The Miracle Strip is Florida's greatest expanse of beach**, and** the sand there is composed of pure white quartz.
2. OK
3. Two of my teachers are male**, and** two are female.
4. The coldest place on Earth is the Pole of Cole in Antarctica**;** the annual mean temperature is –72°F.
5. Kimberly told me about her dream**;** it was about her missing sister.

Editing Practice, 1

Sausage is a popular food around the globe**, and** it has been around for centuries. Nobody knows for sure who first thought of stuffing ground meat into a casing to form what we now call "sausage." Over 3,500 years ago, the Babylonians made sausage**, and** the ancient poet Homer referred to sausage in his classic work *The Odyssey*. Romans were particularly fond of sausages made from ground pork and pine nuts. In fact, the word *sausage* comes from the Latin word *salsus*; it is . . .

Editing Practice, 2

My cousin has never been the overly romantic type, **but** recently he put on quite a presentation when he proposed to his girlfriend. He did so on her birthday; he put the ring inside a toy packet that he placed in a Cap'n Crunch box. It took a bit of effort to get her to open the cereal box and wade through the cereal to the "toy surprise" inside. He carefully timed the proceedings**.** **He** wanted to be sure that she found the ring during half-time of the Dallas Cowboys game on TV, he was. . .

When she found the ring, he gallantly hit the mute button for the TV and said that he would like for her to be his wife. The ring, by the way, was not a real wedding ring; it was a plastic ring with a tiny boot jingling from it. She took it all in stride because she knew he was just trying to make the event memorable by adding some humor. I suppose she appreciated his humor, **but** she . . .

UNIT TWO OVERVIEW

Can You Detect Comma Problems?

Linguists, people who formally study language, have long noted that children learn their native language in similar ways. Although linguists do not fully understand the reason, they do know that children go through similar stages in learning to speak. Children tend, for instance, to go through a "cooing and laughing" stage, which ends at about twenty weeks of age. When they move into the "vocal play" stage, children string together long, steady sounds consisting of a consonant and a vowel, and they move from there into a "babbling" stage. When children are almost a year old, they tend to move into the "melodic utterance" stage, a time when . . .

Around this time, children enter the "one word" stage, which lasts until they are about eighteen months of age. During this stage, they produce one-word utterances**.** **Two** common utterances are "Mama" and "Bye-bye." Children move, subsequently, into the "two word" stage, and they string together pairs of the single words they know. These are not just subject-verb sentences (such as "Daddy gone"); they are also composed of structures not having a verb (such as "There Daddy"). At this time, they are learning grammar, the system . . .

LESSON 3

Diagnostic Exercise

Because Christopher Columbus believed he had reached the East Indies, Native Americans were called *Indians*, and the name is still often used. Actually, there are many types of Native Americans, but they are usually referred to collectively. Along the northwest coast, there were the Haida, Modoc, and Kwakiutl tribes, and these tribes differed considerably from the tribes of the plains. The northwest tribes subsisted largely on salmon$_X$ and built wooden houses and boats. The plains tribes hunted buffalo$_X$ and . . .

Now You Try It, 1

1. Pig iron is refined in a blast furnace$_X$ and contains iron along with small amounts of manganese and other minerals.
2. Piero di Cosimo was a Florentine painter$_X$ and is remembered for his scenes depicting mythology.

3. Tom decided he would walk to class but changed his mind when it started raining.
4. OK
5. OK

Now You Try It, 2

1. Sitting Bull was a famous Sioux chief and appeared with Buffalo Bill in his Wild West Show.
2. The Norman Conquest of England took place in 1066 and brought many changes in English life.
3. My father bought an old sword in England but paid too much.
4. OK
5. Tony is dropping by my place, and I suppose I should clean up a bit.

Editing Practice, 1

Languages use symbols to represent meaning**,** and various forms of language exist besides speech. Braille is a form of language for people who cannot see**,** and it . . .

Each particular arrangement means something different. Grade 1 Braille is a system in which the dots represent letters, numbers, punctuation, and some very short words**,** but in Grade 2 Braille . . .

Editing Practice, 2

Humans appear to be the only animal to use language naturally**,** but there is much about language that we may never know. People have come up with various theories about the origins of language**,** but nobody knows for sure how or why humans learned to speak. According to the "bow-wow" theory, speech began when people imitated the sounds of nature, such as animal sounds. Most languages have a few words (such as "meow") that clearly imitate these sounds**,** but usually . . .

According to the "pooh-pooh" theory, speech arose when humans made instinctive noises resulting from pain, fear, or other emotions. For instance, a gasp, a sigh, or a cry of fear might have been the primitive beginnings of words used to express these emotions. Again, most languages have words (such as "hey" or "oh") that convey emotional responses**,** but . . .

LESSON 4

Diagnostic Exercise

My roommate and I finally had a garage sale**. It** was something we've talked about all quarter to help us get rid of the junk we accumulated since our sophomore year. As our neighbor reminded me one day, it's not a bad idea to get rid of stuff you haven't touched in a year. We sold more than I expected**;** the total sales came out to about $200. Yesterday, I managed to spend most of it on car repairs. I took what was left over and bought some junk food as a "reward" for having uncluttered the house. Maybe we will have another garage sale before we graduate**. We** will probably . . .

Now You Try It, 1

1. My history class is on the other side of campus, **and** I have to run to get there on time.
2. OK
3. My computer seems broken**;** I cannot get it to save this file.

4. OK
5. The Russian cosmonaut Yuri Gagarin was the first person to orbit Earth; John Glenn was the first American to do so.

Now You Try It, 2

1. OK
2. Some companies like résumés kept to one page, **but** other companies are more flexible about the length of résumés.
3. OK
4. Sharon made us some of her salsa**;** it was hotter than I expected.
5. OK

Editing Practice, 1

Many satellites and probes have been launched into space, **but** two of the most traveled probes are the two *Voyager* probes. Both left Earth in 1977, **and** both visited Jupiter and Saturn. Both probes use a "slingshot" method of studying the planets**. The** probes cannot land safely on the planets but use their gravity to pull the probes into a path leading to their next objective. In the late 1990's, the *Voyagers* will be propelled in this fashion completely out of the solar system, beginning a long journey to the stars. Nobody knows when their travels will end**;** they might . . .

Editing Practice, 2

Congress passes hundreds of bills each year**;** some greatly affect the lives of all Americans. The Social Security Act of 1935 is one of the most influential acts passed by the U.S. government. The most important part of this act established the old-age pension system; the original tax . . .

The act created the unemployment insurance system**. It** provided federal grants to states as well so they could give aid to handicapped people, dependent children, and the elderly poor. The original act, however, excluded a great many people who have since been covered by other bills. For instance, the bill did little or nothing for farm workers, domestic servants, and other low-paid occupations. Franklin D. Roosevelt is largely responsible for the act**. He** intentionally . . .

LESSON 5

Diagnostic Exercise

Last Monday**,** there was a fire in one of the dorms. According to the newspaper**,** nobody was hurt. When the fire department finally arrived**,** six rooms were engulfed in flames. A friend of mine had her room filled with smoke. However**,** her room suffered no major damage. Tomorrow**,** school officials . . .

Now You Try It, 1

1. When we got the tests back**,** nobody even thought about sleeping.
2. In France**,** shepherds once carried portable wooden sundials as pocket watches.
3. OK
4. OK
5. Each time my brother or sister calls**,** I seem to be out of the house.

Now You Try It, 2

1. In the middle of the night, our house was burglarized.
2. OK
3. Because the roads are slippery from ice and slush, classes are canceled.
4. OK
5. However, I picked the coat up and gave it to a friend who likes to mend old clothes.

Editing Practice, 1

Although many people may not be aware of this fact, Pearl Buck was the first American woman to win a Nobel Prize in Literature. After spending years as missionaries in China, her parents returned to the United States for a short time in the early 1890's, during which Pearl was born. When she was just three months old, Pearl . . .

During her stay in China, there were many racial problems and protests against the Western governments that had controlled China's economy for years. Her most famous novel, *The Good Earth*, would reflect her compassion for the Chinese and their culture. When Pearl Buck died, President Nixon . . .

Editing Practice, 2

In my never-ending pursuit to be physically fit, I bought a weight machine that I could set up in my basement. I carefully compared various brands and referred to several guides and reports on the models available. After examining my options, I bought . . .

Unfortunately, I forgot to compare two things: the height of the weight machine and the height of my basement. When I finally assembled the metal monster, I discovered that it needed four more inches than my basement ceiling allowed. I was furious at myself. The thing was such a hassle to transport from the store and then to assemble that I did not want to return it. In desperation, I punched . . .

LESSON 6

Diagnostic Exercise

Many places around the globe have universal appeal. They are, however, associated with just one country or another. A twenty-one-member international committee has designated some sites as World Heritage Sites—sites having international value and responsibility. In the United States, for example, the committee . . .

Now You Try It, 1

1. Tecumseh led an attempt to drive the whites from Indian territory. His forces, however, were defeated by General Harrison.
2. Little is known about the Pilgrims' *Mayflower;* we do know, however, that it weighed about 180 tons.
3. None
4. None
5. Mozart wrote many musical works. In fact, it takes 180 CD's to hold all work known to be his.

Now You Try It, 2

1. Sean Connery is remembered most for his James Bond movies. However, he won an Oscar for a different role in *The Untouchables.*

2. None
3. The top position in Britain's army is field marshal. The top position in its navy, in contrast, is admiral of the fleet.
4. None
5. Some countries' names come from unexpected sources. *Brazil*, for example, comes from *brasila*—the Portuguese name for a tree.

Editing Practice, 1

My friend Collett is moving to Oakland, California. Consequently, she wants to fix up her house and sell it. Because she's a good friend, I volunteered to help. A realtor advised her to repaint the living room because this area makes a big impression on potential home buyers. A kitchen, similarly, draws . . .

The biggest task was working on the cabinets. We began, therefore, with taking them apart. Then, we replaced the old knobs with ceramic ones. Two of the cabinet doors had bad cracks. We decided, therefore, to put . . .

Editing Practice, 2

Americans are often proud of their history; nonetheless, there are some unpleasant episodes. One troubling aspect of U.S. history is the many attempts to kill presidents or presidential candidates. The assassinations of Lincoln and the Kennedy brothers are the most famous; there have been, however, many other assassinations and attempts. In 1881, Charles Guiteau shot President Garfield, who died later. Likewise, President McKinley . . .

Political fanaticism has led to many assassination attempts. Others, in contrast, seem to have been the result of pure insanity. John Schrank, for example, tried to . . .

LESSON 7

Diagnostic Exercise

It was strange going back to my high school reunion, which was held last summer. Monica, who was my best friend as a senior, didn't recognize me. I guess she didn't expect to see me bald. I also saw a friend whom I've stayed in touch with over the phone but haven't actually seen in ages. He told me he moved to northern California, where he got married and bought a house. Since I now live in Oregon, we agreed to visit. After the reunion was over, I had a snack with him and Monica, who . . .

Now You Try It, 1

1. OK
2. OK
3. She wanted to go to a place where she could be alone.
4. OK
5. OK

Now You Try It, 2

1. OK
2. OK
3. My mother, who received a degree from the school I am attending, plans to attend homecoming.
4. OK
5. OK

Editing Practice, 1

I went to high school in San Bernardino, which is not far from Los Angeles. I've rarely been back since attending San Diego State University, which is fairly . . .

For one thing, my favorite teacher, who taught world history, is now the principal, and the principal$_{X}$ who was there when I attended$_{X}$ is now the school superintendent. About half the teachers whom I had classes with have left entirely, and several of the ones who are still there are considering retirement. I found the new cafeteria, which . . .

Editing Practice, 2

I am presently rooming with Harold Lee, who is very practical when it comes to buying gifts. We couldn't afford to spend much for Christmas gifts, so we decided to prepare seasonings and can some vegetables. We first made some spicy Cajun seasoning, which was the easiest part of our gift-giving adventure. Then, we made a relish that was primarily composed of tomatoes, onion, and cabbage. The tomatoes, which we bought at the local market, had to be completely green. The jars had to be carefully sterilized, and the directions confused us. Luckily, we received expert advice from my mom, whom I called in desperation. Once we understood the process better, we went on to asparagus, which . . .

LESSON 8

Diagnostic Exercise

Joseph McCarthy, a senator in the 1940's and 1950's, led an extreme movement to guard America against communism, a form of government much feared in the United States at that time. The term$_{X}$ "McCarthyism$_{X}$" now . . .

Now You Try It, 1

1. Admiral Chester Nimitz, the World War II commander of the U.S. Pacific Fleet, has an aircraft carrier named after him.
2. Six thousand people were killed by a hurricane in Galveston, a port in Texas.
3. An emperor penguin, *aptenodytes forsteri*, can remain under water for fifteen minutes.
4. Richard, a guy in my geology class, fell asleep during the lecture.
5. OK

Now You Try It, 2

1. My grandparents recall "Black Thursday," the stock-market crash of 1929.
2. OK
3. OK
4. One of my friends, Pauline, wrote this poem.
5. Victoria Woodhull and Tennessee Cook, two sisters, were the first female stockbrokers in New York.

Editing Practice, 1

Gary, my nephew, called and suggested we throw a surprise birthday party for my mother, who just turned sixty-five. I'm not much for birthday parties, but I agreed to help. We asked my friend Sharon to assist. Sharon, an interior-design major, has an excellent eye for decorating, so she took charge of turning my living room, a very plain room, into a more festive place for the occasion. My mother, who has a notorious sweet tooth, is particularly fond of chocolate, so we ordered an enormous cake made of dark chocolate. Gary asked my oldest sister, Stephanie, to . . .

Editing Practice, 2

World War II, one of the best-known wars of all time, was followed a few years later by a conflict that still is not well understood. The Korean War, a conflict between the United Nations and North Korea, was never officially a war. Harry Truman, the U.S. president at the time, never asked . . .

This war caused many problems for the United States, possibly because its status and purpose were not clear. General Douglas MacArthur, the commander of the UN forces, was removed from office for insubordination to President Truman, the Commander in Chief. After the landings at Inchon, a major turning point, the North Koreans . . .

UNIT THREE OVERVIEW

Can You Detect Punctuation And Capitalization Problems?

Because my **history** class ends at 11:30 and my **math** class begins at noon, I have little time to eat lunch. I can still hear my **mother** saying, "You need a nutritious lunch," so I try to eat something quick that is still filling and at least somewhat healthy, such as~~:~~ vegetable soup, **rolls**, and fruit juice. Luckily, several **vendors** on campus sell healthy food~~;~~ and . . .

LESSON 9

Diagnostic Exercise

In the earlier part of this century, pulp magazines were extremely popular. They were composed of cheap paper (pulp) and contained various types of stories**:** adventure, detective stories, romance tales, and western stories. One successful pulp publisher was Street & Smith; this firm sold millions of magazines. Most issues, however, have . . .

Now You Try It, 1

1. On Friday, there will be a test, one that will be hard.
2. OK
3. OK
4. Sylvia and I went to the same high school, Pine Tree High School.
5. OK

Now You Try It, 2

1. My car wouldn't start this morning~~,~~ because the battery was dead.
2. OK
3. For dessert Amy had a parfait, a dessert made of layers of ice cream, fruit, and syrup.
4. OK
5. Last Friday, our meteorology class traveled to a weather observatory, which was located 20 miles from the college.

Editing Practice, 1

Langston Hughes is one of the best-known African-American poets**,** his reputation having begun in 1915 at the age of thirteen. At that time, he was elected poet of his graduating class, an unusual selection not merely because he was one of only two African American students in his class but because he had never written any poems. Hughes explained that nobody else in the class had written any poetry either. His classmates elected him**,** however, because . . .

Even though such reasoning had an element of stereotyping, Hughes was inspired~~;~~ and wrote a graduation poem that the teachers and students enthusiastically received. He went on to publish many types of writing**:** poems, . . .

Editing Practice, 2

Some science projects can take time. Others**,** however, are relatively easy. A terrarium is a small environment that is built for living plants and animals; it is not terribly difficult to make. It can be built out of containers such as~~;~~ a large glass jug, a plastic container, or even a glass baking pan covered with plastic wrap. A particularly good container**,** however, is . . .

The bottom of the container must be lined with a shallow layer of pebbles; this layer allows for good drainage. A couple of inches of a sand and soil mixture go on top of the pebbles. The terrarium then needs a small dish of water placed into the soil~~;~~ so that the rim of the dish is level with the top of the soil. Then a variety of plants and minerals can be added, including~~;~~ ferns, moss, rotting bark, and a few rocks. The terrarium must be covered with glass or plastic~~;~~ and . . .

LESSON 10

Diagnostic Exercise

The student government announced today the election results for representation in the student senate. Almost half the students **didn't** vote at all, and there **weren't** many candidates running. I'm not sure why, but apathy was widespread. My guess is that many students **don't** think the senators have much real power, or perhaps the candidates' qualifications and goals were unclear. **It's** clear that . . .

Now You Try It, 1

1. Although a friend told me that Mark Twain wrote the poem "Trees," **isn't** Joyce Kilmer the actual author?
2. **It's** a fine time for you to leave me, Lucille.
3. I **wouldn't** do that if I were you.
4. OK
5. "**It's** feeding time for the baby," said Tom.

Now You Try It, 2

1. **Didn't** Fran manage to break her femur while playing soccer?
2. OK
3. My biology class **can't** meet today because the room was flooded.
4. **Haven't** I met you somewhere before?
5. **Let's** meet at the study hall around noon.

Editing Practice, 1

People **don't** think often about where their favorite foods come from, but the subject can be interesting. For instance, there **isn't** much . . .

In France, waffles go back to at least the fifteenth century. Street vendors would sell them in front of churches during religious festivals. **They'd** cook waffles with shapes reflecting religious themes to attract the attention of the celebrators. In modern Mexico, waffles are topped with cinnamon and sugar. In tropical countries, **they'll** often . . .

Editing Practice, 2

Many holidays are celebrated around the globe, but **they're** often celebrated in diverse ways. For example, Christmas is celebrated in many countries, but each culture has **its** own Christmas traditions. In France, for example, the Noel celebration begins right after December 6 (the feast day of St. Nicholas) and **doesn't** end until January 6. Many French have a grand meal that **isn't** served . . .

In Brazil, Christmas **isn't** simply a product of one culture; it represents a blend of Portuguese, African, and indigenous Indian cultures. On Christmas Eve, for instance, a traditional dinner includes a stuffing **that's** made . . .

LESSON 11

Diagnostic Exercise

Two of my close friends were born in Mexico. Paul **Morales's father's** employer relocated to Arizona when Paul was six. Juanita Lopez moved to the United States recently; **Juanita's** goal . . .

Now You Try It, 1

1. In my communications class, we analyzed the **president's** speech.
2. Margaret talked to the manager about the **salesperson's** attitude.
3. **Tony's** favorite meal is ham and lima beans.
4. I strongly recommend going to this repair shop; my best **friend's** father owns it.
5. Paula managed to get three movie **stars'** autographs.

Now You Try It, 2

1. **Bob's** illness lasted almost three weeks.
2. Steve **Martin's** place of birth is Waco, Texas; however, he doesn't have a Southern accent.
3. **Turkey's** population is about the same as that of Iran.
4. Many people would be surprised to know that **Canada's** total land area is one of the largest in the world.
5. I heard that **tomorrow's** weather will be awful, but let's go to the beach anyway.

Editing Practice, 1

Jack **London's** best-known work may be *The Call of the Wild*, the story of one **dog's** adventures in Alaska. However, London was a prolific writer, having published some forty-three books and countless short stories. In fact, this famous **writer's** goal . . .

London also held a variety of jobs during his lifetime. At the age of fifteen, he was an oyster pirate in San Francisco Bay, stealing private landowners' oysters and selling them in the **city's** saloons. Ironically, he then became one of the California Fish **Patrol's** deputies. When just seventeen, he signed on as a sailor for a seal-hunting schooner. These adventures with the sea were the basis for another of **London's** widely read books . . .

Editing Practice, 2

Abraham Lincoln may be one of **America's** most widely recognized presidents, but **Lincoln's** chances as the **Republicans'** presidential . . .

Lincoln's debates with Stephen Douglas gained Lincoln some attention, but some historians believe it was the Cooper Union Speech that propelled Lincoln to the candidacy. When giving this speech, Lincoln was actually in William **Seward's** home territory. Seward was the leading candidate at the time for the Republican nomination, but Lincoln's speech gained the attention of the voters and delegates. In this speech, Lincoln challenged many **people's** belief . . .

LESSON 12

Diagnostic Exercise

Some old **friends** of mine stopped by my apartment for coffee. My roommate's coffee pot was broken, so I made them some instant coffee. I'm not good at making coffee, but everybody had two **cups** apiece. The coffee was pretty old, yet nobody seemed to care. We talked about our **schedules** for . . .

Now You Try It, 1

1. Three strange-looking **guys** are standing outside the door.
2. Gary ate *two* **pizzas** last night!
3. OK **possession**
4. OK **contraction**
5. OK **possession contraction**

Now You Try It, 2

1. OK **possession**
2. OK **possession**
3. OK **special word special word**
4. Janet owns three CD **players**, and she has a huge collection of OK **special word**
5. OK Do you want to ask the Floreses to give us a ride this weekend to OK **contraction**

Editing Practice, 1

My nephew's birthday was a few **days** ago, and I wasn't sure what to get him. Jimmy just turned four, and he likes all **kinds** of . . .

The toy **stores** I visited, however, carried the usual stuff: monster toys, superhero dolls, assorted airplanes and cars, and hundreds of computer **games**. I wasn't terribly inspired, so I decided to look at some of my old toys from the late 1970's. They were all broken. However, I went through my mother's attic and found three old military-type action **figures** from the 1960's. . . .

Editing Practice, 2

Edith Wharton was one of the best-known **novelists** of the early 1900's, but much of her fame in the late 1990's results from movie **versions** of . . .

Undoubtedly, her settings and themes were influenced by her parents' lifestyle. Not only were the **Whartons** well off financially, but their ancestry also could be traced back to prestigious **New Yorkers**. Her childhood was spent among the well-to-do **socialites** of New York City, Rhode Island, and various parts of Europe. Despite her upbringing, Wharton's stories often presented satiric **portraits** of . . .

LESSON 13

Diagnostic Exercise

My history teacher, Dr. Norris, said that we would spend the next class meeting discussing John F. Kennedy's 1963 inaugural address. Kennedy began by saying, **"We** observe today not a victory of party but a celebration of freedom. . . **."** Dr. Norris said that he listened to this speech as a boy and recalled parts of it. He remembers . . .

Now You Try It, 1

1. **Emily Dickinson once wrote,** "Success is counted sweetest by those who ne'er succeed."
   The poet Emily Dickinson noted that success is appreciated most by people who do not succeed.
2. **As Benjamin Franklin put it,** "Fish and visitors stink in three days."
   Benjamin Franklin stated that fish and visitors have one thing in common: they stink within three days.
3. **Gloria Steinem is quoted as saying,** "Any woman who chooses to behave like a full human being should be warned that the armies of the status quo will treat her as something of a dirty joke; that's their natural and first weapon."
   Gloria Steinem, a noted feminist, said that people who resist change are likely to view feminists as though they were dirty jokes.
4. **In the words of Martin Luther King, Jr.,** "Oppressed people cannot remain oppressed forever."
   Martin Luther King, Jr, reminded people that those who are oppressed cannot forever be oppressed.
5. **Just before being executed by the Germans in 1915, Edith Cavell said,** "I realize that patriotism is not enough; I must have no hatred or bitterness towards anyone."
   Just before being executed by the Germans in 1915, Edith Cavell said that patriotism is not enough for her and that she should not hate anyone.

Now You Try It, 2

1. **In a letter to actress Jodie Foster the day he attempted to assassinate President Reagan, John Hinckley wrote,** "The reason I'm going ahead with this attempt now is because I just cannot wait any longer to impress you."
   In a letter to actress Jodie Foster, John Hinckley explained that he was going ahead with his attempt to assassinate President Reagan because he urgently wanted to impress her.
2. **Speaking to General James Longstreet while watching a battle, General Robert E. Lee once said,** "It is well that war is so terrible—we should grow too fond of it."
   Robert E. Lee once told one of his generals that one good thing about the terrible nature of war is that it keeps soldiers from becoming too fond of war.
3. **As the poet Clement Clarke Moore wrote,** "Not a creature was stirring, not even a mouse."

Clement Clarke Moore wrote that even the mice were asleep on Christmas Eve.

4. **In the movie *I'm No Angel*, actress Mae West said,** "When I'm good, I'm very good, but when I'm bad, I'm better."
   In the movie *I'm No Angel*, actress Mae West said that she could be very good, but she was even better when she was bad.
5. **Referring to the Great Depression, President Franklin Roosevelt stated,** "I see one-third of a nation ill-housed, ill-clad, ill-nourished."
   President Franklin Roosevelt noted that during the Great Depression, a third of the American population lacked proper shelter, clothing, and food.

Editing Practice, 1

Many Americans have spoken or written of the need for the United States to provide fair treatment to women. In 1850, for instance, Sojourner Truth, a former slave, said of the feminist cause, **"**If the first woman God ever made was strong enough to turn the world upside down all alone, these women together ought to be able to turn it back and get it right side up again!**"** A few years later, Lucy Stone said ~~that~~ **"**From the first years to which my memory stretches, I have been a disappointed woman.**"** She went . . .

The women's movement became increasingly active after the Civil War. After being arrested for leading the fight for women's right to vote, Susan B. Anthony said, "It was we, the people—not we, the white male citizens, nor we, the male citizens—but we the whole people who formed this Union." She went on to argue that she and all women should be allowed to vote based on the amendments made to the Constitution as a result of the Civil War. These amendments . . .

Editing Practice, 2

The music of the 1960's often reflected a belief that change should—and would—occur if people were willing to act and to work together. Some popular songs of that period became theme songs of the civil rights movement. For example, "We Shall Overcome," which was an African American spiritual song of the nineteenth century, became an anthem of the protest marchers. One key statement is repeated over and over in the song: **"**We shall overcome.**"** That is . . .

"O Freedom" was another African American spiritual that became a protest song of the 1960's. This song proclaims, **"**before I'd be a slave, I'd be buried in my grave.**"** As popular hits . . .

LESSON 14

Diagnostic Exercise

Yesterday, my literature teacher asked, "Who can name three poems written by African Americans**?"** I was able to come up with "Incident," which was written by Countee Cullen. Herman, the guy who sits next to me, named Langston Hughes's **"Harlem."** I started to bring up "Letter from Birmingham **Jail";** however, I quickly recalled that was an *essay* by Martin Luther King, Jr. Then, somebody in the back row mentioned Hughes's "Same in **Blues,"** and somebody else remembered Richard Wright's "Between the World and **Me."** Our . . .

Now You Try It, 1

1. Bill asked, "Will we get our papers back this **week?"**
2. OK
3. OK

4. The title of the next chapter is "Who Runs the Stock **Market?"**
5. Darlene responded, "Why do you **ask?"**

Now You Try It, 2

1. Did you hear somebody say, "The store is **closing"?**
2. OK
3. OK
4. A strange man yelled at the taxi driver, "Follow that **cab!"**
5. OK

Editing Practice, 1

Have you ever heard the song **"Dixie"?** Most Americans have heard this song but have not considered its usefulness as a source of information about the Civil War. Other songs of that time, for instance, the spirituals sung by slaves, offer a personal look at their lives and hardships. In "Go Down, **Moses,"** the lyrics refer to attempts by Moses to free his people from slavery, yet the song is also a poignant cry for the freedom of African Americans. In contrast to this melancholy spiritual is "Dixie." This battle hymn of the Confederacy, with its upbeat tempo, is a celebration of the South. Other songs, such as "The Bonnie Blue **Flag,"** were even more explicit about loyalty to the Confederacy, but the one most remembered today is **"Dixie."**

Editing Practice, 2

Many conflicts have given rise to what might be called "war **songs."** Each war, it seems, becomes the subject of popular music. World War I, for example, had its protest songs, such as "I Didn't Raise My Boy to Be a **Soldier."** This song captured many Americans' desire to stay out of the war. Once the United States entered the war, though, many songs served to rally the troops and the general public. One of the most famous is "Over **There."** All good American parents and "sweethearts," according to this song, should be proud and eager to send their loved one to fight in the war. George M. Cohan received a Congressional Medal of Honor for composing this immensely popular song. In "Oh, How I Hate to Get Up in the **Morning,"** however, . . .

LESSON 15

Diagnostic Exercise

My roommate, who is shopping for a new car, looked at several types, including~~:~~ Fords, Nissans, and Mazdas. She knew which features she wanted, like~~:~~ automatic transmission, cruise control, and leather seats. However, she quickly discovered that such features were not within her budget. To get the best deal for her money, I suggested that she consult sources such as~~:~~ her mechanic or *Consumer Reports* magazine. She did some research, but she seemed disappointed because there was no clear choice. She finally narrowed her choices to~~:~~ a Ford truck . . .

Now You Try It, 1

1. Farmers in this area grow~~:~~ wheat, corn, and alfalfa.
2. Kamilah and Steve saved enough money to travel throughout~~:~~ England, France, and Belgium.
3. This summer, the college will not offer many courses I need, such as~~:~~ English 100 and Speech 201.

4. You will need to buy a textbook, gloves, and a dissecting kit.
5. Some famous actors who changed their names are Jane Wyman, Raquel Welch, and Rudolph Valentino.

Now You Try It, 2

1. During the Renaissance, Greek and Latin were used to form such new words for scientific concepts as *gravity, paradox, chronology,* and *atmosphere.*
2. OK
3. Many languages have contributed to English, including French, Latin, Persian, and German.
4. OK
5. Some slang words that are still used include *cool, dork,* and *geek.*

Editing Practice, 1

In the past, my English teachers discussed various types of writing, including poetry, drama, and short stories. In my present English class, the teacher discussed the writing we'll do this semester. She discussed three other types of writing that my previous teachers had not covered: expressive essays, arguments, and informative papers. She mentioned that there are many ways a writer can develop an essay, such as using narration, comparison and contrast, and definition. For her class, we are required to write six long papers, three fairly short papers, and several in-class paragraphs. Some of these assignments will allow us to pick our own topics, but a few will not. She has already mentioned that we will write about the following: educational reform, male-female relationships, and discrimination. The class seems challenging, but I'm looking forward to it. Next semester, I am looking forward to taking a technical writing class . . .

Editing Practice, 2

Many people try to get rid of "tummy" fat so they'll feel better about their appearance, their self-image, and even their relationships with significant others. However, fat has also been linked to health risks such as heart disease, high blood pressure, and strokes. The most dangerous type of abdominal fat can't even be seen; it's the fat around vital organs like the intestines and . . .

Two factors that determine how much fat a person has are gender and . . .

LESSON 16

Diagnostic Exercise

My sister is attending a **community college** in Kansas City, and we've been comparing our courses. Her **Spanish** class is much different from mine because hers includes discussion of **Hispanic** and **Latino** cultures. Her teacher, **Professor** Gonzales, . . .

Now You Try It, 1

1. My **mother** has a job teaching computer science in east Chicago.
2. Theodore Roosevelt was once governor of New York.
3. Much of the southwestern United States was once Mexican soil.
4. Students write in almost every class at this **university,** even in **physical education** courses.
5. Tenskwatawa was a **Native American** leader who encouraged his people to give up alcohol along with **European** clothing and tools.

Now You Try It, 2

1. The school colors at the **high school** I attended are blue and gold.
2. A nuclear weapon is a general term for various types of weapons relying on a nuclear reaction for their explosive power.
3. Did you say that **Aunt** Mia is arriving today?
4. The **Rhone River** and the **Rhine River** both rise out of the Alps of Switzerland.
5. My **father** thinks we can meet with the Pope during our visit to Rome.

Editing Practice, 1

Mary, also called **Molly**, Dewson was a pioneer in encouraging women to be active in **politics** and the **federal government**. In the 1928 presidential campaign, she worked for candidate Al Smith and helped mobilize female supporters. Smith never became president, but Dewson did not abandon her **feminist** efforts.

In 1930, Dewson continued to mobilize women to campaign for Franklin Roosevelt's successful bid for governor of New York. Later, she worked for his **presidential** campaigns. Perhaps her greatest accomplishment, though, was becoming **head** of the Democratic Party's efforts to recruit women for **government** jobs. She also worked with Democrats in training women to serve in election campaigns. Though she died in 1962, her legacy lives on, and millions of men as well as women have been affected positively by her efforts to involve women in the **democratic** process.

Editing Practice, 2

Last week, the **university** I'm attending announced that all history majors would be guaranteed that they could receive a degree in **history** in no more than four years. As a **sophomore** planning to be a history major, . . .

I spoke with an advisor, **Professor** Hearns, about the guarantee. She said the **college** would do its part in regularly offering courses that are most in demand. In particular, she said that each semester the department would offer several sections of American **History** I and **Cultural History** of . . .

UNIT FOUR OVERVIEW

Can You Detect Problems in Subject-Verb Agreement?

When I was in high school, my family enjoyed camping, so nearly every school vacation, we would go camping. We soon realized that there **are** three completely different kinds of campers. We called them the "nature lovers," the "homeboys," and the "bikers." The people whom we called "nature lovers" enjoy setting up camp in small, isolated sites where there **are** often no toilet facilities. Of course, the food and water **are** a constant concern, especially when all supplies have to be carried in. "Nature lovers" always try to have a minimal impact on the area that they have camped in. For example, their trash and garbage **are** always taken out.

The "homeboys" are people who want to go to the mountains, beach, or desert without ever actually leaving home. They buy a mobile home—an entire apartment complete with living room, kitchen, and bathroom—that **has** been mounted on wheels. There **are** some mobile homes that even come equipped with satellite dishes so that the "homeboys" will not miss any TV programs while they are in the wilderness.

The "bikers" are people who see the wilderness only as a huge empty parking lot. All they want to do is race their bikes and make as much noise as possible. The fragile ecology and unspoiled beauty **mean** nothing to them. The problem with the bikers and all their machines **is** that . . .

LESSON 17

Diagnostic Exercise

The beginning of the first public schools in the United States **dates** from the early 1800's. The pressure to create public schools open to children of working-class parents **was** a direct result of the union movements in large cities. In response, state legislatures gave communities the legal right to levy local property taxes to pay for free schools open to the public. By the middle of the nineteenth century, control of school policies and curriculum **was** in the hands of the state government. As school populations outgrew one-room schoolhouses, the design of school buildings on the East Coast **was** completely changed to accommodate separate rooms for children of different ages. Before this time, all children in a schoolhouse, regardless of age, **were** taught together. . . .

Now You Try It, 1

1. In our recent games, the margin of our losses **has** been agonizingly small.
2. Our response to the accusations made by our opponents clearly **shows** that they have misunderstood the facts of the case.
3. In the opinion of the committee, the type of programs shown during the hours that children usually watch television **is** clearly inappropriate.
4. The reasons for the collapse of the settlement agreement between the union and company management **remain** unclear to outside observers.
5. The time for cooking roasts in ovens **depends** on the type of meat.

Now You Try It, 2

1. Disagreements about the interpretation of the agreement **have** led to considerable unpleasantness among the parties involved.
2. The social aspects of developing of the country's resources **are** often overlooked.
3. It always seems to be the case that the simplest solutions to a complex problem **seem** the most difficult to discover.
4. A group of incredibly noisy children playing outside my windows **delights** in keeping me from doing my homework.
5. Speculation about the nominees for the various Oscars **dominates** today's news.

Editing Practice, 1

The house cat **is** one of the oldest domesticated animals. Researchers who study the history of the cat **believe** that the ancestor of all of today's domestic cats **was** a species of small wildcats found in Africa and Europe. The first group of people to bring cats into human habitations **was** in Africa.

However, the first actual domestication of cats as residents with humans **was** carried out by the Egyptians, who **tamed** cats to hunt rats and mice in grain storehouses. The pet cats of an important official or government officer **were** sacred. When one of these sacred cats **was** killed by a servant, even accidentally, the servant **would** be severely punished, possibly even put to death. . . .

Editing Practice, 2

One of the largest families of vertebrate animals **is** the family of reptiles. Reptiles include alligators, crocodiles, lizards, snakes, and turtles. They **share** the feature of being cold-blooded. Reptiles are among the oldest families of animals on earth. Reptiles played a key role in bringing animal life out of the oceans and onto land through the evolution of eggs. Reptiles evolved from amphibians, the first creatures to come onto land. The great evolutionary advantage of reptiles **was** their eggs. Reptile eggs, with their leathery membrane or hard shell, **have** a great advantage: the embryo is encased in its own self-contained sack of fluid. The ability of reptiles to reproduce away from bodies of water **gives** reptiles an enormous advantage over amphibians and **explains** why reptiles were . . .

LESSON 18

Diagnostic Exercise

Each year there **are** many new movies coming out of Hollywood. Each is designed for a certain segment of the moviegoing audience. There **are** car-crash films aimed at males under thirty. There **are** heart-warming romantic comedies for women over twenty. There **are** even the dreadful "slasher" movies for an audience that it is better not to think about. . . .

Now You Try It, 1

1. There **were** many errands that still needed to be taken care of.
2. Unfortunately, there **are** still some bugs in the new program.
3. There **are** always a thousand things to do!
4. We discovered that there **was** a special tool that we could use.
5. Carl Sagan is fond of pointing out that there **are** billions of stars.

Now You Try It, 2

1. We were all upset about what had happened, but there **weren't** many things we could do about it.
2. There has been a lot of discussion about the problems we will face when we renovate our house.
3. There **are** a couple of openings down at the plant.
4. If you look back at the story carefully, there **are** plenty of hints that tell us what is going to happen at the end.
5. There **are** a museum and a gallery that we would like to visit when we go to Philadelphia next month.

Editing Practice, 1

There **are** two countries in the Iberian Peninsula: Spain and Portugal. Portugal occupies most of the western coast, while Spain covers the rest of the peninsula. There **are** three . . .

Although the coastal plains account for only a tiny portion of the land mass of the peninsula, there is a high percentage of the population in that region. Along the coast, there **are** both a mild climate and fertile soil. In addition, there **are** many rivers that flow into the plains from the mountains in the interior of the country. These rivers provide irrigation water for the fields and orchards in the coastal plains. Especially along the southern coast, there **are** thousands . . .

Editing Practice, 2

The largest distinctive geographical feature in the United States and Canada is the Rocky Mountains. In the lower forty-eight states, there **are** eight states that contain a portion of the Rockies: Idaho, Montana, Wyoming, Nevada, Utah, Colorado, New Mexico, and Arizona. There **are** even branches of the mountains that extend north through two Canadian provinces and into Alaska. There **are** rich veins of minerals, especially gold, silver, copper, lead, and zinc, in the region. Nowadays, however, there **are** greater riches in liquid mining. . . .

The great natural beauty of the Rocky Mountains has made them very popular. There **are** many National Parks throughout the region; two of the best known are Yellowstone and Glacier National Parks. There **are** many winter sports . . .

LESSON 19

Diagnostic Exercise

I work in a busy law office. Even though we now have voice mail, answering the phone and writing down messages **take** up a lot of my time. I am also responsible for maintaining the law library, although most of the time I do nothing more glamorous than shelving. The law books and reference material **are** always left scattered around the library, and some of the lawyers even leave their dirty coffee cups on the tables. I used to have a relatively comfortable working area, but the new computer terminal and modem **have** now taken up most of my personal space; that's progress, I guess. Despite all the stress, meeting the needs of clients and keeping track of all the information required in a modern law office **make** it . . .

Now You Try It, 1

1. In Monopoly, four railroads and both utilities **are** too much to pay for the Boardwalk.
2. A lock and the key that goes with it **are** given to everyone who uses the lockers.
3. When there is a storm, the thunder and lightning **scare** my dog.
4. The debits and credits always **add** up to zero.
5. Lunch and dinner **are** not included as part of the package.

Now You Try It, 2

1. What we see and what we hear **give** us our picture of the world.
2. In a poker hand, aces and eights **are** called a "dead man's hand."
3. The sun and the nine planets **compose** our solar system.
4. His great natural dignity and his consideration for others **were** something that his friends and relatives would never forget.
5. The plants and the animals found in this region **are** adapted to the extreme swings of temperature from hot days to freezing nights.

Editing Practice, 1

In Mozart's opera *Don Giovanni*, comedy and melodrama **are** mixed together in a highly unusual way. For example, the character and personality of Don Giovanni **are** surprisingly complex. His charm and bravery **make** him almost a hero at times. Yet at other times, his aristocratic arrogance and deliberate cruelty to women **make** him a complete villain. The seduction of a willing woman and a rape **are** the same to him.

The role and character of his servant Leporello **are** also unusual. At first, his constant complaining and caustic asides to the audience **make** Leporello seem to be just a conventional comic sidekick. Yet in some ways, his observations and reactions to his master's behavior **become** the center of attention. Leporello's admiration for the Don's charm and his repulsion at the Don's treatment of women **reflect** the . . .

Editing Practice, 2

Barbara Kingsolver is the author of six books and a number of short stories. Her books and stories **have** attracted a wide following. One of her most recent novels is *Animal Dreams*. Codi, her sister, and their father **are** the focus of our attention. The story deals with Codi's reluctant return home to a small town in Arizona to take care of her father, who is dying. The events that take place in the story are seen either from Codi's perspective or from her father's point of view. The past and the present constantly **run** together in their minds. One of the main themes in the book is Codi's discovery of how deeply her present life and actions **have** been affected . . .

UNIT FIVE OVERVIEW

Can You Detect Pronoun Problems?

My friend Richard told me that Clyde, the guy **who** sits next to him in his English class, decided to quit school because he'd rather be a rock singer. Richard and **I** both laughed at **this plan** at first, but maybe it is a smart decision. Clyde has changed his major at least four times this year**, according to Richard.** Although **people** might change their major a few times, changing it too often indicates a good deal of uncertainty and can put **them** back several years.

Clyde usually managed to bring up rock music in class discussions with Richard, our classmates, and **me.** Often, Clyde's comments would seem completely irrelevant, but **his classmates** bit their tongue and let him go on and on about Madonna, Bon Jovi, or another rock star **whom** somehow Clyde managed to fit into the discussion. Of course, **students have** a right to speak up. . . .

LESSON 20

Diagnostic Exercise

"Star Wars" was the name of a military program as well as a movie. **The program** was a large research-and-development program calling for military defense in outer space. This **plan** was initiated by President Reagan in the 1980's, and it had the official title of "Strategic Defense Initiative." The public never embraced that **name** as much as . . .

Now You Try It, 1

1. OK
2. I knew this **problem** was going to happen!
3. OK
4. That **development** is a surprise.
5. A deer poked its head up from the grass where a fawn was resting, and then I saw **the deer** run away.

Now You Try It, 2

1. Alena called today to talk about the antismoking law passed by the city government. This **phone call** took almost an hour of my time.
2. We need a new mayor, but that **change** won't happen anytime soon.
3. OK
4. **The car** was speeding.
5. OK

Editing Practice, 1

Some great books do not become great until long after they were written. This **situation** is particularly evident with a book written by William Bradford. He wrote *Of Plymouth Plantation,* one of the oldest books written by Europeans exploring and colonizing the Western Hemisphere. This **book** was not . . .

This book, written by the governor of Plymouth Colony, chronicles the story of the Pilgrims until 1646. Bradford's book offers considerable detail on the day-to-day lives of the colonists. It contains the oldest-known copy of the Mayflower Compact, which was an agreement among the Pilgrims for a democratic-style government. **The book** disappeared . . .

Editing Practice, 2

Slavery has been a sore spot in the history of the United States. **Slavery** is especially troubling considering the role of African Americans in the founding of the country. In 1774, a group of slaves in the American colonies made a famous appeal to Thomas Gage, who was the royal governor of Massachusetts Colony. **The slaves' appeal** proclaimed that they as slaves had a right to the freedoms that the colonists sought from Britain. This **view** was shared . . .

When the Revolution began, African Americans were excluded from the American army. That **situation** changed, however, when the British encouraged the slaves to join their army. Approximately five thousand African Americans would eventually join the American army. This **development** allowed . . .

LESSON 21

Diagnostic Exercise

Soldiers commit a war crime when they violate norms for acceptable behavior in times of war. Few people want war, but most want their rights and those of others to be respected as much as possible when war occurs. For instance, almost everybody agrees that **prisoners** should have their physical needs attended to and should not be physically or mentally tortured. An officer who orders **his or her** troops . . .

Now You Try It, 1

1. **Doctors have to** have insurance covering them against malpractice.
2. OK
3. College **students have to** pick a field that interests them, but they also have to keep an eye on the job market.
4. OK
5. Anybody who hasn't turned in **his or her** test should do so now.

Now You Try It, 2

1. Not only **do spiders** spin **webs,** but they can do so all their lives.
2. Almost **all students have** to take this course to obtain their degree.
3. OK
4. **Did somebody take my book by accident?**
5. OK

Editing Practice, 1

No other European country has ever spread **its** people and culture around the globe more than the United Kingdom. Each country, of course, has had effects on the world. However, by the end of the nineteenth century, the United Kingdom had its culture firmly planted around the world, in such diverse places as Canada, the Caribbean, India, Australia, and South Africa.

Not everyone in the United Kingdom approved of **its** attempt to colonize the world, but most Britons supported colonization because of the economic benefits of commerce with the colonies. British **citizens** had . . .

Editing Practice, 2

Almost everybody who has taken an English class has written a book report about something **he or she has** read for the class. For one assignment, my English instructor, Ms. Kaplan, asked **us** to read two books that **we** wanted to read. In high school, almost **all my English teachers** made . . .

Ms. Kaplan, though, said that she didn't want to "test" us about the books we read or make us feel that we had to scrutinize each page for **its** "hidden" meaning. She simply asked us to announce the books we read and then be ready to recommend or not recommend them to the rest of the class. Almost everybody seemed to have read **his or her** first selection and truly enjoyed it. One classmate was so enthusiastic about *The Catcher in the Rye*, the novel **she** [or **he**] read . . .

LESSON 22

Diagnostic Exercise

My roommate and **I** visited her friend Jeff, who lives in a cabin he built from scratch. That's a formidable project for **me**. My roommate asked Jeff whether he would mind if **she** and I stayed at his place for a few days in the summer. He said that was fine if we would help him build a new storeroom, and we quickly agreed to help him out. I'm not much of a carpenter, but Jeff said he'd be patient and help me learn. For an inexperienced builder such as **me**, building . . .

Now You Try It, 1

1. The pharaoh visited the burial tomb intended for just **him**.
2. OK
3. OK
4. Huey and **I** went out for pizza late last night.
5. Mom promised to write to us as soon as she arrived in Florida, and today I received a card from **her**.

Now You Try It, 2

1. Just between you and **me**, we are having a pop quiz on Friday.
2. OK
3. OK
4. If not for **me**, you would not be having a birthday at all today.
5. Jane and **I** are going to the women's basketball game tonight.

Editing Practice, 1

Writing has never been the easiest task for someone like **me** who has not written a great deal in the past; however, I am gaining more experience in my technical writing class. Three other students and I are supposed to work on a group paper. One member, Suzanne, and **I** are supposed to write a definition section of our paper, which is on ethical behavior in accounting. I have two friends who are accountants; I don't necessarily agree with **them** about . . .

An objective analysis of the issue is supposed to be included in the section that Suzanne and **I** were assigned. The interviews were useful because the two accountants each presented different perspectives. They also admitted that the issue of ethics was confusing for **them** as well as **me**.

Editing Practice, 2

My roommate, Rusty, asked me to join a money-making enterprise concocted by **him** and his father. The plan they devised sounds simple: Rusty's dad would purchase fifty compact refrigerators that we would lease out to college students living in the dorms. Rusty's dad would supply the capital, while Rusty and **I** would do the labor. When Rusty told me the plan, I was skeptical. I talked it over with **him** and . . .

Rusty's dad lives in town and owns a place where we could store any refrigerators Rusty and **I** could not lease. We placed ads and notices around town and in the school paper. The week before class began, thirty students came by to do business. It wasn't stressful, but we had to stay around all day waiting on people. Rusty and **I** won't . . .

LESSON 23

Diagnostic Exercise

An experience that we all have had is working for a bad boss. One boss **whom** we have all had is the petty tyrant, a person **who** loves to find fault with every employee **who** works in the building. It seems that the petty tyrant is more interested in finding employees **whom** he or she can belittle than in getting the job done. Even worse than the petty tyrant is a supervisor **who** is inconsistent. An inconsistent boss is a person **whom** the employees can never depend on. A game that this kind of boss loves is playing favorites. One day, this boss is your best buddy; the next day, the boss acts as if he or she doesn't know the name of a person **who** has . . .

Now You Try It, 1

1. The young woman **who** answered the phone took my order.
2. Senator Blather ignored the reporters **who** had been waiting patiently outside his office.
3. I called the couple **who** had answered the ad.
4. OK
5. The director repositioned the actors **whom** the camera was blocking.

Now You Try It, 2

1. OK
2. I need to know the name and address of the mechanic **who** supposedly fixed your car.
3. A guy **whom** I knew back in elementary school happens to sit next to me in my chemistry class.
4. Who was the president **who** succeeded Richard Nixon?
5. OK

Editing Practice, 1

I have several teachers **who** use some form of group work. My freshman composition class involves group activities, but Ms. Roberts, **who** teaches . . .

Ms. Roberts believes that we need to become accustomed to working in groups even though they are not effective when they comprise people **who** prefer to learn independently. Of course, any group is likely to have at least one person **who** would prefer to work alone, but usually the group can adjust when it's just one or two individuals **who** learn little from group activities. Early in the course, Ms. Roberts asked us to write a brief essay describing how we have functioned in groups; she then used these essays to help assign us to groups. My group is composed of people with **whom** I can . . .

Editing Practice, 2

Most Americans **who** have a religious affiliation are Christians, but other religions are thriving within the United States. Jews are a relatively small minority in this country, but their religion is one **that** was already established by the time of the American Revolution. Muslims, **who** are a growing presence . . .

Some religious denominations are much smaller in terms of the number of people **who** subscribe to their beliefs, yet these religions have found a niche in American society. For instance, one small religious group, referred to as Ethical Culture, is composed of some 7,000 members and was founded in 1876 by Felix Adler, a humanist philosopher **who** stressed . . .

LESSON 24

Diagnostic Exercise

My psychology teacher, Ms. Crystal, had each member of the class complete a questionnaire that would help **him or her** consider an appropriate career. I had already decided on a career, but she said the questionnaire would offer options. I've always wanted to be an electrical engineer because I like to design things; **engineers spend** much of **their** time drawing designs and writing specifications. Ms. Crystal said my survey results indicated I should consider being an accountant. She also told me, however, that the survey was just one resource for choosing a career. I agree. People have to consider what **they know** better than anyone else: **their** own interests.

Now You Try It, 1

1. A senator has to be responsible to **his or her** constituents.
2. OK
3. We must hire a secretary, and **he or she** has to have computer skills.
4. I prefer **teachers** who **know their** subject material but who **allow** students to figure out some things for themselves.
5. Everybody should cast **his or her** vote in the next election!

Now You Try It, 2

1. OK (The sentence refers to a specific mechanic, not to an abstract, unidentified mechanic in general.)
2. If you ever put your children into day care, meet with the person who will actually watch your children and see whether **he or she** is patient and congenial.
3. Has everyone done **the** homework?

4. **Chefs** rarely **talk to their** customers, but yesterday the chef at my favorite restaurant greeted us.
5. I've never met anyone who brushes **his or her** teeth as often as you!

Editing Practice, 1

College **students have** many options about what **they** might study. I am torn between geology and teaching. On the one hand, I have long been interested in being a geologist in the private sector, perhaps for an oil company. A geologist spends much time outdoors collecting samples, and I like working outdoors. A geologist also works in **an** office . . .

On the other hand, my mother is a teacher and has encouraged me to follow in her footsteps. **Most teachers have** a good deal of stress put on **them** by students, parents, and administrators; however, **teachers also have** many rewards, such as knowing that **they have** helped somebody . . .

Editing Practice, 2

At one time or another, almost everybody has wondered what it would be like if **he or she** were born at another time or place. I don't think a person is necessarily unhappy or out of place simply **by having** such thoughts. Perhaps it's a way to explore possibilities in **a person's** present circumstances.

When I was much younger, I wondered what it would be like to be an early colonist in the Americas. The life of a colonist was not easy; **he or she** had to cope with starvation, the wilderness, and financial ruin. When I was a teenager, I dreamed (like many other kids) of being an astronaut—again, a person who often puts **his or her** life in danger to explore a new world. Even today I think about such adventures, and perhaps it's all a clue that I would not be happy confined in an office. I'm not saying that being a businessperson is dull, but **people need** to find the sorts of challenges and environments that reflect **their** own . . .

UNIT SIX OVERVIEW

Can You Detect Problems Involving Verb Tense?

My wife and I really disagree about old movies. I **love** to watch them, unlike my wife. She would just as soon watch paint dry as sit through an old black-and-white film. The other night, as we **were watching** Hitchcock's 1938 classic mystery *The Lady Vanishes*, she fell asleep. After the movie **had** finished, I woke her up and started telling her about what an **amusing** movie it was. She was not impressed. To her, the poor quality of the print, with its flickering light and uneven focus, **made** watching that movie a chore rather than a pleasure.

LESSON 25

Diagnostic Exercise

Last summer we took a trip to Provence, a region in the southeast corner of France, which **borders** on Italy. The name *Provence* **refers** to the fact that it was the first province created by the ancient Romans outside the Italian peninsula. Today, Provence still **contains** an amazing number of well-preserved Roman ruins. While there **are** a few big towns on the coast, Provence **is** famous for its wild country and beautiful scenery.

Provence **is** especially known for its abundance of wildflowers in the spring. These flowers **are** used . . .

Now You Try It, 1

1. Juan always **gets** a headache whenever he works at the computer without taking a break.
2. In general, the main cause of depressions and unemployment **is** the reluctance of governments to go into debt to stimulate the economy.
3. Last year, we visited George Washington's plantation. It **is** located just down the river from Washington.
4. Last year, I was nearly hit by a taxi in London because I forgot to look to the right when I **stepped** off the curb.
5. Last weekend, we went for a hike on the trail that **goes** through the woods.

Now You Try It, 2

1. The drainage in the area was awful back then; I always **got** my feet wet when I **went** there.
2. It always **seems** to rain when we go on vacation.
3. Painters today are still influenced by the art styles that **came** from prewar Germany.
4. OK
5. One of the things we remember about Teddy Roosevelt is how he always **seemed** to be grinning with those big white teeth.

Editing Practice, 1

A few years ago, we spent a week in Italy on the *Amalfi Coast*, which **is** south of Naples. This mountainous stretch of coast **runs** east to west from Sorrento to Salerno. The name comes from the name of the town of Amalfi, which **is** in the middle of the coastline. Amalfi, which **dates** from the fourth century A.D., was a major city during the Middle Ages. However, much of the ancient city no longer **exists**. It . . .

We stayed in Ravello, a little town on the top of a ridge line that **overlooks** Amalfi. Ravello **is** best known for an international music festival that **is** held every summer near the Palazzo Rufolo. The beautiful palace garden **was** the . . .

Editing Practice, 2

Although William Shakespeare died in 1616, performances of his plays **are** alive and well today. A number of theaters and summer festivals **are** devoted to performing his plays. In England, the Royal Shakespeare Company **performs** in London and Stratford-upon-Avon (the small town where Shakespeare was born). In Canada, there **is** a highly successful Shakespeare festival every summer in Stratford, Ontario. In the United States, there **are** theatrical organizations . . .

Ashland's Shakespeare Festival **began** almost by accident as an outgrowth of the old Chautauqua circuit that **provided** entertainment to rural America before the days of radio and movies. After the collapse of Chautauqua, Ashland **found** itself with a good-sized summer theater facility, and faculty from the college **decided** to stage a few Shakespearean plays.

LESSON 26

Diagnostic Exercise

Every weekday morning at 6 A.M., my alarm **goes** off. By 6:15, the breakfast dishes are on the table, and the coffee **is brewing**. I always **get** the children up next. It is very hard for them to get going. On Mondays, they **resemble** bears coming out of hibernation. While they **are taking** their showers with their eyes still closed, I get [or **am getting**]* everyone's clothes ready. Since the youngest child still **needs** a lot of help getting dressed, I usually **spend** some extra time with her talking about the day's events. By 7 A.M. we all **are sitting** at the table for breakfast. The children **love** pancakes and waffles, but there just isn't time to make them except on weekends. Breakfast goes by quickly, unless somebody **spills** the milk or juice. I **wish** we had more time in the morning, but every morning I am **amazed** when I **look** back and **realize** that . . . (*raises the number of errors to 15)

Now You Try It, 1

1. We had to hurry because a big line **was forming** in front of the box office for tickets to the opening-night performance.
2. When we got to the restaurant, the host **told** us that there would be a twenty-minute wait.
3. The plane **is arriving** right now.
4. The boss **believes** that you may be right after all.
5. The noise **sounds [or sounded]** very far away.

Now You Try It, 2

1. When I was growing up, I always **hated** the uniforms we were required to wear in school.
2. I **think** that it is going to rain all weekend.
3. Right now, that **seems** to be our best choice.
4. They won't hear the phone ring, because they **are working** outside.
5. I am sorry that I can't stop to talk to you right now; I **am going** to an important meeting.

Editing Practice, 1

You all **know** the old joke that research **shows** that the amount of sleep that we **need** is always five minutes more. I never **use** the snooze button on my alarm clock because I **hit** it without actually waking up. In fact, I **find** that I must put my alarm clock clear across the room so that I **am forced** to . . .

I am not a morning person, to put it mildly. I **hate** getting up, and I **am** nauseated by the thought of breakfast. Since I am so dopey in the mornings, I have learned to be methodical. While the water **is warming** up in the shower, I set my clothes out. I fix two pieces of toast while I **am making** the coffee. As I **am leaving** for the office, I grab the morning paper to read on the bus while I **am riding** to work. When I finally do get to work, I almost **resemble** a . . .

Editing Practice, 2

This year, both my husband and I **are going** to school in programs that **require** a lot of writing. We are both pretty good writers and **tend** to get good grades on our papers.

However, we **go** about the process of writing in completely different ways. He is compulsive about how he writes his papers. First, he **brainstorms** the topic and **groups** all his thoughts into clusters. From the clusters, he makes a list of topics that he **wants** to include . . .

I am completely the opposite. I **think** that I would go crazy if I wrote the way my husband does. I **spend** just as much time on my papers as he does, but I write in a completely different way. I **spend** my time thinking about my papers before I ever write a word. I write my papers in my head. When I **feel** that I know what I want to say, I sit down and write a complete draft. I **need** to go over this draft . . .

LESSON 27

Diagnostic Exercise

Unfortunately, most people **have been** involved in an automobile accident at some time. I **have been** involved in several but my luckiest accident was one that never happened. Just after I **had gotten** my driver's license, I borrowed the family car to go to a party. Although it **had been** a very tame party, I left feeling a little hyper and silly. It was night, and there were no street lights nearby. I **had** parked a little distance from the house, so my car was by itself. I got into the car and decided to show off a little bit by throwing the car into reverse and flooring it. I **had gone** about 20 yards backward before I thought to myself that I was doing something pretty dangerous. I slammed on the brakes in a panic. I got out of the car and found that my back bumper was about 4 inches from a parked car that I **had never seen**. Whenever . . .

Now You Try It, 1

1. Senator Blather **has campaigned** in every district for the last six months.
2. It **has rained** every weekend since Easter.
3. Holmes suspected Lord Bumfort because Holmes **had noticed** the unexplained mud on His Lordship's shoes.
4. Holmes **had explained** the clues to Watson three times before Watson finally understood.
5. I **have seen** that movie a dozen times this year.

Now You Try It, 2

1. Before I got sick, I **had been** working about sixty hours a week.
2. The committee **has** met every week this term.
3. The plane returned to the airport after the pilot **had** noticed that fuel was leaking from an engine.
4. In the last ten years, the company **has** expanded into nearly every major market in the country.
5. The defendant's lawyers **had** filed a motion before their time expired.

Editing Practice, 1

America **has had** a love affair with the automobile ever since its invention. However, our attitudes about automobile safety **have** always **been** ambiguous, even contradictory. Over the years, we **have been willing** to pay a lot of money for automobiles that go faster and faster, but we **have** always **seemed** to be unwilling to deal with the safety consequences of this increased speed. An interesting case in point is the recent decision by the federal government to eliminate the 55-mile-per-hour speed limit on interstate highways. We **have had** . . .

Editing Practice, 2

My friend Dale **had been** living on his parents' farm his whole life when he made himself unwelcome at home. Just before Dale got his license, his father **had bought** a new car that was his pride and joy. One day, after Dale and his best friend **had been** out someplace fooling around, Dale got home late for one of his chores: rounding up the cows for milking. Dale drove his dad's new car into the pasture to get the cows, something his father **had** expressly **prohibited**. When he was out in the pasture, the horn got stuck, so Dale pulled out various wires until the horn stopped. That night, after his father **had gone** to bed, Dale . . .

LESSON 28

Diagnostic Exercise

The Smithsonian Institution is an **amazing** system of museums and art galleries in Washington, D.C. The Smithsonian is a **required** stop for every **concerned** visitor to Washington. Recently, I spent a **fascinating** day at the National Museum of Natural History. The only problem is that there is so much to see that the **overwhelmed** visitors find themselves frantically rushing from one **interesting** exhibit to another without taking the time to understand all the information in the exhibits. One solution to this **frustrating** problem is to take a tour . . .

Now You Try It, 1

1. A **watched** pot never boils.
2. We realized that we had a **troubling** problem on our hands.
3. Most good department stores will replace **damaged** furniture if the customer has a receipt.
4. It was a terribly **embarrassing** situation for all of us.
5. Do you know Sherlock Holmes's famous question about the **barking** dog? **[OK]**

Now You Try It, 2

1. We all enjoyed such a **gripping** movie.
2. The **extracted** ore is sent to a mill for further processing.
3. The **sprawling** suburbs went on for miles and miles.
4. The movie was a **smashing** success at the box office.
5. Unable to endure the dentist's silly jokes any longer, the **provoked** patient took matters into his own hands.

Editing Practice, 1

I have quite **conflicting** feelings about the National Museum of Natural History. On the one hand, it is in a **depressing** building. Even a casual visitor can't help noticing the **water-stained** walls and **crumbling** plaster in the remote hallways. Clearly, a **penny-pinching** Congress has not adequately provided the museum with the **needed** funds. One recent report said that repairing **storm-damaged** roofs would alone absorb . . .

On the other hand, the new exhibits are lively and colorful. We can only hope that in these difficult times, Congress can develop a **balanced** plan that maintains the old building and provides for **exciting** new exhibits.

Editing Practice, 2

One of the things that strikes visitors to Hawaii is the **amazing** variation in climate. Waikiki Beach, for example, only has about 20 inches of rain a year. Without irrigation, Waikiki would be a dusty plain, as it was shown in photographs from missionary times. However, Manoa Valley, the valley behind the beach, has gradually **increasing** amounts of rainfall until, at the back of the valley, less then 10 miles from Waikiki Beach, there is an **astonishing** 130 inches a year. Another **interesting** fact about the valleys in Hawaii is that, despite the **astonishing** rainfall at the backs of the valleys, there are only a few rivers. The reason for this **surprising** fact is that the volcanic soil is remarkably porous. The rain is absorbed into the ground before it can run off. In most places in the world, such **overwhelming** rain could not be held by the **saturated** soil and would create streams and rivers to carry off the excess water.

UNIT SEVEN OVERVIEW

Articles with Geographic Proper Names

No articles for specific mountains or small bodies of water; use *the* with the names of mountain ranges and large bodies of water (such as oceans and seas).

Can You Detect Problems Involving Articles?

We live in **a** time of ~~**the**~~ great technological change. The engine that is driving this change is the computer. It is hard to believe how quickly ~~**the**~~ computers have become **an** absolutely essential part of our personal and professional lives. Many of us first used computers as ~~**the**~~ greatly improved typewriters. With computers, we were able to edit and revise ~~**the**~~ essays with a few keyboard commands without going to **the** trouble of having to retype **the** entire document over again. In **the** business world, computers were first used as ~~**the**~~ greatly . . .

As ~~**the**~~ computers have become more common and more powerful, they have begun to redefine what it means to write and to calculate. For example, it used to be that **the** distinction between writing **a** term paper and publishing **a** book was as different as day and night. That is no longer the case. What I write at my computer in my office can be sent out over **a [the OK]** network and be more widely distributed than any published book ever was. It used to be that **the** jobs of **the** bookkeeper and the financial planner were completely different. That is no longer the case. With ~~**the**~~ financial planning software, I can do **an** analysis of dozens of alternative business choices and decide which one works best, and even throw in **a [the OK]** strategy for minimizing taxes at the same time.

LESSON 29

Diagnostic Exercise

The **modernization** of agriculture has meant a huge increase in just a few crops—**wheat** and **rice** for ~~**a**~~ human consumption, **corn** for ~~**an**~~ animal consumption, and **cotton** for industrial **production**. This specialization in a few crops is called ~~**a**~~ *monoculture*. ~~**A**~~ monoculture has some disadvantages: it reduces ~~**a**~~ biodiversity and requires huge amounts of **energy** and fertilizer.

Now You Try It, 1

1. Having a flicker in my computer screen caused me ~~**an**~~ anxiety about saving my **work**.
2. My roommate and I finally unplugged the TV set during the week because we couldn't stand the silly **nonsense** in all the commercials.
3. Most people need to pay a high price for **popularity**.
4. Everyone in the legal profession has an obligation to uphold the **enforcement** of the **law**.
5. A record of traffic tickets is ~~**an**~~ evidence of a tendency to drive dangerously.

Now You Try It, 2

1. After being pursued by a mysterious villain, the hero seeks the **protection** of his friends.
2. The company is trying to prolong the storage of food by treating it with **radiation**.
3. The teacher offered the young people some good **advice**.
4. We assured them of our complete **cooperation** in these matters.
5. To be a writer, you must have lots of good ideas and lots of **information**.

Editing Practice, 1

Gold has long been one of the most valued of metals. **Jewelry** made of gold has been discovered at an excavation in Iraq that dates from 3500 B.C. The high level of **artistry** in the **workmanship** suggests that the craft of working **gold** had been evolving . . .

From ancient times to today, gold has been highly prized for a number of reasons. Its soft yellow color makes it intrinsically beautiful; unlike **iron**, **copper**, and most other metal **[metals**, meaning different kinds of metal, is also **OK]***, ~~**a**~~ gold does not rust . . .
*(raises error count to 4)

Editing Practice, 2

One of the most remarkable Americans who ever lived was Benjamin Franklin. He was born in 1706 in Boston. His **education was** quite limited because his father, who made candles and **soap**, was unable to send him to school beyond the age of ten. It is amazing that one of the most educated men in the Age of **Reason** was entirely self-taught. Franklin learned to be **a** printer, and by the time he was twenty-four, Franklin was the owner of his own print shop in Philadelphia. He began publishing a highly successful newspaper, writing much of the **material** himself as his own editor. Through the newspaper and other **publishing**, Franklin . . .

Adding to his already-substantial **fame** was his work as an inventor and scientist. Two of his most famous inventions were bifocal eyeglasses and a much more efficient stove, called the Franklin Stove. His research on **electricity** made him world famous.

Franklin's great personal **reputation** and knowledge of civic affairs made him a natural political leader. He had enormous **influence** on the Revolutionary War. For example, he helped draft the Declaration of Independence and was one of its signers. However, his most important **impact** on the war ~~were~~ **was** his role in obtaining the diplomatic **support** and eventual military intervention of France on the side of the colonies. After the war, Franklin's **wisdom** and common **sense** played a key role in resolving fundamental conflicts in the **creation** of the Constitution.

LESSON 30

Diagnostic Exercise

Doctors have long known that we need to have iron in our diet. Recently, however, **a** new study has revealed that we may be getting too much iron. The human body keeps all **the** iron it digests. **The** only way we lose stored iron in **the** body is through bleeding. John Murray, **a** researcher at the University of Minnesota, discovered that people who live on **a** very low iron diet may have **a** greatly reduced risk of **a** heart attack. Another study found that diets high in meat have **a** strong correlation with a high risk of heart disease. Apparently, when people have **a** high level of iron, **[the]*** excess iron. . . . *(raises error count to 10)

Now You Try It, 1

1. Reason: Previous mention.
2. Reason: Normal expectations.
3. Reason: Defined by modifiers.
4. Reason: Normal expectations.
5. Reason: Uniqueness.

Now You Try It, 2

1. **The** new airport in Denver had problems with its baggage system.
2. Some people came in and bought **a** postcard and **some** stamps.
3. Just before we landed, an attendant came down **the** aisle and collected **the** headphones from **the** passengers.
4. Most folk tales seem to involve **a** young hero who is required to perform **some** dangerous deeds.
5. During the performance, there was **a** loud cry from the back of **the** auditorium.

Editing Practice, 1

All of us have seen movies that were completely forgettable except for **a** single scene. For some reason, this scene has always stuck in our minds. Often, **the** scene is not even a major part of **the** plot. It is usually some little piece of character development that struck us, or it is **a** funny or whimsical episode. For example, a few years ago I saw **a** French film whose title I can no longer even recall. In this otherwise forgettable movie, there was **a** long scene that showed someone fixing dinner and chopping **a** big pile of garlic while carrying on **a** long and animated conversation with the dinner guests. Everything in **the** scene was perfectly normal except that the cook was wearing **a** mask and snorkel while he prepared **the** garlic.

Editing Practice, 2

My nomination for the Unforgettable Scenes from Forgettable Movies Award is **a** scene in one of Humphrey Bogart's last movies, *Beat the Devil.* **The** movie is set in rural Italy on the Amalfi Coast. Bogart and Sydney Greenstreet are taking **a** taxi up **a** narrow mountain road. Just below **the** top, **the** taxi stalls, and they have to get out to push it. **The** driver walks alongside **the** driver's seat and steers as Bogart and Sydney Greenstreet push from behind. Bogart and Greenstreet get into **a** terrible argument as they are pushing, and **the** taxi driver is dying to hear what they are talking about. All three men get so involved in **the** argument . . .

LESSON 31

Diagnostic Exercise

~~The~~ **scientists** have long known that ~~the~~ **honeybees** are somehow able to tell ~~some~~ other **bees** where to look for ~~some~~ **food**. In the 1940's, Karl von Frisch of the University of Munich discovered that the type of ~~the~~ **dance** that ~~the~~ **bees** make when they return to their beehive is significant. It seems that ~~the~~ **honeybees** are . . .

Now You Try It, 1

1. Advances in ~~**the**~~ technology make it very difficult for ~~**the**~~ school systems to prepare ~~**the**~~ students for the workplace.
2. ~~**The**~~ development is always limited by the resources that are available.
3. ~~**The**~~ sticks and stones will break my bones, but ~~**the**~~ words will never hurt me.
4. We have to be careful driving on ~~**the**~~ wet roads just after ~~**the**~~ summer showers because the oil on the pavement has not been washed away yet.
5. ~~**The**~~ natural gas is formed by the decay of ~~**the**~~ plants and animals.

Now You Try It, 2

1. As a general rule, the cost of modernizing ~~**the**~~ kitchens will be recovered when the house is sold.
2. The key issue in any scientific controversy is agreeing on what constitutes ~~**some**~~ relevant evidence.
3. ~~**The**~~ tropical diseases are poorly understood because so little research has been devoted to them.
4. The appointment of ambassadors requires ~~**the**~~ congressional approval.
5. In many towns, ~~**the**~~ shopping malls have taken ~~**the**~~ business away from older stores.

Editing Practice, 1

The history of ~~**the**~~ furniture reflects the history of ~~**the**~~ culture. Relatively little is known about the furniture of ~~**the**~~ ancient societies, simply because furniture is usually made of ~~**the**~~ perishable materials—wood and sometimes fabric—that have not survived. Our limited knowledge of Egyptian, Greek, and Roman furniture is based mostly on ~~**the**~~ paintings and ~~**the**~~ sculptures. The only actual surviving pieces of furniture are from ~~**the**~~ burials. For example, King Tut's tomb in Egypt contained piles of elegantly decorated royal furniture. About the only surviving examples of everyday Roman furniture are from **the** two cities near Naples that were buried under ~~**the**~~ tons of volcanic ash . . .

Editing Practice, 2

The American linguist Deborah Tannen is best known for her books about the differences in the language of ~~**the**~~ men and women. Her books show that ~~**the**~~ men tend to use language in a very competitive way. For example, ~~**the**~~ conversations among a group of men are marked by ~~**some**~~ competition to be the center of attention.

Women tend to be careful about taking ~~**the**~~ turns in the conversations. Even in ~~**the**~~ animated conversations, ~~**the**~~ interruptions tend . . .

UNIT EIGHT OVERVIEW

Can You Detect Problems Involving Sentence Clarity and Style?

I first went to college some fifteen years ago but decided to stay at home and raise my two children. Back then, I and most of my fellow students wrote papers the old-fashioned way: by typing them. Realizing the need to be more up to date, **I decided that** my goal this year was to improve my word-processing skills, do most assigned papers on a computer, and **learn** how to use a graphics program. My major motivations were keeping up with modern technology and **making** it less of a chore to revise my papers.

However, I noticed all the younger students for whom using a computer was second nature. **These students intimidated me. Although I felt insecure,** my pride wouldn't allow me to ask them for help, go to the computer lab for tutoring, or **ask** my teachers for advice. Then, I began noticing that even many of the younger students were not experts at all. Many, in fact, did not know how to type, turn on a computer, or **insert** a disk into the computer. I signed up for a computer class covering the basics, and by the end of the quarter, I could comfortably do all my papers on computer. Next quarter, **I'll tackle the graphics programs.**

LESSON 32

Diagnostic Exercise

My brother called **today** and said he would travel to Europe. He plans to go as soon as his school is out this summer. A travel agent told him it would cost **only** $400 for a round-trip ticket to London. The agent he spoke with said **enthusiastically** that he should take advantage of this price. My brother asked whether I wanted to go with him, but I have already committed myself to a summer job. He talked for **almost** an hour . . .

Now You Try It, 1

1. OK
2. Hamsters are pregnant for **only** 16 days.
3. We read **almost** thirty poems for this class.
4. My biology teacher said **yesterday** that there are 138,000 varieties of butterflies and moths.
5. We saw a man **gesturing and angrily talking** to an officer.

Now You Try It, 2

1. The woman **slowly skating** asked me to turn off my radio.
2. **Yesterday,** Ira said he found my missing car keys.
3. He bought it for **only** a hundred dollars!
4. We located **only** three sources for our group paper.
5. OK

Editing Practice, 1

My friend Janet **regularly** tells me what her literature teacher discusses. **Yesterday**, Janet . . .

Take, for instance, the popular character Batman. The character today is violent and even scary to law-abiding citizens. The fact that he lurks in the shadows and **frequently** is a creature of the night is interesting. Perhaps readers envy Batman for being outside the law. Indeed, heroes who border on being lawbreakers are **commonly** best-selling characters in the comics—a trend suggesting that readers seem **barely** satisfied . . .

Editing Practice, 2

Generally, a person whose brain is damaged runs the risk of aphasia. Sometimes, this disorder, called *dysphasia*, happens when damage occurs to the part of the brain devoted to language production or comprehension. All people with aphasia have some language ability remaining, but it has been impaired in some way. Strokes account for **almost** 85 percent of aphasia cases. Eating an unhealthy diet, avoiding exercise, or **frequently** smoking . . .

LESSON 33

Diagnostic Exercise

Studying for hours, **I felt** my eyes **grow** tired. I felt I could not read another word. I walked to the store for a drink. When I got there, the store was closed. Deciding against walking another mile to another store, **I found myself thinking** that maybe I would just quit studying and get some sleep. I returned home and tried to decide what to do. Torn between the need to sleep and the need to study, **I heard** the alarm clock go off and **realized that** it . . .

Now You Try It, 1

1. Excited by the fans, the home team quickly scored a touchdown.
2. OK
3. Waving good-bye to his mother, Paul felt his eyes growing misty.
4. OK
5. Running up the stairs, Colleen fell and broke her nose.

Now You Try It, 2

1. Reading the contract carefully, both parties decided to wait a few days before signing.
2. OK
3. Practicing almost every day for a year, Molly improved her writing.
4. Steve revealed his bad temper when he broke the pencil in anger.
5. Feeling hungry because I skipped lunch, I found supper appealing.

Editing Practice, 1

Worried that he would be late for class, **Oliver turned his leisurely walk** into a trot. He quickly entered the science building. His chemistry teacher seemed to dislike late arrivals. **When Oliver met** an old friend who wanted to chat, his chances of arriving on time diminished. Oliver didn't want to be rude, so he left as soon as he could. Thinking about skipping the class altogether, he **considered several options.** He . . .

Opening the classroom door as quietly as possible, **Oliver thought that** his arrival seemed to go unnoticed. But then Dr. Wilson said, "Oh, I hope it wasn't too much trouble for you to join us today, Oliver." Attempting to explain why he was detained, **Oliver realized** his excuse . . .

Editing Practice, 2

Irritated by the recent turn of events, **Jacquita realized that her** day just wasn't going well. She had no control over the virus that plagued her, but she really couldn't afford to miss the study session for her economics test. She decided to ask a classmate to take notes for her. **She called her friend Jerry, but** her . . .

When Jacquita was about halfway to the classroom, the need for a quick detour to the rest room interrupted her. Jacquita soon decided that having a stomach virus was not going to be a crowd-pleaser, so she headed back to her dorm room. **She was overcome** by fatigue and illness, **and** sleep . . .

LESSON 34

Diagnostic Exercise

We all go to college for different reasons—to get an education, meet new people, and **gain** the skills for a job. The best programs are ones that reach several of these goals at the same time. I like to take courses that interest me and **do** things that will lead to a job. For example, it is great to read about something in a class and then **apply** it in a practical situation. That is why I am doing an internship program. I have the opportunity to get credits, develop professional skills, and **make** important . . .

Now You Try It, 1

1. Today, I have to call my mother, write a report, and **pay** my bills.
2. College gives us a chance to be away from home and **to gain** independence.
3. This book will teach you ways to write better, get good grades, and **amuse** your friends.
4. The standard formula for speeches is beginning with a joke and **concluding** with a summary.
5. Student representatives on faculty committees are required to attend all meetings, take notes, and **report** to the student government.

Now You Try It, 2

1. The porters began sorting the baggage and **clearing** a space for the groups to assemble.
2. Before I leave, I have to feed the cat, water the plants, and **lock** the door.
3. This semester I started working at home in the mornings and **doing** my schoolwork later in the afternoons.
4. I don't want you to lose the directions or **get** lost.
5. OK

Editing Practice, 1

It used to be that schools just taught students to read, write, and ~~**to**~~ **do** arithmetic, and that was it. When students left school, there were plenty of blue-collar jobs, for example, on the automobile assembly line. The assembly line required workers who were willing to be punctual, work at a steady pace, and ~~**to**~~ **follow** instructions. These jobs often paid pretty well—well enough for a worker to support a family, to buy a new car, and **to make** the down payment on a house. Because the work was broken down into tiny routines, workers never needed to receive any training more sophisticated than basic first aid or even **to develop** technical knowledge relevant to the industry. The work was designed to be simple, make little demand on the workers, and **ensure** that . . .

Editing Practice, 2

Nowadays, there are far fewer manufacturing jobs around because companies are able to subcontract to the cheapest bidder, get components manufactured overseas, and ~~**to**~~ **do** the same work with fewer workers because of automation. These developments leave Americans jobs that require workers to meet extremely short deadlines, **to produce** customized . . .

These changes in the workplace mean that American workers must become much more sophisticated to function in a high-tech world. For example, they need to learn to read technical manuals, communicate with many different technical specialists, and **be able** to upgrade themselves constantly. What companies need are students who are able to read, write, and ~~**to**~~ **engage** in . . .

LESSON 35

Diagnostic Exercise

Matt's apartment manager called him, wanting to know why he played his music so loudly. **The phone call surprised Matt**; he didn't think his music was very loud at all. He apologized, but he said his radio was playing at only a fourth of its potential volume. Apparently, **this response satisfied the manager. She told Matt** that . . .

Now You Try It, 1

1. Those kids uprooted the flowers.
2. Your yelling frightens us.
3. You broke the television.
4. Your actions hurt me.
5. Eudora Welty wrote the story.

Now You Try It, 2

1. The hungry workers ate the food.
2. On Saturday, a careless driver who pulled in front of me hit my car.
3. The custodians cleaned all the classrooms over the weekend.
4. Another dancer violently bumped my dancing partner.
5. The farmer sprayed the pesticide.

Editing Practice, 1

My parents greatly influenced me to love reading. Both of them are avid readers, yet **they rarely hassled me** to read . . .

Almost every type of reading material has an appeal for me, but **I most often read** science-fiction stories. **I consumed them** during my teenage years; often, **I would read** one a week. Now that I'm in college, I have less time to spend on pleasure reading, but **I carved out some time** from my schedule to devote to reading . . .

Editing Practice, 2

I consider parking on this campus to be a real problem. The school is in the middle of a large city, and **students, teachers, and people working in the city search for** available parking places. When **the school needed** more classrooms, the parking lots it once had disappeared. As the city grew, the parking places gave way to more and more stores. All this growth has its advantages, but **the school or city did not carefully consider** parking needs.

Students can buy parking permits, but the better lots are expensive. **The school and city encourage riding** the bus, but . . .